Seven Years

among

Prisoners

of War

Seven Years among Prisoners of War

CHRIS CHRISTIANSEN

translated by

IDA EGEDE WINTHER

Ohio University Press

Athens

Ohio University Press, Athens, Ohio 45101
© 1994 by Chris Christiansen
Printed in the United States of America
All rights reserved
98   97   96   95   94   5   4   3   2   1

Ohio University Press books are printed on acid-free paper ∞

Library of Congress Cataloging in Publication Data

Christiansen, Chris, 1914–
    [Syv år blandt krigsfanger. English]
    Seven years among prisoners of war / Chris Christiansen ;
translated by Ida Egede Winther.
        p.   cm.
    Includes bibliographical references and index.
    ISBN 0-8214-1069-5. —
    1. Christiansen, Chris, 1914–   .   2. World War, 1939–1945—
Prisoners and prisons.   3. World War, 1939–1945—Personal
narratives, Danish.   4. World War, 1939–1945—Chaplains—Denmark—
Biography.   5. Prisoners of war—Soviet Union—Biography.
6. Prisoners of war—Denmark—Biography.   7. KFUM (Denmark)—
Biography.   I. Title.
    D805.A2C4913   1994
    940.54′77′092—dc20
    [B]   93-45964
                                                                  CIP

To Those Who Paid Part of the Price
That We Could Remain Free People

CONTENTS

PART THREE

Among German Prisoners of War in
Great Britain   151

PART FOUR

Among German Prisoners of War in Egypt   175

Appendix   217

References   219

PREFACE

FEW PEOPLE have any idea of what life was like in a prisoner of
war camp during World War II, and fewer still can imagine the
hardships and humiliations that prisoners of war were subjected
to in the Soviet Union. The book *Seven Years among Prisoners
of War* will, I hope, help its readers to understand what it meant
to have had to live month after month and year after year behind
the barbed wire of a prisoner of war camp.

Time and again friends have asked me to write down my
experiences and memories from prisoner of war camps in the
countries in which I was asked to serve as a YMCA representative. I received the decisive push in October 1987 when the director of the Department of History at the University of Odense,
Denmark, Aage Trommer, Ph.D., invited me to join a group of
researchers working on a project named "The Danish Church
under the German Occupation." The purpose of the project was
to clarify and consider Danish church life during the years 1940–
45 from as many angles as possible, and not only concentrate on
the involvement of the Church in the resistance movement. I
gladly accepted the invitation, and it became an inspiring and
very useful experience to participate in the project and thereby
be able to confirm that the YMCA World Alliance, to which the
Danish Church contributed employees as well as funds, played a
small, yet important role in contemporary history. The interest,
patience, and encouragement shown to me by the University of
Odense Department of History and its director, Dr. Aage Trommer, have been of great value to me and are gratefully acknowledged.

I am grateful for the opportunity to tell the story of the
YMCA work among prisoners of war as I saw it and experienced
it during the years 1942–48. But if I were to name all those to

whom I am indebted for help of various kinds the list would be a long one. My thanks must constantly extend in all directions.

First of all, I would like to thank the Danish YMCA, which already in 1940 asked me to join the YMCA staff as a representative to Allied prisoners of war in Germany. The Danish YMCA leadership gave me the necessary encouragement and thus became instrumental in shaping my later career. My work among prisoners of war as an employee of the YMCA became a good and instructive school for my subsequent eleven years working among refugees in different parts of the world. I am also grateful to the Danish YMCA for allowing me unlimited access to their files of correspondence and reports on camp visits, now held in the Danish National Archives. These files offered very useful and partly unknown information about the YMCA POW Aid during and after the two world wars.

I owe a special thank you to the Danish Ministry of Foreign Affairs for granting me admission to its archives concerning the relief work among prisoners of war, and especially for letting me have the privilege of reading about the many different steps of action which the Foreign Ministry undertook in 1945–46 to try to ease the poor conditions under which I had to live during my imprisonment in the Soviet Union, and to have me released and repatriated as quickly as possible.

I further want to thank all of those former prisoners of war whom I got to know in camps in Germany, the Soviet Union, Great Britain, Egypt, and North Africa—or their surviving relatives—who have written to me and thus assisted me in gathering interesting and important materials which contributed to my completing this book.

Finally, I am extremely grateful to my translator, Mrs. Ida E. Winther, who not only produced an excellent translation of difficult and lengthy Danish texts, but also kindly volunteered to shorten the first two chapters of the Danish edition of the book, "Introduction" and "Background," which were originally meant for Danish readers only, into one chapter in fluent English.

TRANSLATOR'S NOTE

THE TRANSLATION from Danish to English of Christian Christiansen's book *Seven Years among Prisoners of War* included shortening his "Introduction" and "Background" chapters, because these chapters contain a great deal of detailed information about the Church of Denmark, its reaction to the German occupation of Denmark, and its support of the international YMCA relief work among prisoners of war—information of no special interest to English-speaking readers.

This shortened section follows the author's account as accurately as possible in the same objective, detached, and modest manner in which he wrote the original two chapters. This manner has only been departed from where it was felt that the author had given less credit to himself and his work than he deserves.

IDA EGEDE WINTHER

Part One

AMONG ALLIED PRISONERS OF

WAR IN GERMANY

INTRODUCTION

THIS BOOK is an account of the author's experiences during and after World War II—one of many such accounts, you might say, but nevertheless different, because it tells us about a part of World War II which is not included in our history books and which is not common knowledge to most people. Christian Christiansen's book is about prisoners of war (POWs)—hundreds of thousands of them, Allied as well as German—who were unfortunate enough to have been cast away in prison camps all over the world only to wait for the end of the war; and it is about the determination of the Christian Church and the World Alliance of Young Men's Christian Associations (YMCA) to initiate and carry out a dedicated and substantial amount of work to relieve the conditions of these prisoners as much as possible.

Surely such an account is best told by someone who was personally involved, by "a living source," as the author himself expresses it, and Christian Christiansen was very much involved in relief work: he visited countless prison camps and met countless prisoners of war, talked to them, listened to them, and did what he could to help them. Thanks to his authorship, this extensive humanitarian work will not now fall into oblivion.

More than fifty years ago, as a young, newly fledged grad-

uate of theology, Christian Christiansen was asked to take part
in the Christian relief work among prisoners of war; he accepted
and thus became one of the few Danes to be employed by the
YMCA and sent to Germany to work as a field delegate. For
four years he lived in Berlin and worked to do whatever he was
able to do for the Allied POWs in Germany. At the end of the
war he was arrested by the Russians and detained on grounds of
suspected espionage, a quite unwarranted suspicion considering
that his work was purely humanitarian and absolutely nonpolitical. Christiansen spent more than three months in a Russian
prison in Moscow under the most appalling conditions before
he was transferred to an ordinary prison camp. One year later,
practically to the day, he was finally released and allowed to return to Denmark. But because he knew that the need for assistance to POWs was still as urgent as ever, he allowed himself only
a short period to recuperate from his imprisonment before taking on new challenges, this time in Great Britain and Egypt
among German prisoners of war. In 1948 the last prisoners of
war and the last field delegate, namely Christian Christiansen,
were repatriated, and he could retire from seven years of helping
Allied and German prisoners of war.

In his introductory chapters, Christiansen gives an interesting account of the history of prisoners of war. We all know that
the concept of POWs is as old as war itself; every war had its
war captives—its prisoners of war—men who suffered slavery,
torture, and death in the hands of their captors. What many of
us may not know is that until the middle of the last century nobody really cared about these men and the way they were
treated.

One day in 1859, during the Italian War of Independence, a
young Swiss by the name of Jean-Henri Dunant witnessed the
most incredible horrors of war and its consequences. What he
saw on this particularly bloody battlefield made so deep an impression on him that he devoted all his energy to making the
Swiss YMCA recognize the deep need to help future war victims.
He accomplished this successfully, and thus had a large share in
the establishment of the organization which was to develop into
the well-known International Red Cross. The efforts of Henri

Dunant, the Red Cross, and the YMCA World Alliance resulted in the conclusion of an agreement—the Geneva Convention—which was signed by sixteen nations in 1864 in Geneva. This convention governs the amelioration of the conditions of prisoners of war without regard to nationality, and it provides them with a number of fundamental rights. Today, following many amendments and improvements, it has been signed by almost every nation in the world, and it is generally believed that over the years the treatment of prisoners of war has, in general, been in compliance with the Geneva Convention. The reason is obvious: the way any belligerent country treated its prisoners of war would have an almost immediate effect upon the treatment of that country's own prisoners of war in any other belligerent country. One notable exception to this general compliance was the German treatment of Russian and the Russian treatment of German prisoners of war, as Christiansen's own account attests. The Soviet Union did not become a signatory of the Geneva Convention until 1949, and thus Germany did not feel obliged to comply with the convention with regard to Russian POWs, and neither did the Soviet Union concerning German POWs.

The Geneva Convention regulates a range of issues related to prisoners of war: the size of prison camps, the arrangement of quarters, sanitary measures, discipline, punishment, such occupations and activities as education and access to books, musical instruments, and sports facilities, the right to write and receive letters, and the position of chaplains and how they, prisoners of war themselves, should still be allowed to carry out their work as chaplains. The convention stipulates that prisoners of war shall be treated decently and humanely, that they not be submitted to any acts of violence, to indignities, or to public display. Finally, the Geneva Convention contains the provision that both the Red Cross and the YMCA are guaranteed the right during wartime to furnish aid to prisoners of war and interned civilians; it would indeed have been difficult—not to say impossible—to achieve the impressive level of aid for prisoners of war that was provided in many countries had these belligerent countries not been signatories of the Geneva Convention.

But no matter how well treated, a prisoner of war remains

a prisoner, and no one who has not been a prisoner of war is fully able to understand the experience. A prisoner of war is pushed aside, shunted away from the center of activity; he does not count and no longer has any influence on whether his country wins or is defeated. "Ah," many of us might think, "but he is safe, isn't he? He is removed from the dangers of war. Of course he is shut up behind barbed wire, but what does it matter? He can sit back, relax, and just wait for the end of the war and for liberation." Or we may imagine the contrary; we may think of a prisoner of war as a man without any legal rights, somebody who is submitted to whatever highhanded—perhaps even cruel—treatment his captors may see fit; a man who is hungry and cold, perhaps sick; a man who is completely abandoned by his country. Christiansen strongly insists that these two notions are both wrong. The Geneva Convention refutes the latter, and Christiansens's personal experiences demonstrate that the first notion is just as inaccurate.

During his seven years as a field delegate, Christiansen met thousands and thousands of prisoners of war who definitely did not feel safe and secure behind barbed wire; on the contrary, they were possessed by feelings of deep depression, despair, uncertainty, and insecurity. They were deprived of their freedom and of their families, of their usual human relations, month after month, year after year, painfully aware that so much happened outside the barbed wire, so little inside; they lived monotonous lives, with almost no privacy, with daily deprivation and constant friction, in the same surroundings day in and day out, waiting for letters—which perhaps never came—that might comfort them and show them that they were neither forgotten nor abandoned.

Circumstances such as these, which were more than enough to influence both their constitution and their state of mind, often led to so-called "barbed wire psychosis," a mental disorder which, as the expression indicates, resulted from being shut up behind barbed wire. Kindness, understanding, and compassion were the only remedies for this ailment. Prisoners of war did what they could to help each other fight it, and so did their captors. But the International Red Cross and the YMCA POW Aid, of which Christian Christiansen was an employee, were perhaps the two organizations most dedicated to helping prisoners of war recover from barbed wire psychosis, and, because of the Geneva Convention, these two organizations were also in the best position to do so.

In September 1939, when the war was a reality, the leaders of the large ecclesiastical world alliances—the World Students' Christian Federation, the YMCA World Alliance, the World Alliance of Young Women's Christian Associations, the World Council of Churches, the Inter-church Alliance, and the World Alliance of International Understanding—met in Geneva to discuss and delegate the numerous tasks which would have to be performed as a result of the war. The YMCA was charged with taking care of the spiritual and cultural needs of war prisoners and interned civilians, including the procurement of books, educational materials, musical instruments, sports equipment, and so forth. Provisions for their physical needs and welfare, such as postal services and food and clothing, were to be the task of the International Red Cross.

Before the YMCA could actually begin work, however, written permissions from the belligerent countries were required. Great Britain, France, and Germany did not hesitate to issue such permissions, probably because the relief work which had been carried out during World War I was still vividly remembered. The substantial amount of YMCA aid, and the establishment, by national YMCA associations, of soldiers' recreation centers—or YMCA Homes as they were commonly called—with their canteens, libraries, and reading and writing rooms, represented a very valuable and recognized aid, not only to the thousands of soldiers who had used the YMCA Homes' facilities, but certainly, and perhaps more importantly, to the governments of the belligerent countries. Nor had it been forgotten that the YMCA World Alliance had initiated the relief work carried out by volunteer members of the YMCA from neutral countries in service of more than six million prisoners of war in all the belligerent countries. Finally, uppermost in the minds of many government officials was the enormous undertaking of the Red

Cross and the YMCA to repatriate hundreds of thousands of prisoners of war from Siberia to central Europe.

These permissions opened many doors and obtained many privileges: many tons of valuable provisions were dispatched free of charge to war prisoners during the years 1939–48; censors permitted millions of books and stacks of mail and parcels to pass to the prisoners; the Red Cross and the YMCA were given special, very favorable rates of exchange; government officials could be found in all the belligerent countries who looked kindly and sympathetically upon the humanitarian efforts made by the YMCA, and with whom a mutually beneficial cooperation could be established. Without these permissions, and without the assurance of cooperation from the belligerent countries, the YMCA would never have been able to carry out so much of relief work among prisoners of war.

On 15 November 1939 the first YMCA field delegate paid his first visit to a prison camp near Orléans in France; there followed thousands of similar visits to thousands of other prison camps. The number of delegates grew, eventually reaching a total of 278 YMCA representatives working in thirty-eight countries. The funds for such a substantial amount of relief work—more than seventeen million U.S. dollars—were contributed by churches, associations, and governments in twenty-six different countries.

The Church of Denmark and the Danish government had, of course, agreed to take part in and support the POW relief work in the same active manner as they did during World War I; "Active Danish participation is a matter of course" is how the Secretary General of the Danish YMCA and YWCA put it. Consequently, preparations were made to raise funds and to search for and employ people who would be willing to work in prison camps.

In late November of 1939, following a request from the German authorities, the YMCA World Alliance asked the Church of Denmark to employ a man who would be willing and able to take charge of the relief work among almost 300,000 Polish prisoners of war in Germany. The choice fell upon Pastor Erik Christensen; during World War I he had worked in Siberian prison camps for two years, and he was therefore considered the best qualified man for such a job. He was a very intelligent man with substantial administrative abilities and a quiet demeanor. Christensen accepted the call, and in February 1940, after having obtained leave from his job and the necessary permits, he departed for Berlin, where he remained the competent and highly esteemed leader of the POW Aid until 1944.

In the beginning Erik Christensen worked alone, but soon he was joined by a small group of Swedish, Swiss, and Danish field delegates, one of whom was Christian Christiansen. By early 1940, the YMCA POW Aid had established its headquarters in the German capital.

On 9 April 1940, Germany advanced into and occupied Denmark. This raised the question whether the Church of Denmark should continue its participation in relief work in Germany. Some people did not like the idea of giving any kind of support to Germany under these circumstances, but following a report from Pastor Erik Christensen emphasizing how important the relief work in Germany was, and how valuable to the Allied prisoners of war, a resolution to carry on was adopted, and the YMCA POW Aid in Germany thus continued throughout the war.

Obviously the YMCA POW Aid was not meant exclusively for Allied prisoners of war in Germany. German war prisoners in Belgium, France, Great Britain, the Soviet Union, the United States, Canada, Egypt, and other countries—and, when the war ended, in the four German zones occupied by the Allies—had the same desperate need for help. Denmark contributed field delegates who worked in Great Britain, in the Allied zones of Germany, and in Belgium, Egypt, and Denmark.

At the end of 1948, the YMCA POW Aid was finally able to discontinue and conclude its work, because by then the last prisoners of war had been repatriated from Egypt, and with them so had Christian Christiansen.

The huge and selfless work carried out to ameliorate the conditions of Allied as well as German prisoners of war during World War II in the name of the Christian Church helped hundred of thousands of prisoners of war stay alive, endure the hardships of captivity, and avoid any permanent mental or physical injuries. It gave them comfort, strength and hope—it was, literally, their salvation.

"there's a time to keep silence"

A few days after obtaining my theology degree in June 1940, I received a letter from the Secretary General of the YMCA and YWCA in Denmark, Pastor Christian Baun; he asked me if I would be interestd in going to Germany as a field delegate employed by the YMCA. At that time, I had no idea what a job as a YMCA field delegate involved. I only knew that, like most graduates in theology, I would have to find work as soon as possible to earn my living, be it as a pastor, a YMCA field delegate, a high school teacher, or something else. Pastor Baun told me all he knew about the job and the work it involved, and after having thought about it for a few days, I accepted. I suppose a factor in my decision was that nobody seemed to want me for a job in Denmark, although the Danish Church Overseas had asked me to consider a vacancy in Germany, and the Danish Mission to Seamen wanted me as a pastor in Hamburg. So, finally and gratefully, I accepted the first official offer I had received, from the YMCA and Pastor Baun.

It was to be one and half years, however, before I could get my German visa and residence permits. During that time, I earned my living by teaching students of theology Hebrew and other subjects related to the Old Testament, and at the same time I tried to improve my rather limited and at any rate highly theoretical knowledge of English, German and French. My original visa application had been turned down without any explanation, but I think the refusal had something to do with the decision of the German authorities not to grant residence permits to more than six foreigners involved in the YMCA POW Aid at any one time. In 1941, with the number of POWs in Germany rapidly increasing and the prison camps already becoming overcrowded, they even tried to reduce the number of delegates to four. Another reason for the rejection of my application might have been fear on the part of the authorities—fear that they would be unable to exercise sufficient control over the growing POW Aid, or fear that the POW Aid's employees might knowingly or unknowingly be exploited for purposes of espionage. I do not really know, but I do know that the question of the number of POW field delegates was not solved until the World Alliance, through a topranking delegate from Geneva, made the German authorities understand that "if the number of staff in Germany is to be reduced by one third, then the World Alliance intends to reduce the aid to the German POWs in Great Britain and Canada by one third!" Obviously this was not what the German authorities wanted, and the question was never raised again. From spring 1940 until the end of the war, three Swedish, two Swiss, and two Danish citizens therefore remained permanently assigned to the POW work in Germany.

Public opinion was generally in favor of the Danish efforts to help POWs in Germany. However, the "National Socialist"— a Danish newspaper published during the war under the influence of occupying Nazi Germany—was very much opposed to this whole idea. On 25 September 1941, it brought out an article with the caption, "Is It Our Intention To Send Out People Who Dislike And Scorn Germany?" The short article was about the Danish Church Overseas and the Inter-church Aid committee, and it mentioned, among other things, the assistance which Pastor Erik Christensen "receives from foreigners, including Danish employees." The article expressed "indignation" at the recent employment of new field delegates, among them Christian Christiansen, who "declare just how much they want to work among British and French POWs." It was added, and correctly so, that while Christian Christiansen's statements "perhaps do not count much . . . his tone cannot be misinterpreted and is typical of the sentiment which his words conceal." The article ended with the statement that it would be wise "to examine the employees' attitudes towards the 'new times,' before they were sent out, because Germany's confidence in us should not be abused by the poisoning of POWs' mental lives and the relationship between Germany and Denmark thereby become seriously damaged. Christian Christiansen has not yet crossed the border to National Socialist Germany. Perhaps it would be wise for him not to do so."

The influence exerted by the "National Socialist" cannot have been very great; I received my German visa on 5 March 1942, and a week later I took the train to Berlin. My departure either escaped the notice of the Nazi newspaper, or else the editors no longer considered it important news.

I had never been in Berlin before, so I was to cable Erik Christensen and notify him of my time of arrival, and he would have someone meet me. My intention was to go by train and ferry, but the winter of 1942 was extremely severe and ice upon the Danish waters was imminent. In fact, the ferry service across the Fehmarn Belt between Denmark and Germany had been suspended several days earlier, and I had to go via Jutland and Hamburg. Not only did this mean a much longer journey than anticipated, but large masses of ice moving into the Great Belt between Zealand and Funen caused further delays, and the crossing took more than eleven hours instead of the usual seventy-five minutes. I had to stay overnight both in Fredericia in Jutland and in Hamburg. All in all, the journey from Copenhagen to Berlin took forty-eight hours, and if that were not enough, I also ended up at the Lehrter railway station in Berlin and not, as planned, at the Stettiner station. I nevertheless managed to find my way to Wilhelmstrasse quite easily, and there I was welcomed by Erik Christensen, Benedicte Wilhjelm—a Danish YWCA staff member who had been delegated by the World YWCA to assist interned women and children of Allied nationality—and a few other employees of the YMCA POW Aid, all of whom were soon to become my very good friends and colleagues. I was allocated a room at Wilhelmstrasse 34, where Erik Christensen and Benedicte Wilhjelm also lived, and after having settled down I enjoyed a good night's sleep.

The first few days were spent visiting different authorities. The work of the YMCA POW Aid could only be carried out with the approval and permission of the German Ministry of Foreign Affairs and the German High Command, so it was quite natural for Pastor Erik Christensen to introduce his new assistants to these authorities immediately. In the Foreign Ministry,

all matters pertaining to the POW Aid were the responsibility of
Dr. Sethe, a "Geheimrat" or Privy Councillor, and a man to
whom the YMCA as well as the POWs owe a lot for the valuable
help he willingly furnished whenever a sudden crisis arose. And
several crises did occur: the Gestapo constantly sought to jeopardize the existence of the POW Aid by their efforts to suppress
our work and send us back home.

The chief of the department in the German High Command
responsible for POW matters was a Colonel Breier; he was the
son of a clergyman, very sympathetic toward the YMCA, its
employees and its cause, and we all enjoyed a fine relationship
with him. We never encountered any problems with his department, which was in charge of the monthly renewal of written
permits, necessary for us to get access to the camps.

A trip to the International Red Cross was also among the
introductory visits. It was housed in a large villa in one of the
suburbs of Berlin, Wannsee, and throughout the war the YMCA
POW Aid worked very closely with Red Cross employees; they
were all Swiss citizens, and they were always ready to listen and
did not spare any pains when it came to providing assistance to
the POWs.

Naturally a visit to the Danish Embassy, or the Danish Legation as it was called in those days, was a matter of course. The
head of the Danish Mission in Berlin at that time was Minister
Otto C. Mohr, and his closest associate was Councillor Vincens
de Steensen-Leth. The minister did not say much to me when
we met, except "welcome." But the councillor did: he warned
me to be extremely cautious in everything I did in Germany. He
was well versed in the Scriptures, and at one point during our
conversation he remarked, with a humorous smile, "You probably know the words of the Holy Writ, that there's a time to
keep silence and a time to speak." Grateful, I made a mental note
of his kind advice—and felt very young and inexperienced. But
I did not doubt that he was right, and should I forget the seriousness of the situation, I was to be reminded of it every so
often: Each time I traveled by regional trains or the under-
ground, I could not avoid reading the warning posted on the

windows of the compartments, "Vorsicht—Feind hört mit" (be careful—the enemy is listening).

And it was quite obvious that I had come to a country at war: big posters were all over the railway stations. Some reminded people that the trains were running first and foremost for the sake of the war and the victory ("Räder müssen rollen für den Sieg"—the wheels must turn for victory); others demanded that people comply with the rules for blackout ("Licht is dein Tod"—light will kill you); some bore an explicit warning against hoarding and stealing. Most of the advertising pillars depicted a small, bent, black goblin, a dwarf with ghastly luminous eyes in a black face, running away with a sack of coal on his back. The only word on the poster was "Kohlenklau," that is, someone who scrapes coal together tooth and nail. The propaganda machine was working very efficiently indeed and the Germans seemed to be obedient. I had certainly come to a strange and alien country.

In the midst of all this, the Danish Church in Berlin was a sanctuary, a home to me and to many of my countrymen. It was situated on the former Saarlandstrasse, today Stresemannstrasse 57, less than ten minutes' walk from our office on Wilhelmstrasse.

In 1939, when the war broke out, the Danish colony in Berlin consisted of a little fewer than one thousand people, few enough for one clergyman to minister to, even though they lived all over the city. Following the German occupation of Denmark, however, a drastic change occurred: all of a sudden, thousands of Danish workers flowed into Berlin. The Germans needed workers to replace those who had been called up for service, and therefore Danish workers were "encouraged," very persuasively, to enter into contracts with the German authorities for at least six months' work in Germany. At one point, the number of Danish people totalled eight or nine thousand, and a congregation of this size made it impossible for the Danish pastor, Pastor Helge Blauenfeldt, to manage the work single-handed. The problem was not so much the services, but the amount of social work to which he had to attend, such as visits to hospitals and prisons to see and talk to his countrymen. This part of his work took up so much of his time and energy that in the spring of 1941, the Danish Church Overseas decided to employ a young graduate in theology, Axel B. Jeppesen, as an assistant to Pastor Blauenfeldt. I knew Pastor Jeppesen from our years at the Copenhagen University, and our friendship grew even closer when we both started to work in the German capital. It was also in Berlin that both of us were to be taken prisoner by the Russians at the end of the war, and brought to the same prison camp on the outskirts of Moscow.

The Danish Church in Berlin became a home and a rendezvous for hundreds, even thousands of Danes during the difficult years of the war, a much-appreciated place of refuge which allowed many of us a place to breathe. I usually attended the church services on Sunday mornings; but it soon became an established custom for myself, Erik Christensen, Benedicte Wilhjelm, and Axel Jeppesen to spend Sunday evenings at the Danish parsonage with the Blauenfeldts. Pastor Blauenfeldt had been attached to the Danish Legation in Berlin for more than ten years, and he and his wife, Lis Blauenfeldt, had numerous German acquaintances who were interesting to speak with and get to know. I became acquainted with Norwegian, Swedish, and Danish clergymen, Danish foreign correspondents and public servants working at the legation and at the consulate in Berlin, various visitors to Berlin, and numerous other people. I met such people as Dr. Otto Dibelius, Dr. Georg Jacobi, Hanns Lilje, Hans Asmussen, and several other distinguished leaders of the anti-Nazi Confessional Church.

Occasionally some of them dropped by to get the latest news from abroad. They knew that Pastor Blauenfeldt enjoyed diplomatic immunity as a clergyman to the legation, and was therefore able to listen to the BBC without the risk of the Germans starting any legal proceedings. Behind these men's visits to the parsonage was a sincere hope that they would meet with sympathy and that all which they confided to their Danish friends would be relayed to ecumenical connections in Geneva, London, New York, and other places whenever an opportunity arose.

Sunday evenings at Pastor Blauenfeldt's residence were,

therefore, always interesting and profitable. Theology was not the only item on the agenda on these occasions; theology was of course discussed, but even more so was the present situation of the German church under a totalitarian regime. Unavoidable, the conversation would time and again concentrate on the immediate political and military situation: "What do people abroad think about us, do they understand our situation?" asked Dr. Lilje, who became Bishop of Hannover after the war. "We fight to live and to survive, so that our church may remain true to the confession of its creed." Those of us who were young probably did not fully appreciate the deep earnestness and the substantial realism behind his words. But we listened intently, and I think we felt somewhat privileged to have the opportunity to become acquainted with these men. Little did I suspect that in December 1946 I would be acting as Dr. Dibelius's chauffeur and guide during his visit to England and Scotland, where thousands of German POWs would gather around his rostrum; nor that, in 1955 in Jerusalem, I would also for a few days be host to Bishop Lilje, when he visited the Arab refugees in Palestine.

THE WORK OF A POW FIELD DELEGATE

Considering the number of prisoners of war, at that time between two and three million, six POW field delegates were not many to cover the entire territory of Germany. Our ecclesiastical backgrounds were different, our educations, experiences, and nationalities were different. But we were united by a common task: bringing aid to the POWs as best we could, regardless of their race, nationality, or political and religious affiliations and convictions. A pre-defined area of Germany had been assigned to each POW field delegate, and within that area he was expected to pay regular visits to and keep in contact with the many POW camps and hospitals. I was assigned to the provinces Pomerania, Mecklenburg, Brandenburg, including Berlin and its suburbs, and Saxony, an area which stretches from Schwerin in the west to the German-Polish border in the east, and from the Baltic Sea in the north well into Czechoslovakia in the south. Twenty-four prison camps and six field hospitals had been established in this area, and between them they housed many thousand prisoners of war from all the Allied nations. I was at a complete loss as to where and how to begin. And what about my language qualifications? Would I be good enough at speaking and understanding German, French and English? Everything seemed very strange and new to me, and although both Bishop Hans Fuglsang-Damgaard of Copenhagen and Dr. Marius Hansen, chairman of the Danish Inter-church Aid committee, had shared with me their experiences from doing similar work during World War I, I knew that I was in great need of guidance and advice.

"Read the reports on previous camp visits," Erik Christensen advised me, and he dug out a couple of his own for me to start with. "Read German newspapers, increase your vocabulary, speak the language and forget about grammar. That's the way the rest of us had to start. And then," he emphasized, "start visiting camps as soon as possible. Next week! That's not too soon! Throw yourself in at the deep end, gain your experience from the lessons you learn and the mistakes you make!"

The pass issued to me by the German High Command was brief and to the point. It simply stated that I was employed with the YMCA World Alliance, Geneva, and that, as its delegate, I was permitted to visit POW camps and hospitals in defense areas II, III, and IV. That was all the information it contained. At first I thought that it would have been more helpful if a brief description of the purpose of the POW Aid had been included, as well as the tasks, rights, and duties vested in each employee, or "delegate" as we were most often called. For instance, were we allowed to talk to the POWs alone? Could we take pictures in the POW camps? How liberal was the permission to visit the camps? Gradually, however, I began to realize that the brevity of the pass was in fact an advantage; had it established, for instance, an extensive freedom of action, then it might have increased the suspicions of many POWs: "Are you a quisling?" "Isn't it your job to spy on us and make reports to the German authorities?" Such questions were often asked of me, and it took time and a good deal of patience and tactfulness to overcome such suspicions. At the beginning, the prisoners of war were very reserved and cagey in front of a stranger, even a civilian, who suddenly turned up to see them and talk to them. The German authorities, on the other hand, were constantly suspicious of all of us; although we were generally treated respectfully, they always kept a very close watch on what we did and said. We always had to try to steer the middle course, which seemed to be a narrow trough between the waves, with high seas on either side. Too much intimacy and fraternization with the German camp authorities immediately evoked the POWs' suspicions and concerns; conversely, the German authorities would become uncomfortably suspicious if we showed the POWs too much understanding and kindness and provided them with an unnecessarily large amount of help. It was imperative that we gained the confidence of both parties as quickly as possible; in fact, it was half the battle if we succeeded, because we could win concessions from the camp commandant concerning the amount of aid the YMCA and the Red Cross could give.

Some people still think that POW camps and concentration camps are one and the same. This is definitely not true. POWs were captured soldiers wearing uniforms, whereas people in concentration camps were usually civilians who were considered political prisoners. The POWs fell under the responsibility of the German military command and were protected by the Geneva Convention; they were guarded by officers and men from the German Army, Navy, or Air Force. Concentration camps, on the other hand, were run by Gestapo officers and guarded by men from the security police, and neither the International Red Cross nor the YMCA were permitted to visit concentration camps.

It is my impression that, on the whole, the German High Command did what it could to treat POWs from the western Allied countries in compliance with the Geneva Convention of 1929, at least until the autumn of 1942. A lot, however, depended upon the individual camp commandant and security officer. The commandants were usually middle-aged officers, too old for combat, and in several instances they had been POWs themselves during World War I. They therefore knew from personal experience what it was like to be held in captivity. This generally gave them the ability to handle the problems and frictions which invariably arose under such conditions. In other cases, the camp commandant was a young and more inexperienced officer who had probably been assigned to the job because he was not physically strong enough to be a front-line soldier. Most of the camp commandants whom I got to know appeared to behave correctly toward the POWs in their charge. It was not unusual to hear middle-aged German officers say: "Why, prisoners of war are not criminals. They obey orders just as we do." After an attempted escape from one of the camps the commandant said to me: "I don't blame them for trying to escape; in fact, it's the duty of every single prisoner of war to try to escape. But then, it's my duty to try to prevent them from doing so."

Another commandant noted with satisfaction how much the books and the sports equipment, provided by the POW Aid, meant to the morale of the camp's several thousand French POWs, and he once asked me if we could not procure some books and footballs for the Russian POWs in the camp. I had to explain to him that the YMCA relief work was based on reciprocity and that, officially, we were unable to help Russians as long as members of the YMCA were not allowed to enter the Soviet Union and help the German POWs who were kept in Russian camps. The commandant fell silent, but after a moment he said: "Couldn't you then get double the amount of what the French need? I'll take responsibility to see to it that half of the amount is given to the Russians." And so this was the way we did it, and as long as that particular colonel was the commandant, it worked perfectly.

In a prison camp near Stettin, where both British and Russian POWs were in captivity, the German commandant asked the British prisoners of war to consider giving part of their food parcels, which they received regularly from the Red Cross, to the Russian POWs. The British agreed, but on the condition that they be allowed into the Russian compound to personally deliver the parcels. The German commandant agreed, even though it was against the regulations issued by the High Command.

These were some of the good examples of camp commandants who tried to make life behind barbed wire better and easier

for the POWs. Naturally, I also met many commandants who
definitely did not share this sympathy with people in distress.

A visit to a POW camp normally started with a courtesy call
to the commandant, to meet him and his officers and to state the
reason for the visit. Generally there were no problems with older
officers, because in many cases they themselves, had once been
POWs. Perhaps they knew of the German YMCA from the days
before the Nazis suppressed it. But some commandants, especially the young ones, seemed quite ignorant of what the YMCA
meant and what it represented, and faced with such commandants, explanations in great detail were required before they gave
their permission for us to enter the camps. I soon learned how
important it was to be very well prepared for a camp visit: to
read well in advance reports about previous visits to the camp,
to find out what the YMCA had delivered to that camp since the
last visit, and to clarify in my own mind what questions I would
like to discuss with the commandant and his officers, and with
the prisoners of war. Knowing that I was a delegate sent out for
humanitarian reasons, that I had a specific task to perform, and
that I was reasonably well prepared for it always facilitated my
initial meeting with even the most unfeeling camp commandant.
Some commandants believed that we were there to "inspect"
their camps, which was not at all the purpose of YMCA visits.
Other commandants found any sort of aid to POWs "unreasonable, as long as our own men make all kinds of sacrifices." And
some commandants arrogantly claimed that "we don't need the
YMCA; we provide everything necessary to the POWs in this
camp." Or, as one commandant once put it to emphasize his
position, "It's the British and the Americans who are making us
homeless, who are bombing our buildings and our homes, and
then you dare turn up to help those selfsame men with your entertainment, games, and footballs." I always tried to avoid political discussions, and I never failed to emphasize the reciprocity
of our work: the YMCA World Alliance had but one single goal,
and that was to serve both sides—prisoners of war and their
guards—on equal terms.

It always proved useful to stress that the aid furnished by
the YMCA in Germany was equal to that which was furnished to

German POWs in other countries. By doing so, I almost always succeeded in evoking sympathy and understanding for our work. Only once did I meet an over-eager commandant who grabbed the telephone and called his headquarters to find out whether he really had to let a YMCA field delegate enter his POW camp. Gradually, however, as the commandants came to know us, confidence grew, and many camp commandants learned to regard the YMCA POW Aid as a valuable support, and to recognize that, if the prisoners received the means to lead a meaningful life in their captivity, the atmosphere in the camps would improve and so would the morale of the POWs. This, in turn would make it an easier job to be a camp commandant.

PRISONER OF WAR CAMPS IN GERMANY

It is not easy to give a general idea of the daily life in a POW camp in Germany because the camps were so different from each other: they varied in size, construction, and function; their camp commandants and the way they looked upon and treated prisoners of war differed; the POWs were of different nationalities with different religious and political affiliations, different backgrounds and education, and, obviously, different reactions to their imprisonment. Finally, it made a difference whether the POWs were officers or enlisted men, and whether they had served in the Army, Navy, or Air Force. All these differences made it necessary for the German authorities to operate different types of POW camps:

DULAGs	(transit camps),
OFLAGs	(officers' camps),
STALAGs	(regular camps for Army NCOs and enlisted men),
MARLAGs	(camps for Navy personnel),
MILAGs	(camps for Merchant Fleet personnel), and
STALAGs LUFT	(camps for Air Force officers and enlisted men).

As soon as possible after their capture, officers and men of all services were brought to a DULAG. DULAG is the abbreviation of "Durchgangslager" (transit camp), in which they were registered and interrogated, had medical examinations, and were given POW uniforms to wear. Actually they kept their own uniforms, but two diamond-shaped patches were sewn on the back of the jacket and on the left trouser leg; or alternatively two large letters—"K" and "G"—were painted on the back of the uniform and on the left trouser leg just above the knee to signify "Kriegsgefangener"—prisoner of war. When all these formalities were in order they were transferred, either on foot or in good wagons, to one of the permanent camps, according to rank and service.

The large majority of the POWs were army soldiers—officers and men of infantry, engineer, armored, and cavalry regiments—and from the medical corps. Officers were taken to OFLAGs, NCOs and men to STALAGs. One MARLAG and one MILAG were sufficient to accommodate personnel of the Navy and the Merchant Fleet, respectively. The MARLAG and the MILAG were both relatively small camps, and it never became necessary to set up additional ones later in the war, despite a steady growth in the number of captured Navy personnel. The STALAG LUFT was different; very soon it became too small, and additional camps had to be built to accommodate the constantly increasing number of captured airmen, and mind you, these were airmen of the western Allied air forces only; Russian airmen were kept in other camps. In my area of responsibility, there were two STALAG LUFT camps, STALAG LUFT I in Barth (Rügen) and STALAG LUFT IV in Gross-Tüchow (Pomerania).

It is impossible to determine how many POWs were held in captivity by the Germans during the last months of the war. However, the official figures published by the German High Command in May 1944—that is, before the invasion of Normandy—are as follows:

Americans	21,324
Belgians	65,737
British	159,341

French	963,491
Greeks	400
Dutch	9,613
Italians	484,500
Yugoslavs	128,559
Norwegians	1,131
Poles	48,600
Russians	1,141,173

These figures, however, do not include captured airmen of the Allied air forces, because they were the responsibility of the German Air Force and not the German Army; neither does the list include those POWs who were captured outside the German Reich (the various German-occupied areas). Russians constituted a large majority of POWs captured in these areas.

The official figure for Polish POWs is small, because already in 1941–42 the German authorities released most of them; only officers and a few others were detained. "Released," however, did not mean that the Polish POWs were free either to go home and join their families or to remain in Germany as they pleased. On the contrary: they had to stay in Germany, but they were allowed to exchange their uniforms for civilian clothes, provided a big "P" was fastened to the left breast pocket of the jacket or the vest. In other words, they were marked "Poles" and regarded as foreign workers or guest workers in the German Reich. Admittedly they got away from the camps and barbed wire fences and could move around freely, but they were still forced to work for Germany and to live in barracks or similar quarters built for foreign workers.

The treatment of POWs differed from nationality to nationality. It is generally agreed that the British and American POWs in Germany received the best treatment. This is not the same as saying that everything was perfect in the British and American camps, or that their treatment was as should be expected from a country that had signed the provisions of the Geneva Convention regarding treatment of prisoners of war. It was no problem to follow the rules of the game as long as the fortunes of war favored the German armies. But as soon as the tide of battle turned against the Germans on both the Russian and North African fronts, and the shortage of food, warm clothing, coal and other necessities became increasingly serious, then all prisoners of war, including the British and the Americans, were the first to feel the consequences. The closer the end of the war, the more difficult it became for the Germans to comply with the Geneva Convention, at least with regard to providing for the POWs. During one of my visits to a POW camp, a British Man of Confidence told the German commandant that the POWs no longer seemed to get any meat in their food rations. The commandant replied, very quietly and therefore so much more convincingly, "You must remember that we don't even have enough food to feed our own people."

It is my impression that several German officers secretly entertained great respect—even admiration—for the British POWs, because of their calm behavior and ability to adapt to prevailing conditions. "I don't understand these British," a camp commandant once confided to me. "How can they be so calm about everything when they have lost the war?" A German major in that same camp remarked: "It's very strange—as long as the Brits are in the air, we do everything we can to shoot them down. But once we've downed them, we do everything we can to make them feel comfortable." And he indeed proved to be sincere in this opinion.

But while the Germans' behavior toward the British and American POWs was usually very correct, this was certainly not true for Russian POWs: an almost complete lack of respect for international law and human rights was displayed in their treatment—or rather ill-treatment—of the Russians. Russia had asked Sweden to act as its Protecting Power and look after Russian national interests in Germany, but this only applied to civilians and civilian matters, not to the military, and therefore not to Russian POWs in German prison camps. These prisoners were not even allowed visits from the International Red Cross and the YMCA POW Aid. The fact that they did receive such visits from time to time was entirely off the record and only because of the kindness and compassion of a few commandants.

Furthermore, the Nazi propaganda machine had been

working very hard since June 1941 to prepare the German soldiers for a relentless combat on the eastern Front, impressing upon them that Russians were brutes and second-rate men—"Untermenschen"—and the military campaign against the Soviet Union was proclaimed to be "necessary in order to save Germany from the greatest act of barbarism since time immemorial—Russian bolshevism."

During the first few weeks of the war against Russia in 1941 the Germans captured about 360,000 Russian soldiers, and before the end of that year the number had increased to 3,350,000. Entire Russian divisions surrendered, and before the end of 1942 more than five million Russians had been captured. The German Army Command was in no way prepared to provide such an influx of prisoners of war with shelters and food, and the result was what might have been expected: more than half of them died in captivity. All Russian officers, moreover, were immediately executed by order of the German High Command, because they were automatically considered to be party members. Thousands of the Russians were shot on the pretext that they had tried to escape during the long and exhausting marches from the eastern front deep inside Russia to the POW camps in Poland and Germany. Thousands died from starvation, exposure, and exhaustion. If one of them stumbled during a march, he was simply shot, in plain sight of the local population, and left at the side of the road. Thousands caught typhoid fever. Food was in very short supply, but the resident populations in the German-occupied areas of the Soviet Union and Poland were strictly forbidden to give any kind of food to the Russians as they slowly dragged themselves westward. Even so, the number of dead need not have been so excessively high. The fact is that Russian soldiers who were taken prisoner were treated especially brutally and arbitrarily, and they, more than anybody, deserved pity, understanding, and compassion.

In November 1942 I visited STALAG III-C at Küstrin at the river Oder and, shortly afterwards, STALAG II-B at Hammerstein in Pomerania. STALAG III-C, about sixty miles east of Berlin, had just received seven thousand Russian POWs, even though the camp was already overcrowded with several thousand Polish and French soldiers. The commandant claimed that he had not been informed about the arrival of the many Russians and therefore had not been able to make the necessary preparations. No systematic delousing was carried out, neither huts nor tents were available, and the commandant hastily arranged for barbed wire to be put up around the Russian POWs and for a number of watch towers overlooking the fences to be built. That was all. The Russians were forced to sleep in the open, exposed to snow, rain, and cold. There were no shovels, so by means of mess tins and their bare hands, the Russians started to make dugouts for shelters. Death did indeed gather a rich crop from among these Russians; when I visited the camp again two months later, only three thousand were left of the original seven thousand. The commandant allowed me to walk through the Russian compound of the camp, and I shall never forget what I saw on that particular afternoon: a big open truck was driving around, collecting dead, naked bodies from the many dugouts; and the bodies were thrown onto the truck like dead cattle and driven to a nearby field, where they were "poured" into a mass grave. Some prisoners were walking around endlessly, in complete apathy, hollow-cheeked and pale; others were busy building huts, and still others rummaged about in dustbins and rubbish heaps in the hope of finding a few potato peelings or perhaps even a cigarette end. Their daily ration at that time amounted to twenty grams of millet and one hundred grams of rye bread!

In STALAG II-B at Hammerstein the situation was the same: I saw how they lived in the open on the bare ground or in dugouts with a bit of heather for a bed, and how they nosed about in the rubbish, eating grass, flowers and raw potatoes just like animals. Many of them looked like walking skeletons, and many of them had open, infected, and foul-smelling wounds. The worst of it was that the camp actually housed a special POW hospital, staffed by Russian doctors and nurses, but that neither medicine nor dressing supplies were available.

Hammerstein and Küstrin were not the only camps in which the conditions were so appalling; many of my colleagues experienced the same situation elsewhere: the Russian POWs had to build their own camps. A confined area of land was provided, surrounded by barbed-wire fences and watch towers, and it was then left to the POWs to get cracking, with only the most primitive tools and materials at their disposal.

The German Army Command made endless efforts to justify the way they treated the Russian POWs; one of their excuses was that the Soviet Union had not acceded to the Geneva Convention of 1929. But the fact is that the Soviet Union had much earlier ratified the "Convention concerning the Amelioration of Wounded and Sick Soldiers in the Field," so there could be no doubt that Germany was obliged to treat wounded and sick Russian POWs in accordance with that convention. Any improvement in the Russian POWs' conditions during 1942–43 served solely to augment a depleted work force. The Russians were most certainly ill-treated by the Germans. But if anyone were to ask me whether the massive dying of Russian POWs was intentional or whether it was caused by need and circumstances, I could not answer objectively.

Many camp commandants had probably made up their minds that the conditions in the Russian camps were so hopeless that it would be quite futile to try to make any improvements. They just would not know where to begin and where to end. But as I mentioned earlier, some commandants ignored their orders and showed us around the Russian compounds of their prison camps, declaring their willingness to cooperate with any contribution of aid to the Russians, if we were able to provide it. The YMCA was not allowed to provide things like medicine, food, and warm clothing, but we could and did provide simple musical instruments, such as mouth organs, guitars, mandolins, and balalaikas, to a few Russian POW camps. I remember seeing a Russian orchestra consisting of fifteen mouth organs and one saxophone. Sometimes we were also able to get them some tools and wood for carving, modeling materials, and sports equipment, thanks to compassionate and understanding camp commandants. Many of the Russians were extremely good with their hands—some of them were even gifted artists—and could make something useful and pretty out of practically nothing.

The German policy regarding Russian prisoners of war was twofold: First, they were needed as laborers; the Germans used to say about the Russians working in the hostels and in the farming sections that "a Russian is a good worker as long as he gets his potatoes." Second, it was imperative to the Germans to try to disrupt the Russians politically. Specially trained officers were assigned to every camp with the sole purpose of converting the Russians to Nazism. I do not know how many people they succeeded in persuading to join the so-called General Vlassov Army, but it was rumored to be about thirty thousand Russians at one time. Naturally there would always be men who desperately wanted to exchange their rags, filth, and lack of food for a warm green uniform and ample and better food. And it is true that joining did a lot of good for their physical well-being. They paid dearly, however, in their relationships to their countrymen: they were mistrusted, despised, and considered traitors. When they fell into the hands of the Russians after the war, they were treated as deserters and either executed, or—at best—exiled to labor camps in Siberia for an indefinite time.

There is no doubt that the Russians suffered the most at the hands of the Germans during World War II. Other nationalities were treated far better. The officers of the Dutch Army Command, for instance, were held prisoner in Königstein, an old fortress built in the Middle Ages and situated on the top of a steep, rather inaccessible mountain peak at the river Elbe, southeast of Dresden. They were treated, if not well, then at least with decency and respect. And the YMCA was able to render so much help to them that after one of my visits to Königstein, the Dutch Commanding General, General Winkelmann, wrote in a letter to me, "Vi sender vår beste takk for god hjelp af KFUM." (We send you our best thanks for the kind help we have received from the YMCA).

As time went by, fewer and fewer Polish POWs captured in 1939 remained in captivity. Most of the NCOs and men were released and either repatriated or, as I mentioned before, forced into employment as civilian workers in Germany. Those who did not wish to be released could stay in the prison camps, where they received reasonable and correct treatment in accordance with international law. This, at least, is my impression from my regular visits to these camps. However, the conditions in the large Polish officers' camps were definitely not as they ought to be: roundups were often carried out, very thorough ones, including body searches and removal of personal belongings such as precious photographs of families and friends. After each roundup, one or more officers usually disappeared never to be seen again; the explanation was that they had been in contact with their own country or—even worse—with General Anders and his men who were exiled in London.

There were many Yugoslav POWs in "my" camps. They led quiet lives, most of them assigned to farming, where they were normally well liked. Many of them did not know how to read or write, and I could only talk to them through an interpreter. I think they felt a stronger urge to go home than any other nationality. Their most precious possessions were normally photographs of their wife and children at home, especially the Serbs and the Croats who never tired of producing pictures and showing them to me. "I'm like a snail," one of them once said. "I carry my home on my back." The general attitude among these NCOs and men was one of resignation. The officers on the other hand, displayed an enormous amount of initiative; their backgrounds and educations were at a much higher level and their inclination to start up entertainment, training, and so forth was far greater. On the whole, Yugoslav officers were treated the same way as Polish officers.

The French and the Belgians had also, at least to a certain extent, been released and repatriated early in the war. Those who had to remain in captivity right up to the end of the war were allowed to move around outside the camps during the day and go to the small villages surrounding the camps for walks, either by themselves or in groups, without any guards escorting them. This may seem strange, but the reason was probably that the Germans did not credit the French and Belgians with quite the same initiative and zeal to escape as they did the British and Americans, who were never let outside the barbed wire fences without an escort of armed guards.

After the surrender of Italy in autumn 1943, the POW camps in Germany suddenly mushroomed with a large influx of Italian soldiers. The Germans were not prepared for them and they had to go through some very hard times, in conditions similar to those of the Russians. They were, however, given the choice of continuing to fight for Hitler and the Nazi cause or being detained in the camps. At the end of the war, many of the Italians in areas liberated by the Russians were not immediately released, but were transported to the Soviet Union and held prisoner in Russian prison camps. As a prisoner in Russia during 1945–46 I met some of them. One of them wrote in my "guest book": "The tyrants did not want us—Italian men, prisoners of war, and outcasts—to derive any benefit from the YMCA's most blessed work. But, it is enough for us to know that we were close to your heart!" A drawing showed the Italian flag in captivity behind tightly wound barbed wire, and beneath it about thirty Italians had signed their names.

The large officers' and airmen's camps usually consisted of long rows of huts. Some of them were built of wood, but most often asbestos cement was used. Some had tiled roofs, others were covered by sheets of asbestos cement. The huts were identical and had several entrances. Normally a long corridor went all the way through each hut with doors to the rooms on each side. The size of a hut varied. Usually, there were 8–20 men in one room, and 380–400 men in one hut. In each room, a long table with two benches stood along one wall, with three stories of built-in wood-plank bunk beds along the other wall, each with a sack of straw or wood shavings and two cotton blankets. A stove with a pipe going up through the roof or out one of the windows provided a bit of heating. Some narrow cupboards in each room were used to store clothes and food from the Red Cross parcels, but they did not have enough space for everybody, so some prisoners had to make do with a peg or a couple of nails, and the men who occupied the lower bunks had to use the space below the bunks as wardrobes and larders. Those in the upper bunks were more fortunate, because they were able to make a small shelf just below the roof for their personal belongings. Clotheslines stretched across every room. In some of the huts crude decorations hung on the walls: flags, watercolors, and drawings—pictures of Churchill ("our Man of Confidence"), Montgomery, and others. In a room occupied by

British prisoners of war, I saw a handmade poster which announced in large letters: "We have not surrendered." In another
camp, I noticed a watercolor depicting a sunset in one of the
rooms; you could see the camp with its barbed wire fences and
its watchtowers, and the text below it couldn't be misunder-
stood: "One day nearer." The artist had evidently concentrated
on painting a beautiful sunset, but in his mind he had been at
home, a free man at peace with himself.

It was not always pleasant to put your nose inside a room;
it was normally fully occupied, with wash hanging wherever
there was a space for it. Each camp also had a distinct smell,
because of the differences in eating habits and therefore in the
composition of food that the POWs received. If you visited
the British colonial troops—for instance, the Indian POWs in
Annaberg—the smell was like that of the narrow streets of Cal-
cutta and Madras. The Russians and Serbs had their special
smells, too. The Russians ate almost nothing but potatoes, so
there was this awful smell of old potatoes in the Russian huts.
The penetrating smell of carbide usually originated with the
Serbs, and there was absolutely no doubt that the French were
used to garlic in their food. The British, Americans, and others
used their Red Cross parcels in a way more similar to Danish
cooking.

Not only eating habits, but also sanitary conditions caused
peculiar and often foul smells in a prison camp. Water was
sometimes scarce and it was not often the men could enjoy a
proper bath. It often rained during the winter, and the wash
would have to be hung in the rooms where the men slept. Because of the cold, the windows would have to stay closed, and
it is easy to imagine the morning fug. It almost took your breath
away when you entered a room and were hit by this thick fog
of dank air and human exhalations.

A POW camp was usually built in a square around a big
open space with approximately the same number of huts on
each of the four sides. The square was used as a parole field,
where head counts took place mornings and evenings (and
sometimes more often), where sports activities were held, and

where the POWs gathered in good weather for concerts, services and other activities.

As a rule, the POW camps were built away from any other human habitations, often in the forests. But old public buildings, such as deserted barracks, hospitals, hostels, closed-down schools, and medieval fortresses, were also used as POW camps, as were older industrial plants and garages which could no longer serve their original purposes. A former seminary, complete with central heating, tables, and chairs once housed 715 French officers. Other POWs lived in a 200-year-old monastery which had been used as a cadet school; it had very thick walls and could accommodate eighteen to eighty men in each dormitory.

All the camps were confined by double rows of barbed-wire fences, usually eight to ten feet high with each single wire close to the next and lots of loosely coiled barbed wire lying between the two fences. Outside these fences, a number of watchtowers were built so that the guards, armed with machine guns and strong search lights, could survey the entire area.

The camp headquarters was situated very close to the camp. It consisted of offices for the commandant and his staff, huts for workshops, storage rooms for mail and parcels, a hospital, a guard room, and quarters for the guards, as many as several hundred in the large camps. Usually German reserve officers were in charge of administration and camp security. Some of them were responsible for accounts, others for provisions, and still others for censorship of all mail to and from the POWs. The censors were mostly grammar school teachers, lawyers, or young clergymen, because they knew other languages besides German.

In all the regular camps, each nationality elected a prisoner of war to represent them—a "Man of Confidence." This was also done in the hostels, but the Man of Confidence elected in the main camp supervised those of his own nationality in all the hostels. Generally it was the senior NCO who was elected Man of Confidence, and one of his tasks was to negotiate with the commandant, with representatives of the Protecting Power, with delegates of the International Red Cross, and with members of the YMCA POW Aid. It was an extremely difficult job. A Man of Confidence was under constant pressure from the camp's German administration as well as from his own countrymen, and it required substantial tact and ability to strike the balance needed to cope with the diversity of problems. And no matter how well a Man of Confidence performed his task, he never avoided his own countrymen's suspicions of double-dealing and cooperation with the Germans. A few of them were probably guilty as charged, but during the numerous camp visits I made over the years, I can think of only one Man of Confidence who might have been called a collaborator; all others, in my opinion, lived up to the difficult demands made upon men in such positions. I remember, for instance, a British corporal I got to know and learned to admire. He served as a British Man of Confidence in a POW camp at Hohnstein, near Dresden, where a few British together with many French, Poles, and Serbs were held.

This man had called for a joint meeting while I was there to allow me the opportunity to talk about the YMCA POW Aid and the purpose of my visit. Then the discussion period began, and one British POW after another took the floor to express his outspoken opinion about the conditions in the camp, and it became quite clear that nothing was good enough. I tried to explain to them that the YMCA had no authority to interfere in the administration of the camp nor any right to present their complaints to any authority, and I suggested that they instead should approach the Swiss Legation in Berlin or its representative the next time he visited the camp, because as Protecting Power Switzerland had undertaken to handle British interests in Germany during the war. Finally the British Man of Confidence felt that enough was enough, because suddenly he adjourned the meeting by saying: "Now, Friends, will you stop making all those unreasonable complaints about such petty things. Remember, we are British soldiers, and as long as we're wearing British uniforms, we are representing our country and our people at home. The Germans will think that all British are like us, and we have to behave accordingly!"

According to the Geneva Convention of 1929, a belligerent country is allowed to use the labor of all prisoners of war except officers, and in this sense the Germans regarded all airmen as officers. The convention contains very explicit provisions concerning hours of work, which must not exceed those of the country's own workers, and pay, which must not be less than that of the country's own soldiers of equal rank. In practice, however, the pay varied according to the kind of work; not that it really mattered, because a prisoner of war did not have much opportunity to spend his money anyway. The camp's canteen did not provide much, and the ordinary German shops were off-limits to the POWs. But the pay could be saved, and it could be credited to individual POWs to be paid out at the end of the war. The French and the Belgians were even permitted to transfer their savings to their families and relatives in their home countries.

The Geneva Convention also stipulates that prisoners of war must not be employed in the war industry, nor in places of work which might be anticipated targets for air attacks, a provision which was usually rather leniently interpreted, and perhaps rightly so, because what, in fact, is a war industry? Are POWs allowed to repair railway lines? What factories are really not used for the purpose of war? And in the last year of the war in particular, hardly any air attacks upon German territory occurred in which some POWs were not killed along with German civilians.

The big regular camps—the STALAGs—would consist of a main camp and hundreds of hostels: small groups of POWs assigned to work in industry, trade, and farming. Obviously, these hostels provided a cheap and very useful labor force. During the war they were conspicuous sights in daily life all over Germany. You often met POWs assigned to the hostels in the Berlin suburban traffic mornings and evenings, on their way to and from work. Special compartments in the trains were "reserved for POWs." And driving through the German countryside you would often see them working in the fields and meadows, easily recognizable in their uniforms with "KG" painted on their jackets and trouser legs in large, stark yellow letters. They were also employed for such public works as digging and road repair, or for similar work that did not require any particular skills.

Obviously a STALAG constituted a very complicated business. Out of thirty thousand POWs, for instance, only about three thousand would be kept in the main camp; the remaining twenty-seven thousand were scattered around the surrounding area in two to three thousand hostels. The main camp was like the capital of a country of hostels; it housed the "government" which issued all the directives and instructions, and distributed mail and parcels to the POWs. If a hostel was dissolved, the POWs returned to the main camp, and after some time they were sent out to join a new hostel. In the case of serious illness, they were brought back to the main camp for treatment by a medical staff of their own nationality. The administrative network was centered on the main camp's Commandant Headquarters, where employers came to look for workers and where the conditions for work were agreed upon.

In the large hostels, the POWs usually lived in wooden huts containing separate washing facilities, a joint kitchen and dining room, and sometimes additional rooms which served as sitting rooms, a library, a chapel, and so forth for the POWs during their leisure. Other hostels, however, were not as luxurious: the sleeping quarters and the dining room were one—cramped, dark, and humid—and I was often met by a disgusting smell of sweat and filth when I entered the room. The best conditions befell those who were assigned to farming, because they usually lived in one of the outbuildings where they slept on wooden bunks, or perhaps even on some old beds which the farmer had dug out from the attic or some other odd place and furnished with thick mattresses and warm woollen blankets. The farmers were obviously of the opinion that their POWs deserved a good night's sleep after a hard day's work. Furthermore, the food was much better and richer in the country than at any other place, and, as a Serb once told me, "It's quite all right if we boil a few extra potatoes or have a small drink of milk when we're milking a cow."

In factories and elsewhere, where the POWs sometimes outnumbered the German workers, posters had been put up warning the German civilians to be careful about what they said, giving precautionary measures which everybody had better become familiar with and abide by: "Be careful! The enemy is listening! Ignore him! Isolate him!" Only when it was absolutely necessary and in the interest of satisfactory execution of the work was the civilian population allowed to fraternize with the POWs. Any personal or human contact was prohibited and severe punishment would be administered to those who violated the rule, Germans as well as POWs. If sexual intercourse was involved, the punishment was usually three years in prison both for the POWs and for the German women.

There is a lot of truth in the old saying that idleness is the root of all evil. The POWs who were fortunate enough to be put to work were much better equipped to cope with the long years of imprisonment than those who did not work. Work was like a cure; it kept the body in good shape and homesickness and dark thoughts at a distance. Not all places of work, however, were equally inviting, and the sanitary conditions could be appalling. The briquette factories near Leipzig and the cement works at Oschatz, for instance, were surely very dirty and dusty places to work.

Lack of work presented the biggest problem in the Air Force camps and the large officers' camps; these POWs did not have anything to do except what they set up for themselves, so it is not surprising that they were all on edge and often went to pieces; many spent every single day plodding around and around the same barbed-wire fences in the same cramped, often dirty and cold surroundings. Normally they drifted around in pairs, but there were also those who preferred to brood on their own, the "lonely cats" as they were referred to in STALAG LUFT I.

Problems with alcohol did not occur in the prison camps, simply because alcohol was not available. Besides, alcohol could be dangerous: a drunken POW, staggering around and getting too close to the barbed wire could easily get himself and other POWs killed. Some POWs once tried their hands at home brew, but the majority of the POWs were against it, and it was forbidden by the Men of Confidence.

Sex, of course, was a frequent topic for conversation. The overcrowded huts were ideal, I presume, for homosexual activities, but such activities did not take place, at least not openly and not to any known extent. If any kind of homosexual relationship

was discovered, one or the other would immediately be transferred to another camp. As far as I know, no woman ever entered
a POW camp in Germany, and the commandants very effectively
kept the German women away from the barbed-wire fences.

Stealing? Yes, stealing did sometimes occur in the camps,
when need and deprivation became overwhelming and made the
POWs ignore the code of conduct. Hunger was the main reason
for stealing, and even the most honest man was sometimes unable to resist the temptation. But if the culprit was found, his
countrymen—not the Germans—saw to his punishment, a punishment that could be very severe indeed.

So-called "barbed-wire phychosis" lurked just beneath the
surface, ready to strike, especially at those POWs whose imprisonment had lasted a long time. The symptoms were depression
and despair which sometimes led them to engage in rash attempts
at escape which were not adequately prepared. Often the German guards discoverd what was going on along or under the first
row of barbed-wire fences and shot them long before they would
have reached the second row of fences.

Numerous dashes for freedom were made by the POWs in
Germany. In fact, until October 1944, it was the duty of every
British soldier who had been taken prisoner to try to escape and
get back to his own forces, and a lot of them did try. Few, however, avoided recapture. Once, during a visit to a prison camp a
British soldier got up behind me and whispered in my ear, "Pre-
tend not to notice—I'm trying to get out of the camp together
with you!" Fortunately I was able to discourage him when I explained that such an attempt would jeopardize the entire YMCA
relief work. Another British soldier tried to escape disguised and
equipped as a chimney sweep, but at the gate he was stopped by
the German guard who found that his proficiency in German
was rather limited. I also know of two British pilots who dyed
their blankets green, changed them into German uniforms, and
tried to escape posing as German lieutenants.

Some of the POWs thought of nothing else but escape. One
of them was the famous British pilot, Wing Commander Doug-
las Bader, who had lost both legs in an aircraft accident in 1931.

With the aid of two artificial legs and an enormous amount of energy, he had taught himself to dance, play golf, and drive a car, but he had nevertheless been forced to leave the RAF in 1933 due to his condition. I first met him in a prison camp in Saxony; when the war broke out in 1939, he had reported for duty in the RAF, convinced the authorities that he was quite capable of handling an aircraft, got himself a fighter, and participated very actively and efficiently in the August 1940 defence of London, when the Germans launched their extensive air attacks on the British capital. In autumn 1941 his fighter was shot down and he bailed out over German territory, losing both of his artificial legs in the process. When Field Marshal Hermann Göring, chief of the German Air Force, was informed that this man had been captured, and that he had lost his artificial legs when he crashed, he gave his permission for a British Red Cross aircraft to fly over German territory at a specific date and time and drop two new legs for the British pilot. Wing Commander Bader was now able to waltz around the camp at Barth near Rügen and he seemed to have only one thing in mind: to annoy his German keepers as much as possible. He schemed against the commandant and his officers and drove them to exasperation: had they not displayed excessive generosity by allowing this man to get a new pair of artificial legs. And here he was, showing his gratitude by a hostile attitude and constant attempts at escape. After a few months, the German commandant was so thoroughly fed up with the wing commander that he decided to have him removed and transferred to OFLAG IV-C in Colditz, Saxony, which had been set up in an old fortress dating back to the Middle Ages. It really looked like a prison, and it was used only for the most troublesome and industrious escapees. Because the Germans feared that the removal of Wing Commander Bader from the camp at Barth would create turmoil among the POWs, who admired him immensely, they decided to have two platoons of armed soldiers escort him out of the camp. Bader was secretly pleased when he waved good-bye to his countrymen, well aware that they would know how to make good use of an opportunity in which so many guards were concentrating on one single man—a man who did not even have his own two legs.

DAILY LIFE IN THE PRISON CAMPS

The best cure against idleness, homesickness, and mental and spiritual depression is to occupy oneself with something useful and worthwhile. This is true in all circumstances, not least for prisoners of war. And this is precisely what the YMCA POW Aid was all about—providing sound, useful, and worthwhile occupations for the POWs. The YMCA's mission was to help POWs regardless of nationality, race, religion, and political affiliations wherever possible, by negotiating with the authorities as well as by procuring necessary tools and materials: books, writing materials, musical instruments, sports equipment, bibles, hymn books, everything needed for a communion table, and a lot more. Members of the YMCA also made every effort to become friends with the POWs, to win their confidence, to listen to their many requests and wishes brought forward by their Men of Confidence, and to listen attentively to those individual POWs who sometimes ventured to approach them with personal matters and concerns. It proved extremely advantageous to be a citizen of a small country, as I was, and as a rule I did not find it too difficult to win the confidence of the prisoners of war.

Although the YMCA was particularly interested in procuring materials that would benefit the POWs in the fields of education, entertainment, sports, and religion, the organization also replied to numerous individual requests for things like glasses, crutches, hair-cutting machines, special medicine, modeling clay, oil colors, and brushes. If a doctor who was also a POW wanted a cranium to make his lessons more illustrative, he would address his request to the YMCA. It was very easy to detect the nationality of POWs from their needs and wishes, and the YMCA wanted nothing more than to satisfy everybody's needs, although not everybody's wishes were reasonable. When, for instance, American POWs asked for ten typewriters for the teaching of a single class, they asked for the impossible; when, as actually happened, they asked for one hundred footballs, we turned their request down, knowing very well that just one or two footballs would work wonders among the Russian POWs— who by far outnumbered the Americans—if only the commandant would allow us to do so.

The POW camps afforded countless examples of altruistic and unselfish men who spent their time and abilities making life more tolerable and pleasant for their comrades. They did not spare any effort to provide a variety of entertainment, such as concerts, lectures, plays, and sporting events. Gradually the camp libraries became quite well supplied with light literature as well as textbooks, and they were much frequented. The books were studied as intensely and systematically as conditions permitted, and the majority of POWs worked very persistently to gain something positive from their captivity. For such POWs time rarely passed slowly, and when the evening came many of them found with satisfaction that the day had not been wasted after all, and that their studying might prove to be of practical importance in the future. Languages were the most studied subjects of all. Teachers of language were normally plentiful, and the necessary books, dictionaries, and so forth, were provided by the YMCA.

The most diligent POWs appeared to be the Poles, at least in the camps I visited, such as, for instance, a camp in the small town Woldenberg (today Dobiegniew), situated southeast of Stettin, where about sixty-five hundred Polish officers and a few hundred NCOs and men were held prisoner during the entire war. Among the POWs were ten professors and thirty-five highly educated teachers from universities and institutions of higher education in Poland, and already during the winter of 1939–40 these men had taken the initiative to establish a camp Council of Education, and had set for themselves the task of initiating education in various subjects and on various levels.

I visited this camp regularly, every other month, and I am convinced that a better-managed camp university could not be found in any other German prison camp. Each day, more than four thousand men participated in one or more of the many different courses which were arranged and offered by the university, and which continued until the camp was liberated by Russian forces in March 1945. Foreign languages held the greatest interest, but many other subjects in the humanities and sciences were listed in the camp's catalogue of organized studies and lectures. The POWs could choose from among many possibilities: one might prefer to have a teacher all to himself for a few lessons every week, others got together in small groups of three to five men with one teacher, and still others chose to attend the courses and lectures arranged by the Council of Education. The work was just as methodical as in any other school and the teaching was organized on different levels to suit the pupils' background and qualifications.

It took an enormous number of textbooks, dictionaries, notebooks, pencils, and so forth to keep such a university going, but we were able to provide them, thanks mainly to the Swedish YMCA, because Sweden had no paper rationing. The teaching was free, and in their leisure time the POWs prepared themselves or reread what they had been taught in previous lessons. It was even possible, once in a while, to take exams in different subjects, and many POWs did so and thereby obtained a diploma to certify that they had spent their time of captivity in a useful and positive way. The teaching thus filled a large gap in a prisoner's daily life; it broke the monotony and allowed teachers to maintain and supplement their knowledge and capabilities.

In that same camp more than two hundred POWs did research on their own initiative and spent their time writing papers and theses for doctorates. Upon completing these papers they had them censored by the German authorities and, after approval, the YMCA was often asked to take them into custody until the end of the war. In the hope of avoiding their destruction during the last days of the war, 104 scientific papers were handed over to the YMCA by POWs in the Woldenberg camp as late as January 1945, so that they could be safely dispatched and kept with the YMCA World Alliance in Geneva.

One day I asked one of the professors in the Woldenberg camp why the Polish POWs attached such great importance to studies and training instead of displaying more interest in sports and athletics as did, for instance, the British POWs. His answer was, "We know that there will be a day after tomorrow, a day when we shall return to a free Poland, and for that day we want to prepare ourselves, so that we can help build up what the war has broken down and destroyed." His words displayed a wise and optimistic attitude toward the future, and that was a valuable foundation on which to build. The YMCA was happy to try to help these POWs reach their ultimate goal.

The majority of these diligent Polish prisoners of war tried to get home as soon as the possibility arose in 1945, and I am convinced that they played a valuable part in the reconstruction of Poland, which had to be rebuilt on the ruins and destruction caused by the war. But after the war I also met former Woldenberg camp POWs who, in their desolation over the fate of Poland, had sought a new home in Great Britain, and who "are still waiting for the day when Poland shall become a free country." I visited some of them in spring 1947 when I was working in Great Britain, and their feelings could not be mistaken: "When we were prisoners of war in Germany, the Red Cross and the YMCA came to visit us and helped us in many ways. Today nobody seems to care about us anymore. We were needed while there was a war on, and we paid our share for the victory of the Allies. But now we feel deserted, and that Great Britain would prefer to see the last of us; if we want to make our living in this country, the only possibility left to us is to descend into the coal mines." A former lawyer said this to me, very quietly, and he added: "But then, why should I go on living. My wife and my two children are in Siberia—provided they are still alive, that is." After many years of fighting patiently and doggedly to keep up courage, many of these Poles gave up and submitted to pessimism, depression, morbid thoughts, and suicide. "I hate the Germans," a young Polish officer exclaimed, and I could not soothe him by answering that nothing good ever comes from hating, because many of them had very good reasons for their hatred: numerous Polish families, women and children, young people and old people, had been dragged to Siberia during the time Germany and Russia were allies. I have met some of these POWs. Some wanted the YMCA to help them search for their spouses in the Soviet Union. "My parents have disappeared," one said despairingly. "I don't know where they are." In such circumstances as these, it was completely immaterial how many books or footballs I had brought along in my car. I felt utterly empty-handed and helpless, and the only thing I could do was listen to them in silence, and then quietly try to show them my understanding and sympathy.

Interest in the Church and in Christianity varied from nationality to nationality. The Poles, Belgians, and French, being Catholics, showed a great deal of interest, the British a bit less, and the Yugoslavs almost none at all. In some of the Russian camps I saw a few chapels, usually very artistically decorated with crosses and pictures symbolizing the Orthodox Church's icons. On two occasions, I met Russian POWs acting as chaplains in the camps. Unfortunately they knew only Russian, which I did not, so I could not really discuss anything with them. The German commandant, however, told me that small groups of POWs gathered each day in the humble chapel to say their prayers.

Naturally, the Christian activities in the camps enjoyed the YMCA's wholehearted support, and the POW Aid was considered a charitable deed. The tasks of a field delegate did not include preaching to the POWs; this was done by their own chaplains in their own languages. However, it was the task of the YMCA to help the chaplains carry out their ministrations as satisfactorily as possible. The content and execution of church services were left entirely to the POWs themselves. Just as several different nationalities were represented in any one camp, so were a multitude of different religions and ecclesiastical affiliations, and it was an established rule in the work of the YMCA that every POW was entitled to assistance, whatever his race and religion. As many Bibles and other works of religious literature as possible were therefore provided and distributed among the POWs, most often through the chaplains. I remember being asked to procure some copies of the Koran, and receiving a request from a few hundred Sikhs from north India, held prisoner in the POW camp in Annaberg, for some copies of their Holy Scriptures, which we indeed succeeded in procuring.

During visits to the camps, a meeting with the chaplains was a recurring item on the agenda. The YMCA assisted in procuring not only Bibles, hymn books, and religious literature, but also host and wine, vestments, small reed organs, candles by the thousands, and other kinds of church decorations. If too many chaplains lived in one camp, it would normally only take a brief conversation with their Man of Confidence and the German commandant to have one or more of them transferred to other camps, where there were no chaplains and where their work would be far more needed. Within my area of responsibility in Germany, I remember a French camp for army personnel which housed only three thousand POWs, of which no fewer than fourteen were Catholic chaplains, while elsewhere thirty-one thousand French POWs were assigned to 542 hostels almost without any kind of church ministration. Obviously an even distribution of chaplains would benefit themselves as well as their countrymen. Sometimes the distance between the hostels presented a problem to a chaplain who had to minister more than one hostel, but often the problem was solved by making a bicycle available to him, either through the German camp headquarters or, sometimes, through the YMCA POW Aid.

Services held at the hostels were simple: those attending sang a hymn or two, one of them then read from the Bible and perhaps added a few personal remarks, and they finished by saying their prayers together. Nevertheless, because of these services, Sundays did carry the impress of being the Lord's Days, and they helped lift the souls of the POWs up and above their earthly and daily lives so that they were ready to begin a new week of work with sufficient energy.

Most chaplains carried out a formidable and admirable amount of work in those camps, within which they were themselves prisoners. But laymen would also act as chaplains if there were none, or assist resident chaplains in their church work. I remember in particular some British and American teachers and some employees of the Australian and British YMCA whose tireless efforts were much appreciated by all the POWs.

One Sunday I visited a hostel at Bodenbach near the border with Czechoslovakia, where 260 British POWs were employed at repairing roads and railway lines. They were quartered in a former industrial plant which had been converted into two sleeping rooms and one joint sitting and dining room. I arrived early in the day and was invited to breakfast by the Man of Confidence. "You'll attend the service, I hope?" he asked, and I said, "yes, but you don't have a chaplain, do you?" "No," he answered, "but we do have two school teachers who are used to working in Sunday schools at home, and they hold services on Sundays." By the time the service was about to begin, about two hundred POWs had gathered in the sitting room. Whether it was curiosity directed at me—an outsider—or whether it was an urge to attend the service that made so many turn up, I do not know, but I was happy to be able to attend. The service lasted only about thirty minutes and was held in the form of prayers. There were no hymn books and no New Testament; they had all been lost together with the POWs' other belongings when they had been captured. But luckily the two teachers knew some hymns by heart, and they had copied a few of them on empty cigarette packages and other small pieces of paper which were distributed at the beginning of the service. When the first hymn had been sung, one of the teachers related a narrative from the New Testament which everybody already knew—or at least ought to have known—and he concluded with a few personal comments, "what this narrative tells us in our present situation. . . ." No protests, no giggling, no smoking—only quiet attention. The teacher finished by saying a prayer, thanking the Lord for His goodness, and praying for the Church and all its work, for peace in the world, "for our country and our people at home, for our king and all our leaders." We then said the Lord's Prayer together. Finally, the blessing was announced, yet another hymn was sung, and the service was over. Unpretentious and Low Church yes, but to me an unforgettable experience, a day so very different from the other days of the week. It was Sunday indeed, both for the POWs and for their "chaplains."

The lack of a proper church or chapel did not prevent the POWs from getting together to sing hymns and to say prayers. I once attended a service at a big manor in North Germany, where approximately fifty American POWs were assigned to farming.

The service took place in a barn, and the POWs were sitting around on bundles of straw and on some potato wagons which had been pushed into the barn. A couple of mouth organs delivered the music for the hymns. In a hostel nearby, some Polish and French POWs made it their habit to sing a Polish and a French hymn together, say the Lord's Prayer, and make the sign of the cross each night before turning in. Hours such as these, spent with captive men in hostels or in small, narrow and dark huts of the camps, often sitting around a small, crude altar, are hours which I shall always remember.

Most of the large camps had their own chapels, usually built by the prisoners themselves. A lot of care was put into the building of such chapels, and into the decoration of their interiors with beautiful crosses and altars, often ingeniously carved by one of the artists in the camp. A pious Belgian turned the cover of a herring barrel into a finely carved figure of the Virgin Mary; it bore the inscription "Notre Mère de la Liberation" (our Mother of Freedom); by that inscription he expressed not only his own but every POW's great longing and plea: "Lord, Father in Heaven, Blessed Virgin, Lord Jesus Christ, let the hour of liberation be near, and we shall thank You and praise You."

There was no doubt that the camp chapel was the house of God, different from all other buildings in the camp. If there was only one chapel in a camp, a Catholic service, sometimes more than one, was held on Sunday mornings, and Protestant services were held late afternoons and evenings. Mass was normally celebrated every day. The chapel was never closed and there was always somebody in there: one POW after another would walk quietly in, remove his cap, make the sign of a cross, kneel, look at the Virgin Mary, and silently say his prayers. When he had finished, he would get up and go out as quietly as he had entered.

The chaplains' sermons had to be officially censored by the camp's German security officers, and in most cases, as far as I know, that presented no problems. A sermon had to be delivered for censoring not later than noon on Friday, and it was returned to the chaplain on the Saturday, ready for the service on Sunday.

In Prenzlau, services were held in the open if weather permitted. Several hundred Belgian POWs gathered for Mass on the parole field. Everybody joined in the singing of the hymns, which could be heard all over the camp. The chaplain delivered his sermon, which always held immediate importance and much seriousness. It was clear that the POWs listened attentively, and they got down on their knees during the final prayers, which the chaplain spoke on behalf of all of them. The chaplain prayed for their relatives at home: "Father in Heaven, look upon our families with love as we are separated from them. Protect them and keep them from all evil, let them never feel lonely or afraid. Grant Thee that we may return when it is Thy will, without disgrace or shame. Let us, bound together as we are across land and sea by the invisible chains of Thy love, be drawn nearer to Thee and to each other in Thy name. Amen." Then they all said the Lord's Prayer and the service was over. The monotonous wandering around and around the barbed-wire fences could be resumed.

As a visitor from the outside, I was often amazed by the amount of interest which was shown in the services and other Christian activities in the camps. One of the reasons for this may be that during their captivity the POWs had plenty of time to think about the meaning of life. Those who were customary churchgoers were happy and grateful that the Church was there with them and that there were chaplains to hold the services. And on several occasions POWs who had not been used to going to church very often and to whom Christianity meant little or nothing began to feel a growing interest in spiritual matters, and realized that Christianity did, after all, play a part in their lives. The number of churchgoers obviously varied from camp to camp, "depending on the preacher" as we would probably say in Denmark. In some camps the percentage of churchgoers was low, but in others it could be as high as 85–90 percent. Once a commandant said to me, "Every Sunday morning I see one thousand prisoners of war literally running toward the chapel to be able to get one of the six hundred seats available."

Of course the main task of the chaplains was the Sunday services. But the church was much more than a mere Sunday church. Through the establishment of study groups and Bible classes, the chaplains often became actively involved in the educational programs and daily life of the camps. Many chaplains—especially the British and the American ones—had a hand in almost everything that went on in their camps. They often took the lead on the sports field, and as often as not they took the initiative to set up a choir, band, or theatrical group. With a sense of responsibility, solicitude, and perseverance, they did their utmost to divert the POWs' attention from their captivity, and in large measure they succeeded, mainly due to the substantial influence they had obtained through their personal involvement in the daily lives of the POWs.

When spirits were low, the chaplains were often able to cheer up the prisoners. This was demonstrated to me in autumn 1944 during my visits to several Polish camps in Pomerania and Mecklenburg. I entered the gate at Woldenberg, and the first POW I met happened to be a Catholic chaplain. He welcomed me and said: "How good it is to see you. We really need all the help we can get from the YMCA, because in these days we must have something on the program every single hour of the day to prevent us from despairing over the grievous fate that has befallen our homes and our families in Warsaw." Some readers will probably remember that in September 1944 the Poles tried to liberate Warsaw from the German occupation in hopes of bidding the advancing Russian army welcome to a free Polish capital. But the uprising in Warsaw failed terribly and the Poles bled to death. Following sixty-three days of courageous attempts, they had to give up and surrender. The survivors were taken to concentration camps or executed; four-fifths of Warsaw was razed to the ground with such German thoroughness that even the trees in the city parks were cut down. The German attitude was that the Polish capital should be wiped off the face of the Earth. This brutal defeat made an overwhelming impression on the Polish POWs, and some very hard weeks followed during which the atmosphere in the camps was so bad that it threatened to paralyze any kind of activity.

It is hard to determine within which field of activity the YMCA POW Aid was most important. Books—entertaining as well as educational—were always in great demand and normally at the top of the many wish lists the prisoners gave to us. Over a period of nine years, the YMCA World Alliance tried to satisfy the need of thousands of prisoners for reading materials in many different languages, and more than ten million books were distributed in the prison camps. Fortunately there were many sources from which to draw: the Catholic churches of Poland and France, the Christian Students' Movement, and the YMCA and YWCA in many countries all initiated collections and donated thousands upon thousands of books. More than 3.5 million books were printed and published by the YMCA office in Stockholm and donated to the relief work in Germany and Great Britain.

Each prison camp had its own library. The numerous hostels were served by so-called "Wanderbüchereien"—"wandering books"—library boxes containing about fifty books each, which were circulated to all the different hostels. A POW was in charge of the library, and it was his responsibility to see that all hostels that belonged under his main camp were served as well as possible. As a rule, a bindery was attached to the library and a few POWs were occupied with bookbinding and repairing books. We did not have any serious problems procuring the materials for such works. At the beginning they could be acquired locally, and later we had them dispatched from Sweden.

The British colonial troops from Asia and Africa who ended up in camps in Germany, however, suffered from a great lack of suitable reading materials; it was almost impossible to get ahold of books in their own languages. For instance, the more than three thousand Indian soldiers who were prisoners in a camp at Annaberg in Saxony had only one hundred books at their disposal. The Americans and British were more fortunate. Not only were they allowed to have books sent from their relatives at home, but they also received stacks of literature in the English language from the YMCA. A cable forwarded to the office in Geneva and a subsequent contact with London or New York would see to that quite easily.

Second to books came musical instruments. Music and theater meant a lot to many prisoners, and each camp of sufficient size had its own band—sometimes even more than one—and often its own theatrical group as well. The Serbian, Croatian, and Russian POWs were the most modest in their requests for musical instruments, and if the YMCA was able to get them a few accordions, a guitar, or perhaps a few mouth organs, they were most grateful. After working for hours and on Sundays, they often sat together in small groups and sang the songs of their homeland, and you could see from the expressions on their faces that these simple songs absorbed them completely and, for a short time, diverted their minds from captivity. "We sing and we play music and we long for home," one of them said to me.

In the large camps there were normally several bands. In Prenzlau, for instance, a prison camp housed thirty-nine hundred Belgian officers, one of whom was a young lieutenant of the reserve who, in civilian life, had been employed as a conductor at the Brussels Radio. Assisted by the YMCA, he succeeded in setting up a large symphony orchestra consisting of eighty-five musicians. He also took the initiative to establish a choir of more than 250 singers. It was a great experience to be invited to a concert in Prenzlau. The invitation was always written or printed in calligraphic letters, and almost always in Danish. When I arrived, I was handed a program, also done in calligraphy, and reserved a seat right in the middle of the front row, next to the camp's senior officer, General van den Bergen and his personal staff. When I was present, a piece of Danish music would always be played midway through the concert, and when the concert was over the Man of Confidence or the senior Belgian officer himself would get up and, in a few words, express his own and his countrymen's thanks to the orchestra and also to the YMCA for the assistance the prisoners received from the World Alliance. Then, as the guest of honor, I was expected to convey the YMCA's greetings, and I did so with much pleasure, trying to convince the POWs that they were not forgotten and that they could rest assured that friends all over the world were thinking of them, sharing their hopes, and willing to help them until the day when—as free men—they could return to their homes. I always felt that I was shown extraordinary courtesy during my visits to that camp. The POWs' gratefulness apparently knew no limits, and a quite undeserved honor fell to my share. They had a great and unfulfilled need just to be with an ordinary civilian in the midst of their military environment, and I, as a YMCA employee, could help satisfy that need.

Similar experiences in other camps come to mind, especially during my visits to the Polish camp in Woldenberg. Here, too, a professional conductor was in charge of the camp's symphony orchestra, and he also saw to it that the camp could present a well-functioning choir. Early in the war, the Polish YMCA had dispatched music and musical instruments to the camp. I enjoyed the classical concerts and I enjoyed the impressive choir, with approximately 300 male voices. Separately and together the choir and the orchestra were capable of performing in a way which surely compared with the best performances in European concert halls. Conversely, it was sometimes a mixed pleasure to be invited to a concert in a British or—in particular—an American prison camp, because I did not share their love for the saxophone, and the saxophone was really their dominant instrument. I was happy to attend, however, because the POWs had been so kind as to invite me.

Most of the large prison camps had their own theater which was able to provide entertainment to the entire camp; a new play was set up every week and most of them were repeated so many times that everybody had the opportunity to watch them. The quality of the performances naturally varied, depending on the talents of the available "actors." The theaters were often works of art in themselves. In many camps, a hut was converted into a theater and concert hall. In other camps, lack of space prevented the use of an entire hut for this purpose and the stage and theater equipment had to be moved from place to place, but the POWs displayed much ingenuity in making such necessary accessories as curtains, carpets, and lighting effects so that dismantling and reassembling were easy to manage. The actual stage was usually small, but as the hut was long and narrow, there was more than sufficient space backstage for changing and makeup. In most cases, a prompter's box and an orchestra pit could also be set up, and it was amazing, under the circumstances, to see the kinds of entertainment it was possible to offer. The actors, it must be remembered, worked during the day just like the other POWs and had only a few evening hours at their disposal during which they were able to rehearse.

A show would in one way or another involve about twenty men directly, and many more indirectly, in the staging and actual performance: wings had to be drawn, made, and painted; costumes for the performers had to be sewn; wigs had to be made; lights had to be installed, and so forth. Wigs, for instance, were made of untwined hemp rope, and the tailors in the camp worked wonders with such items as coats, dresses, and skirts, which they made from sackcloth and painted in the required colors. The YMCA had to procure an enormous amount of crepe paper for making summer dresses and other ladies' garments, especially for the French prison camps. Women's parts in a play were no obstacle at all; one or several slightly built POWs were always available and brave enough to tackle such parts. In a French POW camp, the POWs were even bold enough to rehearse and go through with the performance of a play that contained female parts only. And it is well that they did, because the play proved a great success!

In a POW camp in Arnswalde, twenty-two hundred Polish officers lived in a military barracks. There were so many actors among these officers that it was possible to set up a show every Sunday afternoon at three o'clock and again at five o'clock. The actors got together in the camp's "dramatic club" and eagerly engaged themselves in doing something valuable, to the delight of all their fellow prisoners, who greatly appreciated their efforts.

I do not think that any activity played a more important role than sports. The camp commandants recognized that football and other ball games were an excellent remedy against loneliness and depression, and in numerous instances they had sports fields established and helped procure the necessary equipment, if not locally, then through the YMCA. The Man of Confidence in one of the French camps told me that they had fourteen football teams in the camp, made up of men from eleven different French provinces. "We have football matches as often as possible; we have tournaments between the teams and we have hundreds of onlookers, including the German guards and the ever present barbed-wire fences, and for an hour or so we forget where we are and why." To a request for more footballs "to replace the ones we have worn out," he added cautiously that, "as a matter of fact, we could also do with some more boxing gloves and Ping-Pong balls."

In a field hospital in Königswartha, I often called on some one hundred British POWs who had contracted tuberculosis. One winter day one of the doctors and the chaplain broke up our conversation by saying, "You must excuse us, but we have an appointment to play football with the boys in ten minutes." There was a heavy snowfall outside, but that didn't prevent twenty-two of the fittest among the patients from turning up for a football match and many more from watching it, standing around in slush and sludge. This made the German doctor in charge of the hospital and the commandant exclaim in one voice: "Yes, they are absolutely crazy, these British. They have to be fatally ill not to play football. But try teaching them how to peel potatoes, that's impossible!"

FROM BERLIN TO SAGAN

During 1943, the atmosphere in Berlin grew more and more tense. Already in the spring the British had greatly intensified their air attacks. Air-raid alarms were sounding almost every evening at around nine o'clock, with the German radio issuing warnings that "strong formations of enemy aircraft are approaching northern Germany, direction—Berlin." Then we knew we would have fifteen to twenty minutes to seek protection before the bombers would reach the city. The searchlights would begin to radiate toward the sky, antiaircraft guns would begin to roar, and the air would echo with explosions. Aircraft were hit and most of them went up in flames; sometimes parachutes opened and we saw men hanging in the air like tiny dots. We were passive spectators to a drama unfolding before our eyes, and it was impossible to be neutral under the circumstances. We were convinced that the day when the Allied forces would be strong enough to direct their intense air attacks against the German capital, and thereby turn the fortunes of war, was drawing nearer and nearer. The violent bombing of Hamburg in July, causing heavy casualties and much destruction, had repercussions throughout Germany: people who had been evacuated and whose homes had been destroyed arrived in Berlin and could tell us about the disasters and horrors which the entire population of Hamburg had suffered. Each day Berlin's newspapers urged the population to keep calm and encouraged Berliners to take all sorts of precautions. At railway stations posters were put up with new propaganda slogans, such as "Unser Glaube an den Sieg ist unerschüttlich" (our faith in victory is unshakable). Nevertheless, this faith was beginning to falter as more and more air-raid shelters were dug out in parks and gardens all over the city.

On 1 August, the Ministry of Propaganda issued a proclamation to the population of Berlin signed by Minister Goebbels himself: all women and children were to leave the capital immediately and proceed to safer places in eastern and southern Germany. The YMCA POW Aid also began to seriously consider moving from Berlin; our office was in Wilhelmstrasse, right in the heart of the city and very close to many of the most important government offices. The decision to try to locate a safer residence was finally made on 24 August, because of what had happened in the late evening of 23 August: several hundred British bombers had launched the war's most vehement attack on the center of Berlin. I had taken refuge in the large air-raid shelter at the subway platforms at the nearby Anhalter Bahnhof. When the all clear sounded I came out into the open and started to walk back to Wilhelmstrasse. I saw houses and buildings on fire all around me. Berlin was in flames: heaps of broken glass and rubble were scattered all over, making traffic in the streets extremely difficult; just outside our office, a bomb had crashed and made a forty foot hole in the ground before it exploded. The blast must have gone straight up into the air, because the building that housed our office was still standing, though it had reeled violently from the explosion and the windows had been smashed to pieces. The bomb must have burst a gas pipe, because out of the bomb crater a flame rose several feet high, straight into the air. Inside the office, typewriters, papers, and files were scattered on the floor, and glass splinters and plaster were cluttered everywhere.

The next morning found Berlin utterly paralyzed. Telephones and telegraphs were out of order. A Swedish colleague who lived in one of the suburbs spent three hours getting to the center of Berlin, a trip which normally took only eighteen minutes by subway. We were very concerned when we started to collect the papers in the office and tidy up as best we could, and rightly so, because the bombers returned and continued their heavy attacks the following evenings and nights. It was difficult to get any sleep before three o'clock in the morning. One particular night I remember taking the shortest route through Anhalter Strasse on the way home from the air-raid shelter at about two o'clock: we saw houses on fire on both sides of the street; it was as light as day and unbearable heat and smoke surrounded us. Here and there the asphalt of the street was burning, and on some streets more than half of the blocks of flats were completely destroyed, leaving thousands of Berliners homeless. Looting became more and more common, unless properties were carefully looked after. The bombing grew in intensity, and we felt an urgent need to move the POW Aid.

By the beginning of September Pastor Erik Christensen had found new premises in Sagan, a small town in the province of Silesia. In a former restaurant, the "Augustinergarten," we settled down in offices complete with storage capacity, much more pleasant and spacious than those we had left behind in Berlin.

Sagan was a small, peaceful, provincial town with about twenty-two thousand inhabitants. It was situated approximately 125 miles southeast of Berlin near the old Polish border by the river Bober, which is a tributary of the river Oder. A beautiful castle dominated the town; during the war it was used as a hospital for wounded German soldiers. Life in Sagan was influenced by the presence of prisoners of war. The town had a paper and textile industry, and the workers were mainly recruited from the POWs. Two large prison camps were situated on the outskirts of the town: a regular army camp, STALAG VIII-C, housing many thousand Allied soldiers, and STALAG LUFT III, where about fifteen thousand airmen were held. Mornings and evenings we would see hundreds of Frenchmen, easily recognizable because of their berets, on their way to and from work. What made Sagan so well-known during the war was undoubtedly STALAG LUFT III. It had been constructed at the end of 1942, and in two years the prison population mushroomed from fifteen hundred to fifteen thousand men.

Our office soon became the center of much activity. The news of our arrival spread, and more and more prisoners of war looked in to meet us. The most frequent visitors were the Frenchmen, because they were free to move about without German guards. But British, American, and Yugoslavian POWs also came visiting; after getting permission from the camp commandants they would come, escorted by an armed guard, to inquire into the possibility of procuring more musical instruments, sports equipment, or books. Sometimes they even came from far away and had to stay overnight. Such occasions were much appreciated by the POWs—and also by their guards—because it meant that for a short while they were able to get away from the daily routine of the prison camps. We had proper beds to accommodate the POWs and we were sometimes able to take them for a drive in the area. We tried to make life as pleasant and varied as possible during the few hours they were "free men." As far as I know, nobody ever abused the YMCA's hospitality by attempting to escape, smuggling letters, or trying any other illegal activities.

It was difficult to receive reliable information about how many POWs from the Allied air forces the Germans had captured. The number grew from week to week, and at least forty thousand British and American airmen—officers and crew—were held prisoner in autumn 1944 in seven different camps. I do not recall ever having met a Russian pilot, and I have no knowledge about what happened to them. Airmen in general constituted an elite among POWs, because the physical demands placed upon air force personnel were among the strictest of all. Many airmen arrived in the camps with heavy wounds following air combat and crashes, wounds that needed extensive care and attention. In all air force camps the Germans set up hospitals, special huts with forty to sixty beds evenly distributed among the available rooms; they were run by German doctors with a staff of POW doctors. Surgical cases were transferred to special hospitals, and if X-ray pictures were necessary, the patients were taken to a local German hospital.

As I have already said, all airmen were treated as officers and therefore not allowed to do any work; they had to pass the time as best they could. As a result, these camps made much greater demands on the YMCA POW Aid than did the regular army camps, and the airmen initiated numerous activities. Although they were ingenious and clever in helping themselves, they nevertheless had great needs which the YMCA had to try to satisfy.

The number of POWs in STALAG LUFT III gradually grew, and it was therefore converted into several compounds. Each compound was organized as a proper camp with its own Man of Confidence, chaplains, doctors, chapel, school, theater, choir, band, sports field, and so forth. For reasons of security, contact between the different compounds in the camp was not allowed. Only the senior American and British officers were permitted to move around freely between the compounds.

In several ways, the Sagan camp was similar to the Polish and Belgian officers' camps. Lively activity prevailed from morning until late evening. Schools and camp universities with highly qualified staffs were established; talent and initiative were abundantly displayed, and many airmen took advantage of the opportunity to study a subject and to graduate.

Theatrical performances were a good remedy against idleness, gloom, and depression. They occupied numerous people, actors as well as craftsmen and workmen. The airmen had, of course, built the camp's theater hall themselves, and they had allowed for plenty of space for the stage and the orchestra. The theater could hold as many as three to four hundred seats, comfortable chairs made of the large containers in which the Red Cross parcels normally arrived. Plays were shown as many times as necessary to enable all the POWs to watch them once. The plays—comedies, tragedies, even operas with music and text—were often written by somebody in the camp. POWs were happy to take part in the rehearsals, and the performances were enjoyed immensely by most of the POWs.

Music, however, was probably the best cure against despair and homesickness; each compound in the camp had several different bands and orchestras. Polish, Belgian, and French POWs favored classical music, the Americans favored jazz, and the British promenade orchestras were also extremely popular. In addition a "record player concert" was broadcast once a week via the camp's speaker system, which the YMCA had helped procure.

The air force camp in Sagan had seven British and American chaplains, Catholic as well as Protestant, who diligently took care of all church matters in the camp. Through their ministrations, teaching, and countless personal conversations with POWs, they gave spiritual comfort to their fellow prisoners. This was highly appreciated by many and looked upon with respect by all. In addition to the traditional Sunday services, there were evening services once a week throughout the year and, naturally, Christmas and Easter services. A lieutenant—an organist who had graduated from the university and had a degree in music theory—provided the church music, and he was also in charge of a choir of twenty to twenty-five volunteer members who participated in the services. Many church concerts were performed during, for instance, the week of Easter, when Händel's "Messiah" was on the program. It was repeated so many times that everybody who wanted to attend was able to do so.

Sagan was the scene of the greatest and most famous escape attempt during the war, when eighty British airmen succeeded in escaping from the camp during the night of 23 March 1944. They had dug a 125 foot tunnel from a point beneath one of the huts to a place outside the barbed-wire fences, escaped through it, slipped into the forests nearby and disappeared in all directions under cover of darkness. Many of them carried railway tickets for different frontier stations; the tickets had been printed in Great Britain and smuggled into the camp in tins and parcels. Digging the tunnel had taken a couple months. Its entrance was just beneath a stove; the floor planks could be removed to allow POWs down for digging and replaced at the end of each night. The POWs had invented an ingenious device by which fresh air was pumped into the tunnel to the men who were working there; electric light had also been installed, and planks from the Red Cross containers served to shore up the walls to keep the tunnel from collapsing. Considering the primitive tools available to the POWs it was an impressive project, and even more impressive was their success in keeping it a secret from the German "snoopers" and carrying through with the escape on that particular spring night.

The escape created much furor, not only in Sagan, but in all of Germany, the Netherlands, Belgium, and France. Roads were blocked and all train travelers were checked numerous times during the following days. The day after the escape I drove from Berlin to Sagan, a stretch of 130 miles, and I was stopped fourteen times by the German police or Home Guard, who wanted to check and recheck my papers. Their suspicion apparently knew no limits. At one point I was confronted with an especially fussy Gestapo man who went as far as opening the hood of my car to see if an escaped POW might be hiding there. I gave a slight smile at this example of German thoroughness, and when he asked me in an irritated voice if I could swear that there wasn't a POW hiding in the back of the car, I answered with a firm yes. Still the man did not seem to believe me, so he went to the back of the car where the charcoal generator was installed and opened its cover to make sure. He should not have done that. As always, when fresh air hit the generator the gas exploded in flames three feet high, and the poor man was left with much less hair than before.

Out of the eighty men who made the escape from the camp, only three reached Great Britain safely; the remaining seventy-seven were recaptured, one of them only a few hundred yards from the Swiss border. With complete disregard for every legal right of the POWs, the Gestapo immediately executed forty-seven of them, a war crime for which the Germans have had to pay after the war.

The German camp commandant in Sagan, Colonel Friederich von Lindeiner, was held responsible for the Great Escape, removed from his post at once, and sent to the front in northern France, where he was later captured by British forces. He was a fine and considerate officer and had, for several years, lived in both Great Britain and the United States as a businessman and representative for his German firm. In spring 1947 I met the colonel in a prison camp near the Scottish-English border. It was an unexpected pleasure to see him again, and he thanked me profusely for the YMCA POW Aid "in Sagan and now also here." Shortly afterward he was taken back to West Germany, still as a POW, where he was accused of war crimes, but former British and American POWs came to their commandant's rescue. They wrote a letter to the court requesting that Colonel von Lindeiner be cleared of all suspicion of participating in any crime whatsoever and that he be released immediately: "No prisoner of war will ever claim that a commandant of a prison camp is a nice, kind-hearted, and considerate person. Nevertheless, we consider Colonel von Lindeiner to be exactly that, a nice, kind-hearted and considerate person," was one of the statements in the letter. The YMCA POW Aid would have said exactly the same had we been asked.

The news of the execution of the forty-seven British POWs aroused a storm of rage and resulted in a very tense atmosphere in the prison camp. The POWs were familiar with the provisions in the Geneva Convention about the treatment of POWs. They knew their rights and obligations perfectly well: it was a gross crime to punish POWs who had tried to escape with death. With the permission of the German High Command the POWs later erected a monument on the camp's small cemetery in memory of the men who had been so callously murdered. The monument was made of sandstone which the Germans supplied, and the YMCA procured a plate of copper which had been engraved with the names of the forty-seven airmen, and with the words: "In memory of the officers who gave their lives." The Germans arranged a formal inauguration in which representatives of the Swiss Protecting Power and the International Red Cross participated. There was a great deal of surprise and also some bitterness that the YMCA POW Aid had not been invited. The reason was probably that the Germans suspected that materials procured by the YMCA POW Aid had been misused in the preparations for the Great Escape.

After the Great Escape the camp in Sagan was never the same, and in the following months the surveillance of POWs was doubled. Members of the POW Aid were still allowed to enter the camp, but now we were constantly watched by German officers who escorted us during our visits and who listened attentively to everything which was said. A Swedish colleague wanted to spend Christmas together with the POWs in STALAG LUFT III. Strong forces, however, worked tersely to prevent it and only after long negotiations with the new German commandant staff and the exchange of numerous letters did my colleague succeed in obtaining the desired permission. Over the following weeks, the YMCA received many tokens indicating that this visit to the POWs just then, at a time of the year when they were perhaps most reminded of their families and homes was greatly appreciated, was an assurance to them that they had not been abandoned after all.

THE YMCA AND THE GESTAPO

The secret state police—the Gestapo—ran very thorough checks on all foreigners in Germany. Those who did not work were considered undesirables and exiled or sent to labor camps. In spite of the Gestapo's hostile attitude toward the YMCA POW Aid, YMCA employees were permitted to work in Germany, because high-ranking officials and officers in the Foreign Ministry and in the German High Command looked upon the activities of the YMCA with sympathy, and they took every opportunity to express their gratitude for what the YMCA did to help German POWs in other countries. Additionally, the High Command saw our work as necessary to divert and relieve the worst dissatisfaction of the POWs; as the Germans themselves were unable to procure materials which were essential to keep the POWs occupied during their leisure time, why not let the YMCA—which had the will as well as the means to procure such materials—do it for them?

The Gestapo worked in secret. Nobody saw their spies, but

we knew they were there, watching us as we traveled by train, stayed at hotels, or called on camps. Even during our work in the camps we could not avoid direct contact with the Gestapo, because to each camp a so-called "Abwehroffizier" was attached, a security officer, normally a party officeholder, who for practical reasons wore the customary army uniform. Most times we were escorted by the commandant himself, but he usually asked his security officer to accompany us too; in security matters, even commandants had to abide by their security officers.

Nothing was allowed into a camp without having passed through the security section; everything was carefully searched. As far as I know, nothing illegal has ever been smuggled into a camp together with YMCA equipment. But I know of several attempts to smuggle in German money, well hidden—though not well enough!—in records mailed by private persons from abroad; the money was to be used for possible attempts at escape. Consequently more or less half of the records which arrived in camps after this case of attempted smuggling were broken to pieces to ensure that no notes or other things had been cast between the two halves of the record. During a few months in 1944 the security people were ordered to open all the tins which the POWs received in their Red Cross parcels. The official reason was that the tins were suspected hiding places for illegal items. To my knowledge the Red Cross parcels were not misused in any such way. What had really happened was that a few privately dispatched parcels containing homemade bread, cookies, chocolates, and so forth, had also contained, for instance, train tickets printed in Great Britain but valid at German state railways, German notes, detailed maps of Germany printed on flimsy silk paper, knives, files, hacksaws, pairs of nippers to cut barbed wire, and many other things which might prove useful during escape attempts. And the innocent Red Cross parcels thus became the scapegoat. Opening all these tins aroused such indignation among the POWs that the order was abolished after a few months.

Similar spitefulness was displayed in several British regular camps during autumn 1944, in the form of a prohibition of theatrical plays. This put a stop to a popular and much appreciated form of entertainment. The result was rebelliousness, dissatisfaction, an increased number of attempts at escape, and refusals to work. The commandants were exasperated; some of them ignored the order and permitted the popular entertainment to be resumed, others circumvented the order by changing "theatrical plays" to "musical entertainment in the form of revues." Finally the order was withdrawn. The reason for this unfortunate order was no secret: since the German civilian population could no longer go to the theater, the British POWs should not be able to enjoy such a treat either!

On the 3 April 1944 the YMCA POW Aid in Germany faced its most serious crisis: early in the morning, the Gestapo arrested Pastor Erik Christensen, the man in charge of the POW Aid, Gertrud Malmquist, a Swedish colleague, and Helle Goudsmit, a Dutch correspondent, and brought them to the prison in Breslau. They were accused of fraternizing with a Jew and found guilty: Goudsmit was sentenced to hard labor and Christensen and Malmquist were ordered to leave the country. The background was that Pastor Christensen had been introduced through the two women to a young Jewish girl who had moved from place to place, staying temporarily with people who, in spite of the danger, had dared take her in. Finally, she had arrived at Sagan, where the POW Aid had its headquarters, and Helle Goudsmit, who lived in a deaconess house, had brought the girl to her room. Erik Christensen had helped the girl get food and had talked a great deal with her; in the end, he had conceded to baptize her. Even as careful as they had all been, the Gestapo got on her track, although the "pleasure" of arresting her escaped them—she was so frightened of torture that she took her own life.

This incident aroused considerable consternation in the small town. We were all very sad when, on that spring morning, we arrived to find that three of our good friends and colleagues had been taken by the police early in the morning, and that they were now in prison in Breslau. The Swedish and Danish ministers in Berlin did all they could to keep the POW Aid going, but everyone in the German High Command as well as the Foreign Ministry was dismayed. Everybody wanted to help, but nobody dared. The YMCA offices in Geneva, Stockholm, and Copenhagen were informed via diplomatic channels, and so were the Swedish and Danish authorities. The Swiss newspapers were even prepared to bring the matter up in the media, but fortunately this was avoided—it would have given the YMCA the publicity we needed least at the time. Secretary General Hugo Cedergren of Stockholm, who was married to the Swedish king's niece, made an unscheduled journey to Berlin and succeeded, through his personal contacts, in having the whole incident treated as a personal matter affecting only the three members of the staff involved. There were thus no implications for the YMCA POW Aid. After four weeks of imprisonment, the interrogations of our three friends were finally completed and they were all released at noon on 5 May. Erik Christensen and the Swedish correspondent had to sign a statement to the effect that they would leave the country within forty-eight hours. During the afternoon they obtained the necessary exit visas in Breslau, and early in the evening they left there together with Helle Goudsmit and arrived in Berlin shortly after midnight. The next day we had a farewell lunch for them at Pastor Axel Jeppesen's parsonage, and a few hours later we bade them farewell at the Lehrter station. Helle Goudsmit was deported to do forced labor at a coal company in Breslau, but she managed to escape and came to Berlin just before the Russians captured the city.

In a report to the YMCA dated 12 May 1944 Erik Christensen himself recounts that during a two-hour-long interrogation he was confronted with six counts of indictment: he had known the identity of the Jewish girl and not informed the police; he had associated with her; he had brought her into contact with Aryans; he had provided her with food; he had let her use his car; and, finally, he had baptized her.

Erik Christensen writes in his report: "Asked what I had to say to these counts, I answered, after a moment of consideration: 'I have to say that altogether I find the treatment of Jews in this country wrong and that therefore, for reasons of conscience, I have felt it my duty to help her; I believe that Jews should be treated like other human beings.' This outspoken answer obviously did nothing to improve my situation. The chief of the Gestapo in Breslau, who later issued the warrant for our arrest, was outraged because I had 'criticized the government,' and he made some very nasty remarks about the Jews: they were 'Germany's worst enemies,' and therefore what we had done had been not only 'a gross abuse of Germany's hospitality and friendship, but also a clear fraternization with enemies of the country.' After this torrent of abuse, I was prepared for the worst. Later, in the prison and after having had time to reflect on my words, I still did not regret that I had not talked myself out of it by referring to a feeling of pity or something like that. Wisdom and caution are of course excellent qualities, but once in a while, the naked truth will out, even though nothing stings like the truth and one may have to pay dearly for speaking it."

Later in his report, Erik Christensen writes: "It is possible that we would not have been arrested had I not infuriated the Chief of Police with my remarks. Nevertheless, I have reason to believe that our friendliness toward the young Jewess was in fact only an excuse, at the most a provocation, but definitely not the real reason for our arrest and expulsion. The real reason in my opinion was the Gestapo's suspicion of our work from the very beginning, a suspicion which deepened when the eighty British POWs escaped from the Sagan camp in March. We had our headquarters in Sagan and it is very likely that we were suspected of having helped in the escape. Two things support my assumption: first, the actual association with the Jewess had already come to an end by the middle of February—she died on 20 February—and already on 25 February a police commissioner from Breslau received a complete report from me about what had happened; second, and most conclusively, the police chief in Breslau had specifically said to me, 'And, by the way, you may take comfort in the fact that the eighty British airmen who escaped from Sagan are now back in the camp again.' The Great Escape had not been mentioned even once during the entire interrogation, so his remark was made without any apparent reason."

Our relief work in Germany was as close to becoming suppressed on this occasion as it could possibly be. The Gestapo wanted to put an end to an organization such as ours which they suspected of having something to do with espionage and which, they were convinced, employed people who worked against the interests of the Nazi Reich. The German Foreign Ministry and the German High Command were well aware of the Gestapo's attitudes, as were influential circles within the German Church, so the Gestapo was unable to carry out its intentions of suppressing the YMCA. But the incident with the Jewish girl made the rest of us tread twice as cautiously in the weeks that followed. It was a serious crime to have anything to do with Jews, and I think that the reason for the comparatively mild sentences given to Erik Christensen and his two colleagues was the immense importance of the work of the YMCA, including its work on behalf of the German POWs in Great Britain, the United States, and Canada.

CHRISTMAS BEHIND BARBED WIRE

I spent the Christmas of 1944 together with twelve thousand British and American airmen in STALAG LUFT IV, which had been constructed almost like a town with streets and houses, and was situated in a softwood forest near Gross-Tüchow, a small railway town between Stettin and Danzig. The camp was the second largest of seven prison camps for airmen in Germany. The name "British" airmen should be taken in its broad meaning to include also captured Canadian and Australian airmen, as well as a number of Polish, Dutch, Norwegian, and other airmen who had volunteered for service in the RAF.

I had paid several visits to the camp and seen how it gradually grew in size. My feelings had always been somewhat mixed prior to a visit because I had encountered an unusual feeling of distrust, sometimes even hostility, on the part of the German commandant staff. Upon each visit the commandant, a young colonel from East Prussia, had made me understand that in his camp all was well and that there was "no reason for international visits or aid of any kind." I found it nearly impossible to engage in any reasonable or pleasant conversation with this man. Although he gradually got to know me, he still insisted on seeing my permission to enter the camp each time I arrived; only then would he get his cap and prepare himself to escort me around the camp. It never occurred to him to leave this task to one of his subordinate officers.

But the Christmas of 1944 was quite different: when I arrived at the camp in the morning of 23 December I went straight to the commandant's office, as always, and instead of appearing inconvenienced, the colonel got up and welcomed me with a few surprisingly kind remarks. He even added, on his own account, "Thank you for all the things you have sent to my prisoners of war since your last visit!" I was wondering what on earth had happened, when he continued: "Since your last visit I have met two German officers who have been repatriated for reasons of health, one from Canada and the other from Great Britain. Both of them told me about the valuable help the German POWs receive in Canada and in Great Britain from the YMCA POW Aid." This was entirely different from what I was used to hearing from this commandant. He welcomed me once more and said: "From now on, it is no longer necessary that I escort you around the camp. You may go wherever you wish without escort. And I'm asking you during the next four days to feel free to move around in the camp and in our German officers' mess as well, just as if you were at home." I asked myself if this could really be the same conceited Prussian whom I had previously wished would be transferred to the front. But he kept his promise. A room was made available to me in the officers' mess during the days of my visit, and I was free to go all over the camp without any escort or guards, and was thus able to speak freely and openly to everybody and about everything I wanted.

I spent the first day in routine discussions with the camp's two Men of Confidence and their colleagues. Although the POWs were under the overall supervision of the German Luftwaffe, the camp was nevertheless structured and run, by the prisoners themselves, like a joint British-American military headquarters commanded by a British senior officer and an American senior officer, with a considerable and well-qualified staff of officers in charge of education, the orchestra and choir, and sports, a librarian, doctors, chaplains, a canteen supervisor, a parcel and postal officer, and many more. During routine meetings each member of the staff had the opportunity to account for the present situation of his particular area of responsibility, and to inform others about what had been received from the YMCA since my last visit. Minutes were taken and new requests which popped up during the meeting were noted. The requests, often long lists, were forwarded to the YMCA offices in Geneva and Stockholm to be processed and carried out. These general discussions were a very useful introduction to a camp visit. Constructive criticism of what went on in the camp was also welcome, and it was often possible to make suggestions for improvements and additional activities based on my experiences from visiting other camps, for the benefit of all the POWs.

My visit to the camp during Christmas that year was extremely gratifying. Spirits in general were usually very high at this camp, but I presume that this year, having received the latest news from both the eastern and the western fronts, the POWs were convinced that it could now be only a matter of a few more months before Germany would have to surrender. Furthermore, everybody had received their Red Cross parcels prior to Christmas with real British and American Christmas food, exactly as they were used to having that time of year: turkey and plum pudding, coffee, chocolate, raisins, butter, wheat biscuits, and lots of other goodies. On Christmas each POW had been required to hand over a little something for joint consumption, and once again I had to admire the POWs' ability to prepare varied gastronomic courses from the otherwise rather unvarying contents of the Red Cross parcels. I watched, for instance, how dry wheat biscuits were pulverized into a kind of flour and kneaded with butter into a dough; making the dough rise was quite easy if you added a bit of tooth powder as it usually contains soda and salt. The dough was then filled into tins and the tins were put in the oven or, if a proper oven was not available, cooked on the stove.

All the rooms had been decorated with chains of fir and the YMCA had provided games, music, Christmas candles, and so forth. So all the physical conditions were in order for a pleasant Christmas. The camp commandant had given his permission for the lights to be on until one o'clock on Christmas Eve, instead of the customary ten o'clock "lights out" in all the huts. In return for this privilege, the British and American Men of Confidence had given their word of honor that there would be no attempts at escape during these two days.

The POWs had prepared for my visit extremely thoroughly, and in such a way that there was enough time to participate in such joint Christmas arrangements as concerts, football matches, services, dinners, get-togethers in the individual huts, and visits to the hospital wards. Everybody seemed pleased to have a visitor from outside and I was shown boundless hospitality everywhere. My room in the German officers' mess was used only for sleep. When darkness fell on Christmas Eve the Christmas trees were lit one after another in all the rooms, hymns were sung, games were played, books were read aloud, and stories were told all over the camp. At about ten o'clock, I entered a hut and found all the POWs assembled in the kitchen, which was the only room that was relatively warm. Some were playing chess, others were having a good time playing cards, one was making a pair of gloves out of the material of an old coat, another was occupied with drawing, still another was absorbed in painting with water colors, and they all drank lots of tea with condensed milk.

In another hut I met sixty-eight Polish airmen from the RAF. I was able to give them the latest news about a Polish officers' camp which I had visited a few days earlier and they were very grateful for that. I also entered a room with two Norwegian airmen, and on this occasion I was met with the question, "Are you a quisling?"

At midnight the festivities culminated. Shortly before, the POWs had begun to gather in the big square in the middle of the camp, the parole field, which was used for daily head counts and sporting events. Four trumpeters accompanied the group singing, which lasted for half an hour. It was cold—5° Fahrenheit—and snow was falling, but there was no wind, so the well-known Christmas hymns could be heard far away. The entire camp was illuminated by the powerful search lights, and outside the barbed-wire fences the German guards marched back and forth with rifles and watchdogs on leashes. The POWs did not seem to notice them, absorbed as they were in the Christmas hymns and the complete silence that prevailed between the hymns, almost like in a church. Thoughts traveled far, to homes and families on the other side of the North Sea and the Atlantic. The entire atmosphere was very special. Half an hour after midnight, the British and American senior officers concluded the evening with a few words and a "Merry Christmas"; the POWs sang the British national hymn "God save the King" as well as "God bless America," and then they all slowly and silently returned to their huts to go to sleep. I could not help wondering who were the most free and happy on that particular Christmas Eve—the POWs or their guards?

One of several services was held at nine o'clock on Christmas Day. The camp had its own church, built by the POWs themselves of wood they had been allowed to collect in the surrounding softwood forests. Well in advance of the service, the POWs flocked to the church, which was soon full of men. To provide as much space as possible, the British chaplain had had all the chairs and benches removed; some sat on the floor, but most of them stood up as close to one another as possible, all the way up to the altar and the pulpit. When absolutely no more space was available, the windows and doors were opened wide, so that groups of POWs outside could join in the hymns and listen to the chaplain's Christmas sermon. The service was as solemn as in a cathedral!

In the afternoon I called on the sick in the camp's hospital. Of course not all cases were equally serious, but some POWs had recently been shot down and were now in the hospital with heavy wounds. One of them, a young American, was so weak that he was unable to speak. I said hello to him and told him who I was, but he only looked at me with uncertainty and did not seem to understand what I wanted. It looked as if it would be impossible to reach him, but then an idea struck me and I pointed to the small international YMCA badge in the buttonhole of my jacket. Almost every British and American soldier knew the meaning of this badge if they had visited the soldiers' recreation centers, and now the sick POW understood: a faint smile appeared on his face. He put his hand under his pillow and pulled out a letter, fervently pointing to the address of the sender. I knew at once what he wanted: I was to write the address and send his greetings to his parents. Two hours later the young pilot died—he was only nineteen years old. It would be a difficult task, I thought, to have to notify his family of his death. But I did it willingly, because it was probably the very last wish he was able to express, and I was convinced that his parents would take comfort from knowing that a YMCA delegate had been with their son on the last day of his life.

One question kept popping up again and again, wherever I was in the camp: "Do you think we shall be going home next year?" Obviously, I didn't know the answer, but I certainly shared their hopes. As it happened, they came true.

I left the camp in the late afternoon of 27 December, and long rows of POWs accompanied me to the gate. I had visited all the huts and seen all the joint assembling rooms and workshops, and I had noticed the POWs' gratefulness to the Red Cross and the YMCA, the only two organizations which had been granted permission, during the war, to enter the prison camps, prisons, and hospitals to provide the help so desperately needed by all the POWs. "Give our best to your family and to the YMCA which sent you here. Thanks a lot for spending Christmas with us," were their last words to me.

NEARING THE END OF THE WAR

When the large-scale Russian counterattack was launched in January 1945, it became obvious to everybody that the war was drawing to its end. Life for the population in the bombed-out cities of Germany became more and more insufferable. Hundreds of American bombers launched their attacks during the daytime, met by almost no opposition from the antiaircraft guns, and during the night the RAF saw to it that the inhabitants in Berlin and other large cities did not get the rest they so desperately needed. Life became more and more aggravating, and the thought of defeat gradually penetrated the mind of everybody. In their fear and panic people began to hope that soon it would all be over.

In the POW camps, everybody was waiting eagerly for the

day when the gates to the camp would be opened and the long wait would be over, the day when their journey home could begin. As early as March 1944 the camp commandants had received instructions that in case of imminent invasion all POWs were to be evacuated from the border areas and the invasion zones. From September 1944 onward this evacuation claimed an incredible number of victims, and the closer the Allied armed forces came to the German borders, the more chaotic and undisciplined was the evacuation. I do not know just how many Allied POWs were killed in the process, but the number of British and Americans alone might be an indication: during the period from September 1944 through January 1945, the evacuations had claimed 1,987 victims, but during the last three months of the war that number increased to a total of 8,348. With so many dead among those who were relatively well treated and who—much more importantly—received Red Cross parcels with food for their daily meals, it can be assumed that the number of dead among the Russian POWs must have been considerably higher. About one hundred thousand POWs from the camps in Silesia were evacuated and marched through Saxony to Bavaria and Austria. Transportation by train had been planned, but had proved impossible because of the rapid Russian advance. Lack of winter clothes, food, and quarters claimed many victims. Over-excited party members and nervous home guard members of the "Volkssturm" decided the fate of the POWs in these last weeks of the war. The German High Command wanted to keep the POWs at any cost to be able to negotiate more favorable peace terms, and it was therefore necessary to evacuate them under these most inhumane conditions instead of just leaving them to await the advancing Allied armies. The POWs in and around Sagan were no exception. On 17 January, the German Radio announced that the Russians were rapidly approaching Steinau, about fifty miles east of Sagan. Day by day, the hope of imminent release grew. The POWs tried to occupy themselves as before, but it was difficult to maintain interest in daily language courses, concerts, and sports activities, for their minds were now preoccupied with what went on outside the camp. They kept speculating on the course of action the Germans would take: would they leave them in the camps where they were or would they force them to march west in the cold of the winter? Just to be on the safe side, the POWs in Sagan speeded up their preparations; they practiced packing bags and rucksacks and made small boxes of wood for their personal belongings. More and more POWs took longer and longer walks along the barbed-wire fences in order to train for the possible march westward. They prepared emergency plans and went through them so that every man knew exactly what he had to do if they were forced to evacuate, if the German staff deserted, or—as many actually feared—if the German staff decided to execute them in the very last phase of the war.

The YMCA's traditional POW Aid actually ceased in January 1945. On 3 February, one of the most fierce and extensive air attacks was launched on Berlin. Life still went on in the midst of ruin and destruction, but everywhere in the German capital the authorities began to establish armored obstructions and place heavy guns at strategically important points.

The Swedish director Gösta Lundin had succeeded Pastor Erik Christensen as leader of the YMCA POW Aid in the autumn of 1944, but at the time of the attack on Berlin he was in Sweden. He therefore instructed me and two Swiss colleagues to go ahead without him and make the necessary preparations to move the YMCA POW Aid's office and warehouse from Sagan to Meissen, where new premises had already been located in case of a possible evacuation. Well in advance of our move we received ten big trucks from the Swedish YMCA, and so at the beginning of February we started to move. One truck after another drove off, loaded to the brim with goods, furniture, and equipment, and headed for Meissen, where we would set up our new headquarters in a castle, "Sieben Eichen," near Meissen and fifteen miles north of Dresden. It was a terrible drive: the weather was very cold with lots of snow and icy roads, and the roads were overcrowded with German military vehicles and with frightened and exhausted refugees and POWs marching away from the battle zones.

While in the process of evacuating the YMCA POW Aid, we continued to receive cries of distress from POWs, either by telephone or by letter. They desperately needed help on the icy

winter roads to have sick POWs and food transported toward
the west. We had no choice but to ignore these cries for help; it
was impossible to break up the evacuation work at this stage,
and it would have been almost impossible to drive east, against
the flow of people and equipment. Besides, we only narrowly
avoided surrendering our swedish-registered trucks to the Germans. The party members who were responsible for keeping order among the large crowds of German refugees on their way
westward made several attempts to requisition our trucks for
refugee transportation. And the further the Russian armies advanced westward, the greater the confusion. All prison camps
situated in Poland or eastern Germany were evacuated and the
POWs were forced to start marching toward southern and western Germany under the most arduous conditions: numerous
POWs died from hunger or from cold. Nevertheless, the Germans pushed on—it seemed that at any cost they wanted to avoid
having the Allied POWs fall into the hands of the Russians.

During the first few days of February, Sagan was a town in
panic, overcrowded by a flood of refugees who wanted to get
away from the battle zones. "The Russians are coming" was
printed on everybody's face; dread, distress, grief, and worry
filled all these unhappy people. Thousands of them were walking
along with their few personal belongings packed in a rucksack
or loaded on a small pushcart, pram, bicycle, or sledge. Thousands of them found room on bundles of straw, on wagons drawn
by thin, hungry horses; they were leaving home and property
behind and moving toward a new and uncertain future in the
west. Along the roadsides, small groups of refugees had built
fires to prepare their meals, or just stopped for a rest. Women
gave birth in the straw on the wagons, and people died from
exhaustion or exposure, quickly to be buried along the roadside
or merely left in the ditch. Every town and village was overcrowded with frightened and homeless people on the run. Words
just cannot describe the inconceivable sufferings we witnessed at
that time.

The refugees came from all corners of eastern Germany and
Poland. Many of them had already been on their way for weeks.
This was the time when Germany did indeed reap the conse-

quences of the agony she had inflicted upon the populations of all the areas into which her armies had once advanced and made themselves masters of.

On 11 February the Russian forces stood only four miles from Sagan. We had not quite completed our move. The thunder of guns was heard incessantly, and the smoke in the distance told us what was about to happen. When evening fell and none of our trucks had returned for a new load we estimated that now was the time for us to get into our car and drive on, and so we had to leave many goods behind which were worth a great deal of money. Early next morning we were woken by the sound of machine gun fire. The eastern sky was red from the glow of many fires, and everybody knew that the Russians were not far away. In the street, I met the chief constable of Sagan, visibly shaken and nervous and very much aware of the seriousness of the situation; he asked me if he and his wife might seek refuge at the POW Aid's office, because, "you see, you are under the protection of the Geneva Convention, and nobody would do you any harm." And as a sort of excuse for speaking so directly, he added: "Please believe me! It's not my fault that I have become involved in all this—our Führer is completely mad, you know!"

Shortly afterward, a military vehicle drove through the main streets of Sagan with its loudspeaker announcing that "Russian tanks are approaching and may be expected to arrive within half an hour." Then we didn't hesitate any longer. With a last glance at our office, we turned the key, started the car, and drove off for Dresden and Meissen.

Our progress was slow because of the armored vehicles and tanks and the countless refugees crowding the roads, and it took us more than two hours to make the first eight miles from Sagan to the wide Berlin-Breslau motorway. Then the going became easier, but at nightfall the car broke down, and as the dark prevented us from doing anything about it, we spent the night in the car. It was freezing cold, but I am sure that this breakdown saved our lives, because during the night the city of Dresden was subjected to a most devastating attack by more than twelve hundred British aircraft, which dropped their full loads of bombs and reduced the entire center of Dresden to a heap of ruins.

The following day, after having succeeded in getting the car back to running order, we arrived in Dresden to be met by the results of the previous night's attack—a most horrible sight. It took us a couple hours to drive the six miles or so from the outskirts to the center of Dresden: tumbled-down walls, fallen cables, and bomb craters obstructed the traffic everywhere. Fires were still burning. Dead people were lying all over: on the pavement, in the gutters, on the streets—crooked, distorted bodies, mutilated and burnt beyond recognition. The hotel where we used to stay during our visits to Dresden had been destroyed by high-explosive bombs, and staff and guests were lying dead under the ruins.

The air attack on Dresden has become especially known; it was so destructive and carried out so late in the war that it seemed quite superfluous, since the war was virtually won already. Dresden was a junction, and the attack had been directed at the railway station, where refugees overcrowded the platforms. Admittedly the operation of trains was stopped for a few days, but no one in their right mind could claim that this attack was necessary to weaken the will of the German High Command to resist or fight, and neither did it hamper the surrounding factories to any substantial degree. It seems that the deliberate intention was to cause havoc among the civilian population. Exactly how many people were killed during this large-scale attack is difficult to say. I have seen casualty lists of up to 220,000 dead. This number may be too high—I do not know—but I do know that I shall never forget the sight of all the dead: men, women, and children, soldiers and civilians, piled on top of one another in high rows the entire length of the railway station just as logs are piled up in the woods, cubic foot upon cubic foot.

The new offices of the POW Aid in Meissen existed only for a short time; in fact, they never became fully operative. Because of the rapid development of military events, we had to move on to Lübeck already at the beginning of March, and there we awaited the end of the war. I myself went back to Berlin and was permitted to stay in the Swedish church on Landhausstrasse.

AMONG DANISH POLICE OFFICERS CAPTIVE IN GERMANY

Some people may still remember the German military operation—almost a coup—against the Danish police force: during the morning of 19 September 1944, the Germans seized and arrested about two thousand Danish police officers from all police branches throughout the country and had most of them transported to prison camps in Germany. At first they were brought to the concentration camp in Neuengamme near Hamburg, but soon after they were transferred to another infamous concentration camp in Buchenwald, near Weimar. Many of the officers, especially the older ones, were unable to manage the hard labor the Germans forced them to do, and they died from exhaustion, hunger, and exposure. Because concentration camps came under the jurisdiction of the Gestapo, neither the International Red Cross nor the YMCA POW Aid had any chance of visiting the officers or of helping them in any way. Several applications for permission to do so were turned down on grounds that the police officers were not prisoners of war, but convicts, a statement which neither the Red Cross nor the POW Aid would accept.

Around Christmas 1944 the Danish Foreign Ministry and the Danish Red Cross finally succeeded in bringing about a change in the situation of the police officers: from then on, they would be considered and treated as prisoners of war and not as convicts. This resulted in the transfer of those who were well enough to be moved, from the Gestapo's concentration camp to the prison camps under the jurisdiction of the German High Command. And it meant—at least in theory—that they were no longer without legal rights; they were under the protection of the Geneva Convention.

As soon as the change in status of the police officers had been implemented, the YMCA POW Aid requested permission to call on them to assist them in the same manner in which the

Allied soldiers in German prison camps received assistance. However, we had to wait until 4 March 1945 before we finally received the German High Command's written permission.

I left the following morning and spent the next ten days visiting three prison camps, one field hospital, one prison, and five hostels, all in the area of Dresden-Leipzig. The joy at receiving visits from home was great, and everywhere I answered questions as well as I could about the present situation in Germany and at home. I explained the relief work done by the YMCA in the POW camps and suggested that those who wanted me to call the national YMCA office in Copenhagen to ask the office to call their families and tell them how they were should write down their names, home addresses, and telephone numbers. The list turned out to be a long one, and as soon as possible I forwarded it to the national office via the Danish Legation and the Foreign Ministry. A modest contribution, perhaps, but the police officers understood the situation, and they were very grateful that their greetings to their loved ones would be passed on in this way. Their greetings were plentiful, their wishes few and modest. There was only one thing that they really wanted—their freedom. "We'll keep going for the short time that we still have to endure" was the general attitude. But there was also mourning because of the loss of the many colleagues who had been in no physical condition to bear the hardships of the disease–infested huts in the concentration camps.

The generous help which the Red Cross had sent in the form of food parcels was immensely appreciated and much praised by the police officers. "With these parcels, the Red Cross has surely saved a lot of us from dying of starvation!" Reading material was in very short supply; the Danish Red Cross had already dispatched a couple thousand books, which had arrived while the police were still kept in Buchenwald, but when they were transferred to different prison camps and hostels they had to leave almost all the books behind, so only between five and ten books were available at each place, and they had, of course, been read and reread by everybody a long time ago.

I saw only one musical instrument—a small mandolin—in one of the hostels, and everywhere I was met with requests for a record player and some records. A few asked for a mouth organ, a guitar, and a violin. No particular interest in studying any kind of subject was shown: the long hours of hard work forced upon the men exhausted them and they did not feel up to the mark when they returned in the evening. However one officer was interested in drawing and painting, and the YMCA would have liked to procure the necessary materials, if they had been able to make contact with him much earlier in his captivity.

Everywhere I went I was met with the same request: to have a Danish chaplain come to Germany under the same conditions as had a Danish police doctor, that is, to willingly submit to internment and share the conditions of the police officers. I was told this every Sunday, in every camp, in every hostel where a service or prayers were held. The police officers themselves supplied a few volunteers to be responsible for the services at each place. I forwarded the request for a chaplain to the Danish Church Overseas, which certainly would have done its best to meet it. But before anything decisive could be achieved, the joint Scandinavian cooperative effort for the release and repatriation of all Danish and Norwegian prisoners of war had begun, and so the Christian aid which would have been quite natural did not—fortunately, I might add—become necessary.

My first visit to the Danish policemen was to those interned in Mühlberg, 128 men led by a detective from Copenhagen, in a prison camp that housed thousands of other Allied war prisoners. They lived in one hut, unheated and with no electric light, and they had to sleep on the floor. My visit had not been announced, but as soon as they heard that I came from the YMCA I was met with confidence, trust, and warmth. On this occasion I was not able to remain quite as neutral as the Germans normally demanded from a member of the POW Aid staff. It was quite impossible for me to discuss only books, note pads, footballs, and other kinds of material assistance, when all these men were my own countrymen. "What's the news from home?" "How long do you think this is going to last?" Nothing seemed more important than the answers to these two questions.

Upon leaving the camp in Mühlberg I paid my customary respects to the German camp commandant. He was a middle-aged colonel whom I knew well from earlier visits, and who had shown me his confidence by letting me move around in the camp without any escort. One of the things he said to me was: "The Danes don't cause any problems; they never complain of their fate, and they possess a national awareness—they make it a point of honor to keep their uniforms nice and clean to a much greater extent than the other POWs. Their hut is always tidy and clean, and I never hear any commotion or yelling, which I sometimes do from some of the other huts in the camp." As an afterthought, he added, "Besides, I believe that we're doing them an injustice by keeping them here at all." This opinion I could support wholeheartedly.

Incidentally, the request to get a Danish chaplain was most strongly and spontaneously expressed in this camp at Mühlberg, and so was a request for some copies of the Bible and the Hymn Book. I was told that a Dutch chaplain held regular services for the Danish police. He did not know any Danish and his sermons were in German, but he had made the effort to teach himself so much Danish that he was able during prayers to pray for Denmark, the Danish people, and its Royal Family; as for the Lord's Prayer—it could be prayed by everybody. "At home, the church wasn't of too much concern to very many of us, but here we've come to realize our loss, and now we miss it," a policeman told me in a sad voice.

In Grosszössen at Espenhain, I called on a hostel housing 132 police officers. When I got out of the car at the entrance, one of them called out to me through the barbed-wire fence, "Don't enter—you're sure to catch lice." I did enter all the same and asked the men in one of the huts how they passed their time; the answer was prompt: "Twelve hours a day we work in a briquette factory, and twelve hours a day we pick lice!" And I am sure he was right; never before had I seen men so verminous as these Danish police officers. Most of them had suppurating wrists, forearms, and necks from lice bites. Not even during my own imprisonment in Russia did I see anything like this, and in the prison where I was kept there were plenty of bugs. These men needed nothing more than to go home to be nursed and cared for properly.

While I was there, the evening meal was brought in a large metal container: the usual thin vegetable soup which the POWs had every day and which in fact consisted of water rather than vegetables. One of the police officers went quietly to his bunk and pulled out a mangold from beneath it; he peeled it and cut it in four, one for himself, and one for each of three colleagues. Then he said dryly, "Now we can start calling this vegetable soup."

After a couple hours I had to say my goodbyes, and almost all the police officers accompanied me to the gate of the camp. I could leave, they had to stay behind. I told them that I was sorry I had to leave without having been able to help them, but one of them assured me, "Don't you worry—thank you for coming to see us at all, and believe me, we're going to stick it out for as long as it takes!" I left with their last words echoing in my ears: "Give our love to Denmark!"

In Park Meusdorf near Leipzig, I visited 448 police officers led by police inspector Niels Hovang from Copenhagen. Half of these men had been put to work at the Leipzig cemeteries, where they had to help bury the many victims from the British-American air attacks on Leipzig. The other half were employed with clearing operations in the streets, many of which were quite inaccessible due to collapsed buildings, burnt-out vehicles, and fallen streetcar wires.

The atmosphere in this camp was quite optimistic: everybody had recently received Red Cross parcels from Denmark, and I was asked to stay until the next day, a hospitable offer which I accepted with thanks, because it would give me the opportunity to talk to many of the police officers individually. And several of them did approach me about personal matters which they asked me to handle in Denmark through the Danish YMCA. After the evening meal I had the chance to tell them about the YMCA POW Aid in general, and about the conditions in other POW camps as I saw them during my visits. That gave rise to an interesting discussion and, if nothing else, it was a welcome change in the camp's monotonous routine. It seemed quite natural when one of the police officers suggested that we sing a hymn. I asked which one, and the answer was the well known hymn, "A Safe Stronghold our God is Still" which most of us knew by heart—at least the first and third verses. Later, someone else suggested the Danish national hymn, then followed the Danish king's hymn and "Altid Frejdig" (Be Undaunted in Your Doings). Finally, police inspector Hovang said, "Good night and thank you for a pleasant evening."

In Park Meusdorf, the police slept in bunks—lower, middle and upper. I was installed in a middle bunk with the apology, "we are sorry, but we don't have a proper guest room." But before I was ready to go to bed, two officers came up to me and asked me to please hold Communion for them and twelve other police officers. At that time I had not yet taken holy orders, but I could not refuse, so we all gathered in the police inspector's room (a private room was the privilege of a camp leader). Thus, at midnight we celebrated Communion, a Communion that none of us are likely to forget. A small table covered with a towel was our altar, the "bread" was small pieces of Danish crispbread from the Red Cross parcels, and the "host" was water from the camp's water pump in a white mug. I read the fifty-first Psalm of David and proceeded in accordance with the liturgy in the Hymn Book, while the communicants knelt on the cement floor before the provisional altar. It was long after midnight when we finally settled down; I got into my bunk and some police officers thoughtfully covered me with their uniform coats. I slept like a log, protected by the world's finest police officers.

The next morning, a young police officer gave me a drawing he had been working on the previous evening. It was a drawing of a prison camp surrounded by a three foot barbed-wire fence; inside the fence sat a Danish police officer, securely planted on top of a thick book entitled "Danish Law," which he was clearly looking after very carefully. In the distance, on the other side of the fence, the contours of Denmark could be seen—Jutland and the Danish islands—and two large trucks, one marked Red Cross, the other YMCA, were heading south toward the main gate of the prison camp. Behind the trucks was a drawing of myself as the YMCA field delegate, and underneath it the artist had written, "Best regards and thanks to our beloved Denmark from the Danish Police Force in Park Meusdorf, Leipzig." Just as I was leaving the camp, another police officer came up to me and said the same thing in different words: "Thank you so much for visiting us and for all that is done for us from home. It's enough for us to know that we're not abandoned or forgotten, and we look forward to the day when we can resume our work at home for the good of our King, our country, and our people."

From Leipzig I went straight to Berlin to report to Minister Mohr and Councillor Steensen-Leth in the Danish legation on the situation of the Danish police officers in Germany, and the minister later arranged for me to make the same report to Count Folke Bernadotte in the Swedish Legation. The count had made extensive preparations for an operation designed to bring Norwegian and Danish POWs home from Germany, and he was now able to carry it out successfully. This visit to Danish police officers in German captivity was thus to be the only one, and the aid which the YMCA had already planned became unnecessary, and fortunately so.

THE LAST WEEKS IN BERLIN

On 18 March the YMCA POW Aid held its last staff meeting before the end of the war. It was hosted by Pastor Erik Myrgren of the Swedish Church in Berlin, where premises had been made available. The meeting was held in agreement with the World Alliance headquarters in Geneva, and Secretary General Hugo Cedergren participated, together with the entire staff of the YMCA POW Aid. The purpose of the meeting was to discuss what had to be done during the days and weeks immediately following the cessation of hostilities.

It turned out to be a very peculiar meeting: before we even got around to business, the air-raid alarm sounded and the radio announced that "strong formations of enemy aircraft are flying over northwest Germany and approaching Berlin." Shortly afterward, the first echelon of British and American aircraft could be heard as well as seen. Later in the day BBC radio stated that about twelve hundred heavy bombers and one thousand fighter-bombers had directed their attack mainly toward the northwestern part of the city; this was true, because we saw

enormous clouds of smoke that from time to time completely
darkened the sky and bore witness of the intensity of the attack.
In such a sinister atmosphere of horror, doom, death, and destruction, it was impossible for us to discuss any plans for work
in the near future. So we agreed that every one of us was free to
do what he thought best—whether he felt that it would be right
to remain in his job, or whether he felt that he ought to go westward during this very last phase of the war.

When our "meeting" was adjourned we returned to our individual jobs in western and southern Germany, and the chief of
the YMCA POW Aid, managing director Gösta Lundin, went
back to Lübeck, where he had started setting up his new headquarters. I remained in Berlin, because at that time it looked as
if the prison camps in northern and central Germany, to which
I had paid so many visits and for which I had arranged for des-
perately-needed aid for more than three years, might not, after
all, be evacuated. As it was, the Germans had already evacuated
the camps in eastern Germany and Poland, causing the POWs to
march incredibly long distances to western and southern Germany, because these areas were thought to be safer. But gradually, as the war drew toward its end, Germany grew smaller and
smaller in size; the Allied forces advanced from the east and from
the west, gaining territory more and more rapidly, and the time
was getting near when the German High Command could no
longer transfer POWs to other and safer places. Apparently, a
feeling of resignation was beginning to prevail. So I decided to
remain in "my" area, where there were still several camps and
hospitals and thousands of POWs. It was still possible to call on
them and also, to a degree, to be of assistance, especially with
the distribution of the almost vital Red Cross parcels.

At the beginning of April I made a three day journey to the
area between Berlin and Stettin, and I visited as many camps and
hostels as time permitted. I saw many POWs, easily recognizable
because of their uniforms, moving around quite freely, waiting
for the Russians. The civilian population had vacated most of the
villages to escape westward, and there was almost no one except
German soldiers and POWs around. I got as far as the outskirts
of Stettin; combat was going on as near as the eastern part of

Stettin, and I had to assume that the large POW camps in Stargard and Woldenberg had already been liberated.

In the center of Berlin was a large depot of Red Cross parcels meant for distribution to the POWs who were assigned to hostels all over Berlin. But the German authorities could no longer make any means of transportation available; I had a car as well as gasoline at my disposal, so naturally I offered to help with the distribution. I drove around for the next ten days or so, accompanied by a French POW, and delivered as many of the much-needed parcels as possible.

On 20 April Russian artillery guns started to fire on Berlin, and the air-raid alarms and the usual warnings over the radio of imminent air attacks ceased completely. Now it was your own responsibility if you walked around in Berlin. A strange atmosphere of doom pervaded the city. In all main streets trenches were dug, barricades were built, and antitank blockades were positioned. People began to wonder why the Americans did not arrive: "They're there, aren't they? Just outside the city!" At least that was what they hoped for. Not one Berliner wanted to surrender to the Russians, and they all prayed that it would be either the Americans or the British who would be first to arrive in Berlin. The fact was that the Americans were indeed just outside Berlin, but the Russians, following a special agreement, had been given the sole right to conquer the German capital, something the Berliners found very hard to understand.

On Sunday 22 April the Russian guns really started to sound. As usual, we attended a service in the Danish church in Saarlandstrasse, but this was to be the last one. I suppose about twenty-five or thirty of us found our way to church on that Sunday. The windows had been blown out a long time ago by the air blast of a bomb that had exploded nearby, but at least we had a roof over our heads. From time to time, Pastor Jeppesen's sermon was accompanied by the fierce sound of guns, which made it difficult to hear his words. The service was concluded with Communion and the hymn, "A Safe Stronghold our God is Still." After the service I resumed my work of distributing food parcels, this time in eastern Berlin to a number of French POWs.

On 24 April, I began the day by going to the Danish church to help Pastor Jeppesen distribute food parcels to old Danish people sitting around in air-raid shelters in eastern Berlin. We loaded the car and distributed the parcels; we knew we were behaving recklessly, because several times Russian aircraft passed over our heads so low that we had a clear view of the pilots, and it was probably sheer luck that nothing happened. After this "adventure" we took the Danish church register to safety in Pastor Jeppesen's temporary residence at Dahlem.

On the morning of 25 April, a French POW told me about fifty-two Frenchmen in the neighborhood of Neukölln who were in desperate need of help because they had no food at all. I immediately loaded the car, and together with the French POW we also completed this expedition without mishap. But it was a near miss, because at one point a shell exploded so close to us that the car was completely covered with sand and gravel, and we realized that we were seriously endangering ourselves by remaining in the open.

I therefore returned to my temporary residence in the Swedish church in Wilmersdorf, and in the evening I moved into the Swedish Legation's bunker in the Tiergarten neighborhood together with Pastor Myrgren and two of his colleagues. I got there with much difficulty, because I was continuously stopped by nervous SS soldiers who would not allow me to pass and wanted to confiscate my car. They would probably have succeeded had I not persistently and stubbornly referred to my Danish passport and the Swedish registration number of the car. It was no longer possible to get past the barricades, and men from the "Volksturm" armed with old rifles were guarding the narrow openings through which a small car like mine could barely pass.

The Swedish bunker was a solid cement colossus constructed ten feet below the ground and protected by a ten-foot-thick cement roof. During the last eight days of the war I found shelter in this bunker together with some twenty people, primarily the staff of the Swedish Legation and the church. Each day was one long continuous air raid, with few and short breaks. Endless noise came from aircraft, shells, exploding bombs, and artillery guns. The bunker received several direct hits, some light and some heavy, which made it reel and shake once in a while, but it held. We were adequately stocked with water and food, but the electric light had failed, so we were sitting, lying, or groping our way in the dark, waiting, waiting, and hoping for an expedient liberation. We had candles, but we used them sparingly because we had no way of knowing how long it would be before we could leave the bunker. A powerful receiver helped keep us informed about events outside, and we were told about both Field Marshal Göring's dismissal and Count Folke Bernadotte's attempt to negotiate peace. We stayed in the bunker the whole time, though, because it would have been highly dangerous to go out into the open.

On 2 May, at half past seven, we were finally liberated. After a couple of hard knocks on the steel door, two Russians entered and shined their strong lights at us. "Are there any soldiers or weapons about?" one of them asked. The answer of course was no; they went on to inspect our papers and, after having made sure that none of us were German soldiers who, in the last hours of the war, had exchanged our uniforms for civilian clothes, we were allowed to go out into the open, into fresh air, daylight, and—under more peaceful circumstances—a beautiful summer morning.

The guns had ceased firing and a deadly silence prevailed. All around us we saw the appalling consequences of war. The Tiergarten had turned into a battlefield: the ground was marked by shells and bombs, hundreds of trees had fallen, and not one house was standing as far as our eyes could see. The legation had burnt down, and everywhere in the streets we saw armored and other military vehicles completely destroyed. We took a short walk later in the day and it proved a terrible experience: bomb craters and shell holes covered the ground, dead soldiers and horses, victims of the last days of the war, were lying everywhere. I watched some women cut out large pieces of meat from the dead horses, and in front of the legation I saw the remains of what had once been a German soldier; his dead body had been run over so many times that all that was left was a flattened, red and wet substance in the remains of a green uniform—a most gruesome and terrible sight which I have never since been able to get out of my mind.

I soon made contact with the Danish Legation, which was not far from the Swedish Legation, and also with Pastor Jeppesen and some Danish Berlin correspondents. We considered ourselves extremely lucky that no harm had come to any of us, and during the next few days we went about the city as much as we wanted. We were often stopped by Russian soldiers who wanted to put us to work clearing the streets, burying the dead, and so forth, but as soon as they saw our foreign passports they usually changed their minds and let us proceed. I even obtained permission to use my car again. It had received several serious bruises and dents and not a single window was whole. Pieces of glass were all over inside the car and the body showed signs of many rifle shots. It seems incredible, but the engine was in perfect running order, and I was thus able to resume my visits to the French and Yugoslav POWs at their former hostels, at least for a little while, until I ran out of gas.

No change in our situation occurred until the afternoon of 18 May, when two Russian officers came to the bunker and told us that the necessary preparations had now been made for us to be repatriated. We would be picked up that same afternoon at around six o'clock and would be traveling via Moscow and Helsinki to Stockholm and Copenhagen. "What about my car?" I asked. Although it did not represent a fortune, it was still the property of the YMCA. The reply came promptly: "The Russian authorities will confiscate your car and the question of damages will have to be referred to Moscow via your own Foreign Ministry."

GOING HOME TO DENMARK—VIA MOSCOW

It did not take long for us to pack our things and, as promised, we were picked up, and after a long drive in an open truck through the ruins of Berlin, we reached the suburb of Lichtenberg. In Lichtenberg we were installed in a large block of flats whose occupants had simply been turned out to make room for the many foreigners whom the Russians wanted to repatriate via

Moscow: about 30 Italians and 150 Japanese, my 11 Swedish friends from the legation and the church, what was left of the staff attached to the Swiss Legation, a few Hungarians and Greeks, 3 Norwegians, and 30 Danes, 10 from the legation and the consulate, 4 journalists, myself, and 15 others whom we didn't know, but collectively called "Germany Workers." One flat, consisting of three small rooms, was allocated to the group of Danish people. The four journalists and I stayed together in one room and had to share a single bed with no mattress. Pastor Jeppesen and Pastor Christian Bakmann Christensen installed themselves in the small kitchen—one on the kitchen table and the other curled up on a kitchen shelf. We did not sleep much that night, and we were tired and worn the next morning; in fact, Pastor Bakmann Christensen felt so bad that Pastor Jeppesen suggested to Councillor Steensen-Leth that we ask the Russians permission to go to the legation and get some medicine for him. The councillor's reply was sharp and to the point: "We don't have any sick people among us!" It sounded very much like a rebuff, but he was quite right; the Russians were so used to seeing people die that to them one more or less would not really matter, and we would get nothing but problems if we told them about Pastor Bakmann Christensen.

Progress was slow—we waited all day Saturday 19 May to be told to move on—but Russian trucks continued to stop in front of the block to unload more people who were also supposed to go east. We were not allowed to leave the building except to walk in the yard, so the neighborhood and the city of Lichtenberg remained unfamiliar. The block was surrounded by military police armed with machine guns. The food, however, was good—almost too good—with genuine tea and fresh bread. For dinner we had soup with macaroni and plenty of meat from a large Russian goulash container placed outside the block. After several weeks on a spartan diet we suddenly had plenty of very rich food, which resulted in several of us suffering from stomach trouble, much like dysentery.

The next day, 20 May, was Whitsunday. At six o'clock in the morning we were told to get ready to depart, and after a hasty breakfast we all walked the short distance to the railway station in Lichtenberg. All our luggage had been loaded on trucks and taken to the station, where passing Germans were ordered to unload it and carry it to the waiting train. An old carriage was reserved for the Danish group. We noticed at once that the German eagle and the words "German State Railways" had been removed and replaced by the corresponding Polish markings. The Russians seemed to have plenty of time; we spent all morning waiting on the platform without anything happen-, ing. The sun was shining from a clear blue sky, it was baking hot, and a bit of wind filled the air with ashes and dust from the surrounding heaps of ruin. At half past twelve we had potato soup, and finally, one hour later, we were ordered onto the train and it began to move eastward. We rubbed our tired eyes, determined to keep them wide open, and steeled ourselves for the long impending journey. We were going home!

We had no idea of the duration of the journey. Some of us guessed that it would be eight days, whereas most of us reckoned a couple of weeks would be likely. But it really did not matter much—we were happy. "We're going home," we told each other. At the beginning the going was very slow, and we were told that this was the first train to carry people east after the surrender of Berlin. The wake of the war hit us as we proceeded mile after mile. Traveling toward Frankfurt via Strausberg at the river Oder we went through the area where the last fierce battles had been fought before the surrounding and siege of Berlin. Only one of the two railway tracks could be used; the other was completely destroyed by shells and at several places the metal bars stuck into the air in all kinds of distorted shapes. Villages and fields had been destroyed, either by fire or by the weapons of war, and along the railway tracks we saw heaps of wrecked tanks, burnt-out vehicles, and dead horses.

Over a distance of about sixty miles, from Berlin to Küstrin, I did not see one single human being, nor a single horse. A destruction more total than the one we witnessed cannot be imagined. A frail-looking provisional wooden bridge carried us across the river Oder and into the completely destroyed city of Küstrin; we proceeded via Landsberg to Poland, going through parts of the country which were so very familiar to me from my countless visits to the POW camps.

It was almost impossible to get any sleep. There were not enough seats for all of us, let alone couchettes. The heat was oppressive and so were the dirt and dust. We could not wash or shave properly—hot water had to be fetched from the engine, and by the time we would return to our carriage it would have turned lukewarm. A few of us who were brave enough ventured up into the brake towers on the goods cars to wash there.

We had entered Poland, the country which, measured against its number of inhabitants, had suffered the most and paid the highest price for the victory of the Allies; the country whose soldiers I had met by the thousands in the camps and admired and respected because of their diligence, their urge to perfect their knowledge, and their belief that "Poland is not yet lost." All the railway stations we passed were full of waiting people; some were walking around, others were sitting in groups with their few belongings wrapped up in blankets and stuffed into sacks. Some were waiting for an opportunity to get on a train; others, I suppose, were hoping to do a little business with the train passengers, or begging for a bit of food, or hoping to snatch the odd cigarette end which the Russian soldiers threw out of the windows of the train as it passed the station.

We arrived in Warsaw the next morning where we had a twelve hour stop. We were told not to leave the railway station, and that made us feel rather annoyed, because in spite of all the destruction, some of us would have wanted to take this opportunity to see the Polish capital. We had to content ourselves, however, with walking up and down the platform, preparing a meal over an open fire, and doing a bit of business: I got some hot water for my instant coffee in exchange for a handkerchief, and a Polish woman prepared our evening meal for a pair of socks for her four-year-old daughter. The surroundings had developed into a slum area, where the Poles lived in empty train cars— husband, wife and children in one end, a cow and a calf in the other. We talked to some people and they told us that about three-fourths of Warsaw were in ruins.

In the evening we proceeded, and by morning we had

crossed the Polish-Russian border at Brest-Litovsk. It was exactly the same as in Poland: many poor people, women, children, and old men walking, barefoot and poorly dressed, up and down the platform along the carriages, offering homebaked bread, milk, and hard-boiled eggs in exchange not for money, but for clothes. Then the train continued through Minsk and Smolensk and, at last, on the morning of 25 May at about seven o'clock, we arrived at one of the stations in Moscow. "How exciting it will be to see Russia's old capital!" we exclaimed and looked at each other happily when the train pulled up at the station. "We'll probably stay here for a couple of days," one of the journalists said in a hopeful voice; I am sure he had nosed out some good stories for a series of articles for his newspaper at home.

We had left Berlin in sunshine and almost tropical heat. Here in Moscow the weather was foul and cold, with heavy lumps of sleet falling. If any one of us had been so naive as to expect a beflagged city to welcome us, he soon discovered he was mistaken. Only the Swedes had reason to be happy that morning: members of the Swedish Legation, headed by Minister Stefan Söderblom, had shown up to welcome their countrymen from Berlin; all the Swedes were to go with him and stay at the Legation. But where was the Norwegian diplomat? And where was the Danish minister, Thomas Døssing? We did not see them. What was the meaning of this? The Swedes took a hearty farewell of us and left together with their country's official representatives in Moscow, while Norwegians and Danes were accompanied to a waiting room on the second floor of the railway station and asked to wait there. So were the Japanese, but that seemed more understandable; after all, Japan had been an ally of Germany. But what about us? Both Norway and Denmark were Russia's allies!

One of the journalists asked the Russians for permission to telephone Minister Døssing, but that was denied him. Later in the morning, however, the minister showed up on his own initiative, because the Swedish minister had informed him about our arrival. When he got to the door of the waiting room, he was stopped by armed guards, and to our dismay he was not allowed to enter.

Part Two

A PRISONER IN RUSSIA

INTERNED

NOTHING HAPPENED for the next seven hours, except that we got more and more worried and confused—what was going on here? Large pictures of Stalin and Molotov and a couple of other powerful men were hanging on the wall; their eyes were fixed on us and they seemed to be saying, "*We* won the war!" and, "You'll just have to put up with it, sooner or later, so relax and stay calm!"

Finally an interpreter came in and told us in French that, regrettably, it had been impossible to get in touch with the legation, which we knew was not true, and that, therefore, we must be prepared to wait "until tomorrow." The interpreter added that she had been instructed to accompany us to a small "maison de campagne"—a "country house"—a few miles away, where we would have to stay for a few days while some administrative matters were being cleared up, "so please take your seats in the busses which are waiting in front of the entrance."

The drive to the "country house" was something of a trial. At the beginning the road was quite good, but after a while the busses left the main road and we proceeded along a branch road full of holes, and shortly afterward it developed into a genuine mud field. Again and again we got stuck in the mud and had to get out and push. The wind was straight in our faces and so was the sleet. The worst, however, awaited us as our bus was about to cross a temporary and fragile-looking wooden bridge which had been built across the river Moskva. The driver either did not know the weight of the bus or overestimated the capacity of the bridge, because suddenly it began to give way; he accelerated desperately, but the bridge started to break. The rear wheels of the bus went right through the surface and did not stop until the bodywork rested on the wooden planks. We looked down and stared into the cold and turbid water and then, very carefully, began to edge our way toward the door. Luckily we managed to get out safe and sound, and after that experience we decided to walk the rest of the way. The so-called "country house" was no country house at all but a real prison and internment camp with barbed-wire fences and armed guards. The heavy entrance gate slammed behind our backs. We were locked up. We did not know exactly where we were, nor—more importantly—did the Danish Legation. Near the gate was a white, oversized statue of Lenin. German soldiers—prisoners of war—got out some camp beds for us, and we told them not to bother too much, because "tomorrow, we continue our journey"; this statement made them smile indulgently as if they knew better than we what exactly "tomorrow" means in Russia.

What a strange "country house," shut up behind barbed-wire fences. One of the POWs told us that it used to be a "hunting seat," a kind of a luxury prison camp which, during the entire winter the previous year, had housed a number of German generals, including Field Marshal Friedrich von Paulus, the strategist at Stalingrad.

The POWs were right about "tomorrow"! We were to spend the next couple of months in this place. The German POWs acted as our cleaning ladies and our servants, and I am certain they were also told to spy on us and report to the Russians what they heard and saw going in and out of our rooms. The rooms were numbered and I shared room number 13—a very modest room, but clean and tidy—with Vice Consul Erik Munch-Andersen, two Danish journalists, and pastors Axel Jeppesen and Christian Bakmann Christensen. The food was nothing to write home about, but probably as good as the present circumstances allowed: cabbage soup and porridge, porridge and cabbage soup, which the German POWs prepared. Nobody really liked the soup; it was always watery and tasteless. The porridge alternated between oatmeal, millet, barley, and rice. I think most of us preferred the oatmeal porridge. For breakfast we had tea, bread, and a tiny nut of butter; for lunch soup and porridge, and in the evening soup again, this time with a slice of bread. There were no tablecloths in this grand country house, and the only eating utensil we were allowed was a spoon, because a knife and a fork could be used as weapons. Our food rations, we were told, were larger than the average ration in the Soviet Union at that time, and that was probably true.

The first interrogation was easy. It took place the day after we had arrived, in the commandant's residence, which was situated outside the fences. The interrogator was a young policeman wearing a "NKVD" uniform. One after another we were summoned. In a quiet and relaxed manner the officer asked my name, where and when I was born, the names of my parents, their date, year, and place of birth, my father's occupation, my education and occupation. Most of the information was stated in my Danish passport, but that did not seem to interest him at all. Did he perhaps believe that the information was forged? Anyway, after these introductory questions, a whole series of other questions followed:

—Is your father a rich man?
—How many heads of cattle does he have?
—What kind of training have you received?
—What languages do you know and what is your proficiency?
—Were you abroad while studying?

After I had listed, not without a certain amount of pride, the countries I had visited during my summer holidays, he immediately fired off the questions:

—Which intelligence service did you report to?
—How did you get involved in POW work?
—How and why did you come to Germany?

—Why did you not go to Germany right after you
graduated?

—What did you do prior to obtaining a German entry
permit?

—What exactly is the YMCA POW Aid?

—How is it financed?

—Name the leaders in Geneva, New York, and Stockholm.

—When were you last in Stockholm?

—Whom did you see when you were there?

—Did you visit foreign legations in Stockholm?

—From where did you procure materials for the prison
camps?

—Do you have any friends or acquaintances in the Soviet
Union?

—Have you been able to help Russian POWs, too?

—Why did you help the Poles?

—Are you a member of any political party?

—Have you ever been to Buchenwald?

—Can you provide a list of all the prison camps in
Germany?

—What was the attitude of the German High Command
toward your relief work?

—Have you also been to Switzerland?

—What are you going to do now?

My reply to this last question was that it would be for the YMCA
World Alliance to decide. Personally, I would be happy to continue my work, if the YMCA wanted me to.

Life in the camp was boring and monotonous. We were
awakened at seven o'clock in the morning, made our beds, and
had breakfast; lunch was at two o'clock and supper at six thirty.
To pass the time during the day we played patience and cards
for hours, or took walks in the camp area, or taught each other
languages—Italian, French, and English. Our two Danish pastors were free to hold services every Sunday, and together with
one of the journalists, Mr. Jacob Kronika, they recruited a small
group of men and made a study circle, which met every morning
to go over the Acts of the Apostles, and later one of the Pauline

Epistles. The camp had a small library with about fifty books, German translations of Russian works that glorified Lenin and Stalin.

One or two evenings a week we were able to watch a movie, but we soon discovered that the intention was not entertainment but propaganda—an attempt at reeducation and indoctrination which could not be misinterpreted. The movies were supposed to give us an impression of Russia outside the barbed-wire fences, but it was an impression, mind you, which the government wanted to impose on us.

One night Councillor Steensen-Leth gave a lecture on the occasion of "Valdemarsdagen," a Danish national holiday, and another night I was asked to say something about the YMCA POW relief work. Four weeks later I was asked to expand on the subject, but somebody must have mentioned it to the camp commandant, because fifteen minutes before my lecture I was summoned to his headquarters. He told me that "it's not desirable that you explain anything about your work to these Hitler-legations, because they won't believe you anyway, and if you are to present an objective picture—and you are!—then you also have to explain just how atrocious everything was, and that serves no purpose in front of these people."

The commandant took this opportunity to ask me about my plans for the future. I told him that I hoped to continue my employment with the YMCA and allowed myself to express my surprise at being detained in Russia at all, considering that I had taken part in the international relief work to benefit Allied prisoners of war. "Don't worry," he answered in a soothing voice. "You're young, you have experienced a lot of things in Germany and you have seen more than most people your age. I'm sure you'll have no problem finding work when you return to Denmark. Now the only thing you need is a bit of patience."

Given that we must be detained, I suppose that life in the camp must generally be considered tolerable, at least compared to what I experienced a few weeks later. The Russians took some pains to help us keep up our spirits, although everything would have been so much easier if only, just once, they had disclosed their intentions. As it was, the never-ending attempt to put us off with talk and the uncertainty of the length of our stay in the camp were a continuous mental strain. Why were we not allowed to call the Danish ambassador? Why was he not allowed to visit us? We were allowed—even encouraged—to write to him, and many of us did, but we doubted very much that he ever received our letters, because we never received any replies from him.

Sunday 1 July was warm and sunny, and on that day something unexpected happened. We were told to remain in our rooms. The building had been surrounded by soldiers and guards were posted at every door. All our luggage was to be searched. No such search had been carried out before, not when we left Berlin, not at the borders we had crossed, not when we arrived at Moscow, not at the camp, and not once during all the weeks we had stayed in the camp. But now, out of the blue, all our luggage, papers whether printed or written, notes, diary entries—simply everything, was to be delivered to the commandant.

Among my papers was a letter, the content of which was unknown to me because I had been foolish enough not to read it in advance; it was written by a former Russian citizen who had lived in Germany for several years and had served in the German Ministry of Propaganda. In his letter, which was addressed to the Secretary General of the YMCA, he offered his services to the American YMCA. The man had approached me in the Swedish church in Berlin at the end of March and asked me to arrange for the letter to be given to the Secretary General. I had promised to do so, but as I did not meet the Secretary General before the end of the war, the letter was still lying among some other papers in my luggage.

This small incident resulted in another interrogation in the office of the commandant one of the last days of July. Apparently, the contents of the letter had reinforced the Russians' suspicion that some people were prepared to use the YMCA POW Aid as a tool to promote personal political interests, and I was therefore asked to explain how that letter had come into my possession. I was also asked to translate several pages of my diary into German, and I took this opportunity to emphasize, once again, the non-political and neutral character of my work.

"That's *your* opinion," the commandant retorted, "but we in the Soviet Union are of the opinion that all acts are political, and although it seems as if you personally have only the purest motives and the best intentions, we still believe that you have been used as a tool to promote a political system."

In the evening of 2 August we were in our rooms as usual when suddenly the commandant entered, accompanied by his interpreter. He greeted us kindly and said that he had come to tell us "which of you have won the prizes in the lottery." He then proceeded to read out the names of twenty Danes who were to make themselves ready to return to Denmark early the next morning. The names included the entire staffs of the legation and the consulate, the four journalists, and six of the "Germany workers." I was terribly upset that my name was not mentioned; in fact, I was so disconsolate that I could not even cry—not to mention sleep; my mind was reeling; What was the reason? Why was I not going home? What was going to happen to me?

The following morning at five o'clock everybody was aroused, and two hours later our twenty Danish friends departed. It was a sad experience to be left behind at the gate and watch them get into the waiting bus and take their seats, without being able to do likewise. But in some ways it was good that some of us were able to leave that day, because it meant that they could bring our love to our families and let them know that we were alive and well—at least moderately so.

Of the ten Danes now detained in the camp all, except myself, had been working in such German organizations as the "Waffen SS" and "Todt." I just could not understand how it was possible for me to be included in such company, but after awhile I made up my mind that from now on, I would refer only to what I had said earlier. I would not say any more, I would not say any less! As it was, however, my stay in the so-called country house was to last only a short time longer.

IN PRISON IN MOSCOW

Ten days later, mid-morning on 13 August, a guard came to my room to escort me to the office of the commandant. I thought that another interrogation was about to begin, but he asked me to get into a car which was parked in front of his office. Surprised, I asked if I should not bring my luggage along, but he answered, "No, you'll be back again tonight." I learned later that my luggage had been picked up that same afternoon and that my countrymen in the camp had been informed that I had been taken to the Danish Legation in Moscow.

I got into the back of the car, a young officer got in next to the driver, and we proceeded toward the city. I was absorbed in deep thoughts about where I was being taken. It would never have crossed my mind that in fact I was on my way to prison, though I could not understand why I had had to leave without my luggage; I assumed that perhaps I was to be interrogated by someone in Moscow who did not have time to go to the camp. The traffic grew heavier as we approached the center of the city. I did not get the chance to see any of the sights of Moscow, though, because we left the main street, proceeded along a narrow, cobbled street, and reached a sinister-looking, four-storied building, with iron bars in front of the windows and a guard posted in front of the main entrance. My nervousness made me remove my wristwatch and put it in my pocket. The escort officer jumped out of the car and showed some papers to the guard. The gate was opened and we drove into the yard. The sound of the gate slamming shut behind us made me jump in my seat. I looked around and realized that I had been taken to the state prison, the "Butyrka," which was considered a kind of a forecourt or a subdepartment to the far more infamous and well-known "Ljubjanka" prison.

The officer beckoned to me to get out of the car and led the way into a big room, almost like a waiting room, with green tiles on the walls and with lots of doors. A guard or prison officer in an "NKVD" uniform opened one of the doors and ushered me into a small cell the size of a telephone booth, about five square feet and too small for me to lie down in; I alternated between standing up and sitting down on the floor. I was beginning to feel frightened. The cell was bare except for an electric light. In the door there was a tiny observation hole, one of those judas holes which enables the prison staff to look into the cell, but not the prisoner to look out. After some time, the door was opened and a female prison guard pushed in a small iron bowl of cabbage soup and handed me a big round spoon of dark wood. The soup smelled awful, but it did not really matter, because I was quite unable to eat anything at all.

Sitting on the floor, I suddenly began to feel the coldness creeping into my body. The hours passed and nothing happened. I could hear footsteps in the "waiting room," and now and then a guard peeped through the judas hole of my cell. Finally, when darkness fell, the door was opened and I was summoned. At last, the reception formalities were about to begin: Filling out forms—name, birthday (year and place), names of parents, and so forth. Then there was the body-search where I had to strip naked; an electric torch was shoved into my mouth and my lower parts were searched just as thoroughly as everything else; my armpits in particular were under suspicion, presumably because the Russians were used to finding letters and small pieces of paper there. My watch was removed and so were my pen, my belt, and even my shoe laces—supposedly to prevent me from killing myself. I had to sign my name to a list of all the confiscated things. Everything was put into a large envelope which was sealed and put away. And that was all for now.

On our way back, I learned that a prisoner often had to stop and wait with his face against the wall, that he was not supposed to look around him when he was escorted up and down the corridors. My guard led the way through long, brightly lit corridors, up a number of stairs and into another wing of the prison. The stories were connected by a system of iron stairs with banisters and strong wire netting to prevent prisoners who had become weary of life from committing suicide by throwing themselves down the stairwells. I was taken to the second floor to a corridor with numbered doors. The guard stopped in front of number 92, opened the door, and signaled to me to enter. I shivered when I heard the heavy door slam behind my back.

I looked around me and saw about forty men, cowering on the floor as close to each other as possible. The air was almost unbreathable. No one seemed to notice me, so I sat down on the floor near the door, feeling quite sick with worry, and looked at the men among whom I suddenly found myself. At last, one of them spoke: "You're not German, are you?" I explained who I was and where I came from, and I learned that they were German soldiers or officers, with the exception of two—one a Dutch merchant, the other a German engineer and an expert on V-1 and V-2 bombs.

Cell number 92 became my residence for the following four months. It was certainly not equipped with any unnecessary luxury, and the furniture was very primitive: to the right of the door was a soil tub with two handles and a lid. A long table with shelves and two long benches were placed in the center of the cell. The big solid iron door had the usual judas hole and a small hatch which could be opened from the outside and positioned horizontally, and upon which the prison guards would place the daily rations of bread. We slept in two long rows on the hard cement floor on each side of the table, with less than two feet of space allocated to each of us. It was impossible to sleep on the back, and if we wanted to change positions during the night because it hurt to lie on the same hip all the time, we would invariably wake up either of the men beside us. The gangway between the door and the table was kept clear for possible soil tub visits during the night. The only window had solid iron bars and was placed high, opposite the door. To prevent us from looking out, a frosted piece of glass had been affixed to it. Above the door, an electric light was on twenty-four hours a day, obviously because the prison staff would then be able to watch us through the judas hole. As the last arrival, I was told that my place would be the one near the soil tub "until one of us is taken away; then you may move closer to the window." The first few days were like a nightmare. The stench from the soil tub and the constant pool in front of it was appalling. Any use of the tub during daytime was much frowned upon, because the last arrival had to eat and sleep at that very spot.

On the day of my arrest, the weather had been mild and warm and I had been wearing light summer clothes: a short-sleeved shirt and thin underwear. But from 8 October onward, it snowed incessantly and we had severe frost. I was not allowed to get my luggage which contained clean and warm clothes, and soon the cold began to bother me, and so did the filth. Until the end of February I wore the same shirt—I could not wash it—I did not have a haircut, and I did not shave—not once!

The days in the prison began at 5:50 in the morning when a prison officer yelled: "Dawai, bistré!"—"Now, get up, on the double!" The yell made everybody jump up from the hard floor, because the object was to be the first to reach the washing room, where there were only five lavatories and a few taps available. Not that it was any pleasure to use the lavatories: They were holes in the ground, with no partitions at all and nothing to sit on. A couple of cement bricks or tiles for your feet were built into the ground, one on each side of the hole. I am sure it is not difficult to imagine what it felt like to have to squat down to relieve nature—on command—while the rest of the prisoners were queuing up in front of you, waiting impatiently and staring at you. Toilet paper was unheard of—not even an old newspaper could be found. Unfriendly and vicious jeers to hurry up, so that the next guy could get his chance, flew around the room. The queuing up was resumed in front of the taps. Thirty minutes for forty men were obviously not sufficient for a proper wash. In the afternoon, at the same time, the same procedure was repeated; consequently, if one of us suffered from stomach trouble, or for some other reason was unable to manage with two visits to the lavatory a day, then he had to resort to the repulsive and stinking soil tub.

The food never varied: Each morning we had a thick slice of dark bread, about five hundred grams, fresh, solid, and sticky, served with as much cold water as we could drink. The bread ration was not bad—it was probably even more than ample—but it was very wet and I do not think its nutritive value was very high. Three times a day we had a small iron bowl of warm cabbage soup—not soup in the usual sense of the word, but boiled water with a few pieces of cabbage leaves thrown in. We never had any other kind of vegetable, nor did we ever get any meat. On rare occasions a couple of small fish heads had been added to the soup, but they were so over-cooked that it was quite impossible to detect any meat, only a few bare fishbones. Margarine and lard, not to mention sugar, coffee, and tea, did not exist.

Bread and water—that was all. It took me some time to get accustomed to such a spartan diet, but I was soon so hungry that all of it—even the evil-smelling soup—was eaten, down to the very last bit.

A couple times during the week, a middle-aged woman, wearing a white kerchief, would come into our cell. She would carry a bucket containing a white liquid, looking very much like milk—though it was not, as I realized when I saw her pour a bit of it into the soil tub with a ladle. Then she would disappear without a word. It was chlorine and she used it for disinfectant. When we were talking about her we simply referred to her as "Milk-Auntie."

Twice a week we were allowed fifteen minutes of exercise in the prison yard. These exercises were the height of luxury during the entire prison stay, because for those short periods we did not have to sit and crouch on the floor but were able to stretch our legs, get some fresh air, see a bit of blue sky, and sometimes hear the distant sound of traffic from the street outside. Watched by two prison guards, we could look at freedom, walk around, and allow our thoughts to travel; we did not talk much while walking around; instead, we concentrated on enjoying the fifteen minutes as much as possible.

Every three weeks we got some books from the prison library; its collection of books was limited and consisted of literature in German only. Some of the books were old and torn, printed in the eighteen hundreds, but were nevertheless reasonably good and entertaining books. Sometimes we were lucky to get a translation of one of the old Russian classics, but mostly the "book girl" brought us Communist propaganda books. We used to call her "Kniggi" because she always stuck her head through the hatch and called out "Kniggi," the Russian word for books.

Kniggi's rare visits with her limited number of books was in fact the only diversion the Russians offered. So we had to be inventive in our efforts to find other things to pass the days with. One of the prisoners, for instance, drew up a chessboard on the reddish floor with a piece of chalk which one of the prisoners had somehow got hold of—had "organized," as we called it. The chessmen did not present any problem, although it meant a cut in our bread rations, but that was gladly sacrificed knowing it would enable us to keep ourselves occupied during a few long and drab hours. Even without any particular artistic ability, it was quite easy to shape the solid and wet bread into some reasonably nice-looking chessmen. We left them on the window sill for a few days so that they would become dry and hard, and then they were ready for a game of chess. In order to tell black and white chessmen apart, a shred of newspaper was tied to the white ones.

In order to keep track of time, we had drawn up a calendar on the wall, and each day was ticked off very carefully with our piece of chalk.

The cell was kept moderately clean. We did it ourselves according to a list that we had made. But there was not anything we could do about the bugs, so at regular intervals, when they got so impertinent that we could not sleep, we notified the prison staff and they immediately sent a middle-aged Russian—the "bug killer," we called him. He was armed with a large blowpipe which he turned and let its bluish flame lick every corner of the cell where there was the remotest possibility of these ugly "partisans" having established their permanent residence. After such an operation, the whole cell smelled horribly—of burnt bugs—but it helped, at least for a while.

The interrogations usually took place at night at about eleven o'clock, just when we had fallen into a heavy sleep. The hatch would be opened and a name called, followed by "get ready and leave your things behind"; sleepy and confused, we would start looking for our shoes, and then the door would be opened, and each time we would hear the same hard and cold words: "Dawai, bistré!" I believe that these two Russian words were the words I heard most frequently; at least, they were the words I first learned to understand during my Russian imprisonment. A prisoner might wait for weeks, months, even years, but if he was wanted for an interrogation in the middle of the night, then he had to tear along like mad: "Dawai, bistré!"

It took time to get used to life in a Russian prison cell. The light, which was constantly on, prevented any kind of undis-

closed movement. Even worse than that was the constant physical contact with human bodies, although it sometimes proved an
advantage, because the colder it was, the more you felt like moving closer to the man next to you to try to get a bit of warmth
while lying on the cement floor. The cell remained unheated, and
an extra blanket, or even just a mat, was completely out of the
question. We had to put up with things as they were.

The lack of privacy was equally difficult to get accustomed
to. Not only did we not receive any newspapers or any other
kind of news, have no possibility of sending or receiving mail,
and no contact at all with our families; we also did not know
who we could trust and confide in. I did not know a single one of
my cell-mates; I knew that there might very well be one, perhaps
several "cell spies" among them, men who would listen to what
we said and try to pump us, especially new arrivals, for information which might be of interest to the Russian authorities, and it
was assumed that the Russians, just like the Germans and others,
allowed these prisoners to enjoy a number of small privileges, if
they would inform against and thereby betray or "blow" their
cell-mates.

When I had first arrived in the cell, I had explained that I
was a theologian employed by a Christian organization, and it
therefore seemed very natural when one of the German officers,
a Lieutenant Koch, introduced himself to me and told me that
he was from East Prussia and that he, too, had studied theology,
but that the war had prevented him from graduating. He said that
he had a Bible which I was most welcome to borrow whenever I
wanted to. This alone aroused my suspicions, because the Russians had already in the internment camp taken my Bible and
hymn book away from me. I naturally did not decline his offer,
but I became very cautious and knew that I had to be on my
guard against his friendliness, and in particular against his pious
stock phrases. I was confirmed in my suspicions, because it soon
became apparent that he was treated differently from the rest of
us: he was taken to interrogations much more often than anybody else, and one night when he returned to the cell and I happened to be awake, I saw him pull a bar of chocolate from his
pocket and eat it. That confirmed my suspicions to my full satis-

faction and I confined our conversations to a minimum. Not that I could give him any information the Russians were not welcome to have, but I just did not feel like talking to him. Anyway, a few days later he was taken out of the cell and never returned as long as I was there. Most probably he had been transferred to another cell to do his informer's work. This incident, however, had shown me how difficult it was to have complete trust in one's fellow prisoners.

I had been in the cell for two days when I was summoned for my first interrogation. The walk from the cell to where the interrogation was to take place took about five minutes; the prison guard walked a few paces in front of me and constantly beat upon the iron buckle of his belt with his big bunch of keys. It struck me that it must be a signal to his colleagues who happened to be walking in the prison corridors: "Watch out! I'm here with a prisoner, don't let your prisoner come within sight!" It seemed that the prison authorities wanted to prevent us from knowing who else was kept prisoner. And everywhere along the long corridors were small, dark cells, into which a prison guard could quickly push a prisoner to prevent him from meeting another prisoner. We reached a wide and brightly illuminated hall with lots of doors leading into different rooms for interrogation. I was ushered into one of them and asked to wait there; apart from a desk and two chairs, the room was bare. Soon a young lieutenant appeared, sat down at the desk, beckoned me to sit down in the opposite chair, and started to question me.

The interrogation was rather brief and formal, and it was confined mainly to the usual personal information which I had already given in the internment camp, my family details and a couple of questions about the YMCA's "political affiliations." The lieutenant spoke a passable German and at no point was he unfriendly. Toward the end I ventured to ask him if I could talk to his superior, and he answered somewhat bemused, "Don't worry—you'll get to meet him soon enough." He finally asked me how I was, and I answered quite truthfully that I was not well at all and that I did not understand why I was in prison. He looked at me and answered in a sympathetic voice: "Don't take it so hard—you're a young man passing through Moscow on

your way home from Berlin. Think of yourself as someone staying in a hotel in Moscow for a short time." I could not help it:
"In Denmark, we don't use barred windows in our hotels, and
we are not in the habit of having armed guards in front of the
doors, either!"

The first proper and more serious questioning took place a
few days later, again in the middle of the night. The interrogator
during this and all subsequent interrogations was a colonel—a
tall, barrel-chested giant of a man, about 250 pounds. I was not
sure about his name, but he was referred to as Colonel Lüttich
by my fellow prisoners. A young Jewish woman acted as his
interpreter. He put his questions to her in Russian, she translated
them into German and then repeated my answers to the colonel
in Russian. While she asked me a question, he would just sit
there—huge and heavy—and stare at me, intent on noticing even
my smallest reaction to his question. At first he seemed kind
enough, but after a few questions about my well-being, he
started to question me straight from the shoulder:

"Why are you collaborating with the Nazis?" I was completely stunned and tried to explain the purpose of the YMCA
POW Aid and their methods of work, and I emphasized that my
cooperation with the German authorities had been carried out
only to the extent necessary to be able to help the Allied POWs
in the best possible way. "Why did you collaborate with the Gestapo?" "I did not! The YMCA dealt only with the German Foreign Ministry and the German High Command!"

Then the colonel directed his attack from another angle. He
raised his voice and said: "We have proof that both the YMCA
World Alliance and the International Red Cross have worked for
the British Intelligence Service. You are a spy! You have done
illegal work in Germany, and you have helped prominent Nazis
escape to Sweden and Switzerland with forged passports." He
did not explain how working for the British and helping Nazis
to escape could possibly be compatible, and I rejected both these
accusations as being quite unfounded and untrue. I asked him
instead why I had not been allowed to continue my journey
home together with my countrymen. He ignored me and said:
"Together with three Swiss employed by the International Red

Cross you're one of the few persons detained in Berlin who were frequenting the German Foreign Ministry. You had the opportunity to visit prison camps, prisons, hard labor camps, and hospitals all over Germany. You associated with many foreign diplomats in Berlin. And you can tell us much, much more than you have done up to now."

"I'm not aware of having done anything illegal, nor of having worked against the interests of the Allies. I've done nothing that I wouldn't want to be revealed. My conscience is clear and I've nothing to hide. That is why it's so terribly wrong and unjust to have me locked up in a prison." He interrupted my outburst in a loud voice: "We know all about you and your work, and you're not going to get out of here, before you have confessed!" And he emphasized his words by slamming his fist against the desk with an enormous bang. After a little while, he said: "Now, you go back to your cell and think carefully about what I've said, and if you don't come clean, I shall invite you down to the cellar and show you the things we use to get people to talk!"

He was threatening me. If you could not break a man and humiliate him by means of hunger, cold, filth, and loneliness, you could always resort to physical terror—torture—in the cellar. But certain as I was that there was absolutely no basis for his untruthful accusations, I told him: "I know of course that you can beat me and torture me as much as you please, and that you most probably are able to bring me to the point where I shall admit to being Hitler himself, or Goebbels. But as long as I am in possession of my right mind, I shall go on repeating that you do me a great injustice by locking me up. I haven't done what you accuse me of, and I'm convinced that none of my colleagues in the Red Cross and the YMCA have been involved in any kind of illegal work either." "You can answer only for yourself," he interrupted, "go back to your cell and come to your senses, and the next time I call you for questioning, I would advise you to tell me what you know."

The colonel had finished with me for now and I was escorted back to the cell. I remembered a drawing I once saw in a hotel room in Germany; a small black cat stands in front of a vicious, yapping dog, its sharp teeth bared in a threatening way; the cat arches its back and spits out "Bange machen gilt nicht"— to scare does not count. Somehow, I took comfort in these words after having left the colonel that night, and I felt at peace with myself.

More than three weeks went by. Then, on 19 September, I was summoned for another interrogation. On this occasion the colonel did not ask me about my well-being, but went straight to the point: "Make a list of all the prison camps in Germany!" I told him that I could easily make a list of the camps and hospitals in the four provinces that had been my area of responsibility—Pomerania, Mecklenburg, Brandenburg, and Saxony, whereas the camps in the remaining part of Germany and in Austria and Poland had been the responsibility of my colleagues and were therefore not familiar to me. In a few minutes I had made up the list and handed it to him. After having glanced through it for a few moments, he said, to my amazement, "Soon now, you shall return to Denmark." He looked hard at me and continued, "We count on you, once you are home, to be an excellent advocate of democracy." I told him that I had never been a greater supporter of democracy than at this very moment. "Yes," the colonel said, "I'm sure you'll be a good associate to Russia when you get back to Denmark." His remark made me feel uneasy; if I said no, the colonel would definitely become displeased and threatening again, and I could not say yes, because I did not want to serve the Russians in any way. After a moment's hesitation, I said, "I don't think I possess the qualifications to become a good associate to you."

The colonel's reaction was just as I had anticipated; he slammed the desk and shouted, louder than ever before: "I knew! As soon as you're back in Denmark, you'll start working against the Soviet Union. But you won't be going home—you'll sit here for years; and don't you think that any diplomatic step from Washington or Copenhagen is going to save you—it won't!" His last words, which he probably meant to be a threat, pleased me greatly, because I guessed that the YMCA World Alliance as well as the Danish Foreign Ministry were making every effort to have me released and sent home.

I was proved right when years later I had the opportunity to read the Foreign Ministry's files on the matter. Under the circumstances, the Danish Foreign Service did all that was possible—by personal appeals to the Russian authorities, and by so-called verbal notes—to ease my conditions during my imprisonment and to have me released and repatriated. I regret that it is no longer possible to convey my gratitude to those diplomats who were personally involved in my case, and whom I knew well from my time in Berlin, as they have all passed away.

The next interrogation took place two weeks later on 25 September and lasted from eleven o'clock in the evening to four o'clock in the morning, interrupted, however, by several small breaks. Whether the colonel was questioning someone else in another room, I do not know—he would just suddenly disappear without a word, usually together with his interpreter, and leave me alone for twenty to forty minutes. Only once did the interpreter remain with me, and she started to talk to me about wind and weather in Denmark—did we have good skiing snow, did it rain much, and so on, and I actually got the impression that she liked me and wanted to be kind to me. I ventured to ask her name, but that was apparently going too far, she looked at me and shut her mouth tight, violently shaking her head. I understood exactly what she meant.

Long though it was, the questioning was carried out in a reasonably friendly atmosphere without the colonel blowing his top or making threats. At the beginning, many of the questions were a repetition of earlier ones, and I suppose that they served to determine whether my answers and explanations corresponded to those I had given earlier. Later on, the colonel turned the questioning to the YMCA in Denmark and Sweden. He also wanted to know about the POW Aid's cooperation with the Red Cross and about the funding of the YMCA relief work. He disclosed a certain knowledge of the YMCA in Denmark when he asked me: "Who is Christian Baun? And what are his responsibilities in the YMCA?" I wondered how the name "Baun" could be familiar to him, if he did not know of this man's excellent leadership of the YMCA and YWCA in Denmark.

I was asked why I had not joined the Danish resistance

movement. I replied that I found it rather difficult considering that I worked and lived in Berlin. Finally, the colonel said: "Actually, you could go back to Denmark, provided you resigned from the YMCA both as a member and as an employee." I shook my head and explained that I had been a member of the YMCA since I was a boy, and that I had had nothing but pleasure from that membership. And I went on: "This organization has given me a job which interests me tremendously and gives me much pleasure, and you want me to give it up—I can't do that!" "I don't understand," he said, "how can you possibly be a member of an organization whose leaders now stand trial in Nuremberg, accused of being war criminals?"

I found his statement an unfair and quite unreasonable accusation against one of the world's largest relief organizations and told him so. "The International Red Cross and the YMCA World Alliance," I emphasized, "are practically the only two organizations that helped the POWs in Germany regardless of their nationality, color of skin, and religious and political affiliations." And I added, "You'll have to prove such an allegation!"

"You're an acquaintance of Count Folke Bernadotte. You've been together with him in Berlin as well as in Sweden and you know, I take it, that he is a member of the Swedish YMCA, and that his sister, Elsa Bernadotte, is one of the leaders of the Swedish YWCA, married to Hugo Cedergren, chairman of the Swedish YMCA and director of the World Alliance's POW Aid in Geneva." He paused and then continued: "Bernadotte is a war criminal. He negotiated with the Nazi leaders, Himmler, for instance, in the last weeks of the war, intent on obtaining a separate peace between the Western powers and Nazi Germany, thereby excluding the Soviet Union."

I told him that I did not know Count Bernadotte very well. It was true that I had met him in Berlin in the Swedish Legation five weeks before the war ended. I knew that he was there to negotiate with the German authorities about release and repatriation of Norwegian and Danish POWs, but I knew nothing about a conciliation between Germany and Great Britain.

At this point the colonel got up and left the room; he returned a little later carrying a small tray with a cup of tea and two slices of white bread which he placed in front of me, muttering something in Russian—presumably something like, "There you are, this is for you." I was surprised, but I certainly enjoyed this unexpected luxury. Now he seemed quite another person. He talked to me in a quiet and normal voice, chatting about this, that, and the other, the Russian winter and the excellent skiing snow. I became so encouraged by his apparent friendliness that I ventured to ask him if I could have my warm clothes back and if he could possibly expedite the conclusion of my case. He promised that in the future he would summon me for questioning "at least twice a week." I believed him and, feeling much better than before, I returned to cell number 92.

He did not keep his promise, for I was not summoned for questioning until three weeks later, from eleven o'clock in the evening of the 19 October until about three o'clock the following morning. On that occasion I had to make an account—down to the last detail, verbally as well as in writing—of the incident in April 1944 during which the Gestapo arrested and exiled Pastor Erik Christensen, in charge of the YMCA POW Aid in Germany, and our Swedish correspondent, Gertrud Malmquist, an incident which had placed the POW Aid in Germany in its most serious position ever. At the end of the interrogation, I took the liberty of asking the colonel why he had not kept his promise to summon me twice a week. He explained that he had been away on duty and therefore had been unable to see me until now, but in the future he would be sure to send for me more often.

When yet another three weeks passed without any interrogations I began to lose faith in Russian promises, but what was far more serious, I began to lose heart and to take a pessimistic view of the future. My nerves got frayed. The German prisoners' never-ending discussions about the lost war, which used to be very interesting, tended to become infinitely boring. The bugs and the filth were a regular curse, but worse than that were, I think, the hours just after midnight, when the prisoners returned one after another from the interrogations, and—consciously or subconsciously—began to express their reactions, even their pain. Most of them hunched themselves up on their allotted narrow spots without speaking; some cursed and swore softly, others lay shaking all over, and sometimes somebody was weeping silently. I was dismayed by all this misery; there were times when I myself became terribly frightened, not because I had a bad conscience—I did not; I knew in my heart that the Russians had no basis for their accusations against me—but because I could not help thinking of some of the atrocities I had heard were taking place in Russia, and I was afraid that in the end they would simply make me "disappear."

On top of all this, my stomach began to act up because of our unvarying, scanty, and vitamin-deficient diet, and as I mentioned, it was not looked kindly upon if you had to use the soil tub in the cell—the air was foul enough as it was. And then my back started to hurt; the cold and the cement floor which we had to sleep on without any mattresses gave me rheumatism, and the cell was still unheated in spite of the snow and the cold outside. It was beginning to be extremely uncomfortable having to wear the same dirty clothes, not being able to wash or change them. Every morning when I woke up, my eyes were glued together by yellow puss to such a degree that I had to use water to get them opened, and my first bite of bread made my gums bleed. Gradually I became weaker, and by the middle of November I was so exhausted after just a little walk in the prison yard that I had to cling to the banister as I returned to my cell on the second floor. In the end, I reached the point where I could not keep anything down at all and I made a perfect mess of myself.

After another three weeks without being sent for I was convinced that the colonel did not give a hoot about me, and so, after a few days of reflection, I decided to call a hunger strike. "If there's anything the Russians respect, it's definitely hunger strikes," declared the German colonel, Freiherr von Sass, who was sitting next to me. "Then why don't you do it more often?" "No," he answered, "It is not unreasonable that we are here, because we started the war. You didn't!" The following morning I refused to take the bread that was handed to me through the hatch, and when the soup was distributed a little later, I did not touch it. I continued this for three days; the second day was the worst—I really felt hungry that day—but then it passed, and I actually did not mind not getting any food.

On the morning of the fourth day, when I again refused the bread and the soup, something happened. A young officer entered the cell and asked me what on earth was the meaning of this refusal to eat. I ought to consider my health and start eating again. I told him not to worry, because it really was none of his business. He asked why I was refusing food, and I told him to put that very question to the colonel who used to question me, and if the colonel did not know, I would be more than happy to give him an explanation, the next time he sent for me. The officer did not know what to do, so he left. Half an hour later, however, he returned and shouted through the hatch that I should pack my things quickly and get outside. Packing my things was no problem, because I had only a towel, which I put into my pocket, and then I was outside in the long corridor. I was ordered to take off my jacket, my socks, and my shoes, but was allowed to keep on my trousers and my thin short-sleeved shirt which I had been wearing since the beginning of August. Barefoot I was escorted through several corridors to another wing of the prison and locked up in a dark cell, probably no larger than ten square feet, with no windows, no light, no furniture. The door banged behind me and I was alone. I fell to the floor, feeling terribly dismayed and terribly cold, and deeply worried what would happen next, and how long I would have to be shut up in this small cell. The darkness made it impossible to know the time of day; at one point, somebody handed me the usual bowl of soup, but I did not eat it and it went out again untouched. A little later I heard a man wailing and moaning in the cell next to mine; it sounded as if he had been beaten or even tortured. Whether this was true or not I did not know; it might very well have been something which the Russians had staged to test my nerves; if so, they certainly succeeded—I was very frightened that something similar would soon happen to me. On the other hand, I was determined not to give in. I wanted out! I could not stand life in prison much longer.

In my heart I knew that I had not done anything wrong or illegal in Germany; I knew that the relief work that I had helped carry out in the prison camps was not something that I had taken upon myself to do, but a task which others had given me, and slowly I began to calm down. When the evening soup was brought in, I once again refused to eat it. Later that night I was summoned for questioning, and I stumbled barefoot along the corridors and up the many stairs to my interrogator—the colonel. He was walking back and forth, wearing his large military coat, with a thick scarf around his neck and a fur cap on his head.

The cold made me shiver and I must have been something of a sight, because his immediate reaction was, "Man, you look terrible!" No chatting about the weather or the skiing snow this time. I said hotly, "Of course I look terrible—when a man is treated the way in which I have been treated now for several months, then he is bound to look terrible." "It's your own fault—you stopped eating. Why on earth did you do that?" "I stopped eating, because I don't think you care one little bit about me. I can assure you that the food you give me at this place is much worse than what we give our pigs on my father's farm, and the way you treat me is much worse than the way the Nazis treated the Allied POWs in Germany. If I can't go home to Denmark, I have no interest in life anymore." "Now listen, don't take it so hard," he said. "You'll be able to go back to Denmark—don't worry."

I told him that I did worry—he had given his promises so often, and "You've never kept any of them so far." "A Russian officer," he shouted, "always keeps his promises!" But I remembered, precisely, the dates when I had been questioned by him, and shouted back: "On 5 September, you promised me that I would be allowed to send a postcard to my parents to at least let them know I was alive. On 16 September, you promised me that I could have my luggage so that I could get some clean clothes and have a shave. You promised me that I could have a medical examination. More than once, you promised me better food. At the end of September you promised to question me at least twice a week. You repeated this promise on 19 October, and here we are, with three weeks having passed already. Promises, promises, promises, and you haven't kept one single one. How can you possibly expect me to believe you when you say I'm going home soon?"

I paused to get my breath, but the colonel did not have anything to say to my outburst; it would have been very difficult to, because the dates and the content of his promises were quite correct. He turned and left the room, but was back almost immediately, carrying a tray with a glass of tea, two slices of bread, some cheese, an apple, and a small bar of chocolate, which he placed in front of me. I got up and moved it away to the farthest end of the table. He looked at me, incredulous, for a moment or two, then he left the room, and I was alone with this luxurious repast. Nothing happened for two long hours, but finally he returned, and when he saw that I had not touched the food, he became so outraged that he started screaming at me and abusing me in a manner which he had never done before.

"Just who do you think you are?" He swore at me. "Do you think, perhaps, that you're able to force your will on the Russian authorities, eh?"

"No!"

"Then get started—eat!"

"No! Not until I'm out of prison."

After ten minutes of complete silence, during which we both just sat there, staring at each other, he tried something different: "Now listen to me," he reasoned, "you must think about your health, you just cannot keep this up, you know, not in the long run." "Why are you suddenly so concerned about my health," I asked him, and remembering, went on in an agonized voice, "I have been suffering from diarrhea for weeks now, and that hasn't seemed to bother you at all!" He pretended not to have heard me and continued, "You must also think about your old parents; it would be so tragic, you know, if we had to inform them that their son died during his stay in Russia." I got angry: "Till now," I retorted, "you have shown absolutely no interest in my parents, and it's not necessary that you should do so now. That's not what all this is about. If you think that I have done anything illegal, then prove it. If not, then set me free and let me go home. That would be the best consideration you could show my parents." Again the colonel ignored me and asked instead, "What do you really think you're going to achieve by this hunger strike?" "That you release me," I immediately replied, "or that I die!"

The colonel got up, took a few paces around the room, sat down again, and then slammed the desk with his enormous fist and shouted, right into my face, "If you don't stop this foolishness of yours at once, and start eating, I warn you that I have means and ways enough to make you eat." In a threatening voice he added, "provided of course we are interested in keeping you alive after all." Thoughts flashed through my mind; what was the right thing to say now? But before I could say anything, the colonel went on: "You're lying to us; we are well informed about you and your activities. I'll have you remain in your cell for months or until you come to your senses and see reason!"

His words gave me a peculiar feeling of calmness and I thought to myself, "Go ahead, scare me as much as you want— I have done nothing wrong!" And my voice was very quiet when I said: "I know perfectly well that I'm at your mercy and that you can do what you want. You may force me to eat, if that's what you want, but I shall not eat of my own free will until I'm out of this prison. And if you would be honest with yourself, you know very well that, to the best of my ability, I have tried to do a decent job in Germany to help the POWs, including the Russian POWs, and you also know very well that your treatment of me is wrong." This time the colonel was listening. He did not speak for a little while, but then in a quite normal, even kind voice, he said, "Now, go on, eat, and I give you my solemn promise that soon you'll be out of prison."

Somehow, I had the feeling that this time the colonel was honest with me, that he was almost begging me to stop the hunger strike, and I said: "If you will let me call Minister Døssing at the Danish Legation and talk to him, either in German or in English, so that you understand every word I say, then I shall regard that as a token of your being honest with me, and I shall begin to eat." "No, no," he exclaimed. "That's out of the question; never before has a prisoner been allowed to contact his legation." "In that case, I must take that to mean that in a Nazi prison, a prisoner is treated far better than in a Russian one: when a Danish citizen was arrested by the Gestapo in Berlin, the Danish Legation was informed about it within twenty-four hours of the arrest, and the minister, his representative, or a

Catholic open-air service held in Stalag II-B, Hammerstein

Polish officers at Oflag II-E, Neubrandenburg

Title page from a book of lithographs given to author by four Polish officers. The lithographs that follow illustrate the daily life in the overcrowded camp at Woldenberg, Oflag II-C.

We patient crew of ships-barracks, which seldom catch friendly winds, over sky, land and sea we constantly seek signs foretelling a moment which will suddenly arrive.

It is unproductive to be imprisoned: some carts bring food packages, others take out to the neighboring fields the only product of our inactivity.

Every night is the same all over again—they crawl out of hiding, sneak into dreams—neither coffee nor tea nor lysol work—fleas, bed-bugs, and memories as they once bit they now bite.

They fry, smoke, chatter, blow into fireplaces, always lacking water but never music. Everyone has a sad sigh when remembering the bathroom: life there floats in total harmony.

Winter is too long, Fall too despairing, Summer is too short, and Spring is too wet—and besides, constantly from all corners of the world wind blows in prisoner's eyes throughout all the seasons.

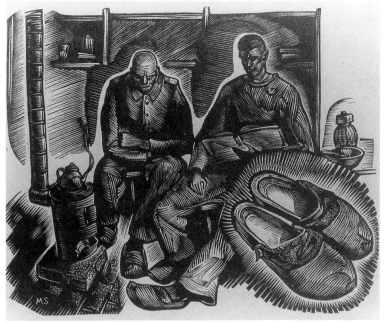

Prisoners cannot live without clogs, although they can live
without women, but clogs are really only the floor, which
we carry along.

Behind the camp wild fields, meadows, freedom—but we
here take walks slowly by the fence; sometimes someone
stops, glances quietly: what do you think sir? a year? or
two? or three?

Constantly waiting for our bad lot to end, we play games . . . Players as well as fans watch, but without us there goes by a much more important game—unfortunately still spectators.

Each year for the last time, ever since four years ago, a colorful row of regiments observes its holiday: For those who are not living—a prayer and a tear, but for those who still live—coffee and a cake of grits.

Drawing by R. Fryszowski. An overcrowded room at Oflag II-C. The camp accommodated over 7000 Polish officers and other soldiers.

A corner of the camp library at Oflag II-C, Woldenberg.

A British officer and a Polish cavalry officer, drawn by a Polish artist in Oflag II-C, Woldenberg.

chaplain to the legation was permitted to see the prisoner in his cell on the following day. Apparently this is not so in Moscow; apparently, it's much worse to be arrested in Russia than it was to be arrested in Nazi Germany."

The colonel continued to try to persuade me to have the tea and the bread, but I refused to touch it. As time passed, I grew calmer, because he neither beat me nor seemed to want to carry out his threats about forcing me to eat. I think he found it extremely embarrassing to be confronted with this stubborn man and his hunger strike, and finally he said, in a convincing voice, "I guarantee that you'll be released very soon!" And he emphasized his words by once more slapping his fist on the desk. Knowing very well that he was so much stronger than I was and that, in the long run, I would be the one to have to give in, I conceded: "I am willing to trust a Russian officer's promise one more time, so if you promise me that I shall be out of this prison within two weeks, then I'll believe you and I'll start eating." "I guarantee!" he answered firmly. I asked for a piece of paper and a pencil and before I began to eat, I made a written statement to the effect that I now put an end to my hunger strike because the colonel had promised me that I would be out of prison not later than two weeks from now, and I added that "if I am not out within the specified period, I intend to resume my hunger strike and I will not discontinue it until I have been released from this prison." I printed my name and the date, signed it, and handed it to the colonel. Only then did I drink the cold tea and eat the bread and cheese; the apple and the small bar of chocolate I stuffed in my pocket for later.

I was then taken back to my dark cell. Twenty minutes later, two women doctors entered and gave me a thorough examination. I swallowed some pills which were probably meant to help cure my indigestion, I got my jacket, socks and shoes back, and then I was brought to another cell, similar to number 92. I felt that I had been through a strange kind of hearing, a travesty of justice, a kind of endurance test between an enfeebled, hungry man and the mighty state machine.

I was never again summoned for interrogation. I am sure my hunger strike had had its effect. Perhaps it helped to show that the accusations against me were wrong. I did go to the interrogation room every day, but not for questioning; the colonel was not there, but his interpreter explained that she had been instructed to give me a glass of tea and some bread every day. Of course, this helped to put me in better spirits and regain some of my strength, and I let myself begin to believe that things were going in the right direction.

And so they did. Ten days later, I was finally able to walk through the gates of the prison. Suddenly one morning at about three o'clock the cell door was opened, my name called, and I was told "to get ready for transportation." The packing of my things was soon accomplished because I still only possessed one towel. Hastily, I bade my cell mates farewell, telling them not to lose courage. I shook as many hands as I possibly could and looked into as many faces—faces so full of sadness and worry. Some of the prisoners handed me the addresses of their wives in Germany and one of them begged: "You probably have a better chance of being liberated than I have. Please give my love to my wife and try to help her if you can!" Another prisoner, a German colonel, was waiting for the execution of his sentence to death. He was not afraid to die; he awaited his fate with resignation and calm. Four weeks later he was hanged in public in the square of Weliki-Luki, a town in western Russia where he had served as a town commandant during the German occupation. He had always treated me in a friendly and sympathetic way, and it was hard for me to believe that he had been guilty of any kind of war crimes.

In the corridor outside the cell, a prison officer was waiting to take me on the nightly walk through the prison, accompanied by his bunch of keys beating his buckle; he did not lead me out of the building as I had expected, but downstairs to the cellar where he shut me up in a solitary cell. I felt all my old fears rise inside me again: What had gone wrong? Why was I here? My earlier speculations about whether the Russians would simply let me "disappear"—were they true? At last, at five o'clock in the afternoon, after twelve hours of pure agony, I was led into the prison yard.

To my great surprise I heard a calm, Swedish voice exclaim:

"Well now, Christian! What on earth! You're here too, are you?" The voice belonged to Edward af Sandeberg, an editor and a very good friend of mine from my days in Berlin, where he had been a correspondent for a Swedish newspaper, the "Stockholmstidningen." I'd had no idea that he, too, had been in prison; I had not even known what had happened to him in Berlin after the capitulation. It goes without saying that the joy of meeting each other again was immense. Shortly afterward, a Russian captain came up to us and said encouragingly: "On behalf of Colonel Lüttich, I regret that we have had to keep you imprisoned here. However, I am pleased to inform both of you that we have been able to establish the fact that you're not guilty of anything which could be held against you. Now we're going to take you to a camp where you are to stay for a few days only, while the last details in connection with your journey home are taken care of."

The captain looked so trustworthy and nice and spoke in such a convincing and friendly voice that both of us believed every single word he uttered. I do not know why I had not been taught by my bitter experiences. I do not know why I did not know enough about broken Russian promises. But I had not and I did not! In a most naive way, I trusted this officer completely when he told us that soon we would be going home. I was already beginning to imagine: Who knows—we might even be home for Christmas. We were not! It was to be five and a half months before I could finally turn my back on Russia!

Shortly afterward we were asked to get into a waiting car. I must say that the preparations for our departure had taken some time. I had been awakened at three o'clock in the morning, and it had been dark a long time before we finally drove through the prison gates—the very same heavy gates which I, filled with presentiments of evil, had heard slam shut in August.

With this, my one hundred days in the Moscow prison were over, and together with Edward af Sandeberg, who was to be like a brother to me the following months, we were driven to a large POW camp about ten miles northwest of Moscow in the outskirts of the village Krasnogorsk; the official name of the camp was Camp number 27. During our ride, Edward related how he had experienced and survived the fall of Berlin, how he

had been picked up by the Russians and transported to Moscow
a month later than the rest of us, and how he had spent a couple
of months in the Krasnogorsk camp before he was imprisoned.
He told me that the camp housed about three thousand German
POWs and that it consisted of three different sharply divided so-
called zones, yet was managed by a joint commandant headquarters and administration. Now, Edward told me, the big question
was to which of the three zones we were to be taken. He hoped
very much that it would be the so-called "generals' zone," because this was where he had been earlier, and he was of the opinion that the food was better there than in the other two zones.

IN A PRISON CAMP IN KRASNOGORSK

Edward's hopes were dashed, because we were in fact assigned to zone 3, or the work zone, as it was also called. But
before anything else, we were taken to the "banja," the washing
room, and told to scrub ourselves clean. What a delight! For so
long I had been forced to live in filth and unable to have a proper
wash, and here I was, standing next to a wooden tub filled with
hot water which I could use freely. While we were washing, our
clothes went through the delousing oven, and when we had finished they were ready—quite warm and smelling pungently from
the delousing treatment, but absolutely free from any living
bugs, at least for a little while. After the washing and the delousing, we were escorted to the so-called "officers' hut" which, in
spite of the name, did not differ much from all the other old
wooden huts in the camp. Our arrival aroused a great deal of
attention. The inmates soon realized that we were civilians and
that one of us was even a citizen of neutral Sweden, and so we
were bombarded with all sorts of questions: "Where are you
from?" "Have you been in the Butyrka prison?" "In which cell?"
"Who were you together with?" "For how long?" "Did you
meet Mr X?" "Mr Y?" And so on.

We had a hard time finding a place to get ourselves installed
and lie down. "The hut can only accommodate 60 men and at
the present time we're 185," one of them said protestingly. However, we were lucky enough to be able to squeeze into one of the

long shelves, although we had to be separated from one another. I found myself between two German officers, which was quite all right except that one of them snored terribly. I did not sleep much that first night, even though I was exhausted after having been awake and tense since three o'clock in the morning. It was not so much the officer's snoring that bothered me—it was the bugs; besides, I was musing on the words which were printed in big letters on the wall: "Long live the great and mighty Soviet Union—Guardian of peace and freedom." It seemed to me that the barbed-wire fence, the watch towers, the searchlights, and the guards did not quite fit into the picture of peace and free-dom—What freedom! During the months to follow, I had plenty of time to reflect on this question.

The POW camp in Krasnogorsk, like all other POW camps, came under the jurisdiction of the secret police, and it was staffed with officers and men of the NKVD. As I mentioned, it was subdivided into three zones which held different types of prisoners.

Zone 1 was a transit camp to the Moscow prisons. German and Hungarian officers who were considered politically dubious were taken to zone 1 for interrogation and closer examination of their past. If they proved to be harmless they were quickly transferred to an ordinary camp and put to work like tens of thousands of other German POWs. If, on the other hand, a POW had been accused with good reason, or if he was unwilling to give information about his past, he was transferred to one of the three large Moscow prisons to be "softened up," as it was called, by more and tougher interrogations. Months later—sometimes even years—such officers might suddenly reappear in zone 1 and stay for some time, before finally being transferred to an ordinary prison camp, or sent to prison again to serve a sentence. About two thousand officers and a large number of interned German civilians—engineers, chemists, technical experts, diplomats, and so on—were held in zone 1 at that time.

Zone 1 was also referred to as the "generals' zone," because it housed a couple hundred German generals. It was claimed that they enjoyed certain privileges, such as better food and exemption from forced labor, which did not extend to enlisted men and

lower-ranking officers. After his defeat and capture at Stalingrad, the famous field marshal Friedrich von Paulus had been
taken to the POW camp in Krasnogorsk, and it was here, in the
"generals' zone," that he had formed the "Free, German National Committee." Together with fifty-five German commanding generals of corps and divisions—all of them willing to
promote the fall of Nazi rule—he had prepared a manifesto that
encouraged German army forces to ground their arms. Over a
powerful radio transmitter the National Committee continued,
night after night, to encourage a national upsurge against Hitler
and the Nazi rule.

Zone 2 was quite unknown to me; I only knew that it was
referred to as "the anti-fascist school." I had been told by German POWs who had attended the school that the teaching consisted of several courses, each of about four months' length and
attended by approximately one hundred pupils, Germans and
Hungarians, officers and men—all of them exempt from forced
labor. The purpose of these courses was to train the pupils to
become Communist leaders so that they could be used as propa-
gandists in other POW camps, or sent to Germany and Hungary
to take part in the reconstruction work as qualified leaders. The
teachers were mainly German Jews and other refugees who had
fled to the Soviet Union during the Hitler era. Upon the conclusion of a course, the pupils were to take an oath under the witness
of a high-ranking Russian, and in doing so they confirmed that
with all their might they would work against fascism in all its
shapes. The pupils were brought in from camps all over Russia
and Siberia.

Zone 3 was a typical labor camp which, at that time, housed
three thousand German soldiers and fifty officers, including two
generals. The officers claimed to have no idea why they had been
sent to this zone—a regular soldiers' camp. All officers of the
rank of major and below were assigned to daily work. They usually worked within the boundaries of the camp, whereas the enlisted men worked in the aircraft and tank factories nearby.
Officers worked in two shifts, one from six in the morning to
six in the evening and the other from six in the evening to six in
the morning. They were responsible for cleaning the camp, peel-

ing potatoes in the kitchen, and working in various workshops, the largest of which was the carpenter's shop where furniture for Russian firms was manufactured. Neither men nor officers were paid for their work, but the officers' food was a bit better than that of the men, and the generals got the best food of all.

All the prisoners lived in old wooden huts, very similar in appearance and arrangement. They were said to have been used as quarters for homeless people before the war. They were incredibly dirty, in bad need of maintenance, and full of bugs. But the worst was the cold—the huts were unheated, and there was a horrible draft from every corner. Outside there was snow on the ground throughout March and half of April, and often the temperature dropped to 6° Fahrenheit.

We had only one blanket—no mattresses and no pillows—so during the extremely cold nights we had to lie very close to one another to keep just moderately warm. A few dim bulbs lit up the long room and made it appear very gloomy in the evenings and at night. Because of the cold we could not open the windows, and with 187 men sleeping in the hut the result was a disgusting smell; upon entering you were almost knocked out, and much tempted to remain outside in the cold, but fresh, air. The smell of chlorine, sweat, wet clothes, filth, and extinguished bugs was more than I could bear, and I do not think I shall ever be able to get that foul smell out of my nostrils.

Sometimes I woke up in the middle of the night, and if I looked around I would be sure to see one or several POWs sitting up in bed; they had pulled off their shirts and were hunting for the small disgusting beasts hiding in the seams. Once I heard a POW mutter to himself: "Man—whew—I've never seen such a partisan in Russia before!" I guessed he'd just come across a particularly large specimen.

Edward af Sandeberg and I were not the only civilian prisoners in the labor camp. One other was a Spaniard by the name of José de la Cruz. He had been a very convinced and active Communist for many years and had spent a lot of time in prisons and concentration camps in Spain, France, and Germany. He, too, had been "liberated" by the Russians in Berlin and taken, he thought, to the paradise of his dreams, the Soviet Union. But things here had not lived up to his dreams and expectations, and now he shared his fortunes with us, locked up behind barbed-wire fences. His Communist convictions and dedication had faded away like morning dew.

Another civilian was a young, very blond man from Finland named Ström. He spoke good Swedish and told me that at the age of eighteen he had gone to America, and for ten years earned his living as a driver and a car mechanic. He had been lured to the Soviet Union when he was twenty-eight and had indeed done well as a mechanic. But during the Winter War and the Russian attack on Finland he had been interned due to his Finnish citizenship, and since then he had been transferred from camp to camp. He was a nice man, and we had many enjoyable games of chess together. I am sure that today he is very grateful that he retained his Finnish citizenship and did not become a Russian citizen; if he had, I hardly think that he would have been able to build up his prosperous delivery business in Finland, which I understand he did after his repatriation.

On 30 November, a week after my transfer from the prison in Moscow to the POW camp in Krasnogorsk, my interrogator from Moscow—the colonel—came on an unexpected visit. I was summoned to the office of the commandant. Without a word, the colonel pulled a packet of biscuits from his pocket and handed it to me, and soon after a guard came in with a cup of coffee which he placed in front of me. I really had difficulty restraining myself from smiling or in any other way showing the colonel my amusement when I noticed that both the cup and the saucer bore a picture of a typical German railway station and the name "Bahnhofrestaurant Stendal." Stendal is a large railway town situated between Berlin and Hamburg. After having taken the town, the Russians must have brought the restaurant's chinaware, and presumably many other things, back with them to the Soviet Union.

I was not questioned on that particular occasion; on the contrary, in a friendly tone of voice the colonel told me that "now, finally, we've found out that you have done excellent work to help Allied POWs." He continued, "From this day, we shall treat you properly, and it won't be long now before you can return to Denmark." He bade me goodbye and assured me that "you'll be back in good time before Christmas." And again, as so often before, I was gullible enough to have faith in Russian promises.

Shortly afterward, Edward af Sandeberg was taken to the commandant's office, too. To his disappointment, he did not get any coffee or biscuits. However he, too, was promised that he would be going home before Christmas. And so, during the following days, that was *the* subject of discussion: "Do you really think we'll be home before Christmas?" "Are we going to make it?" "Do you truly believe that what he said is really true?" And on and on.

Both of us regarded the short meeting with the colonel as an encouragement, and in spite of our present situation we felt happy and very optimistic. We were not forced to work and we could take walks along the barbed-wire fence as often as our inclination and strength allowed us, and the fresh air was good for us. At the beginning our walks did not last very long—we were too weak following our long stay in the Moscow prison—but gradually we gained strength, and our walks became longer and longer. We knew each other from Berlin and we trusted each other completely, and it was such a relief to be able to talk to one another, to share one another's worries and hopes. Occasionally we discussed politics, but only among ourselves and only in Swedish and Danish, so nobody understood a word of what we were saying. We knew that there would be POWs in the camp who served the Russians and informed on their fellow prisoners; "Feind hört mit!"—the enemy is listening—also applied to the Soviet Union.

We had the opportunity to borrow books from a modest library—heavy stuff by Marx, Lenin, Engels, and the like, no books of fiction, drama, or poetry. I managed to finish one single book while in the camp, a German edition of Karl Marx's "The History of the Communist Party," an extremely bulky book of several hundred pages which I do not think I would have enjoyed reading under normal circumstances.

Because of this lack of reading material, I came up with another kind of diversion which I certainly would not have thought of had I been living a normal life. I began to go through some of the subjects which I sat for when I graduated. Obviously I did not have the relevant books, but I found myself able to picture them page by page, and I passed many hours asking myself "What's in Chapter One of the Gospel according to St. Matthew? Chapter Two? Chapter Three?" I covered all the chapters, one by one. And after that, I proceeded with St. Mark and the other two Gospels, all of which were expected to be familiar to students of theology about to graduate. After having gradually repeated the entire contents of the New Testament in this way, I went on to Lorentz Bergmann's six-hundred-page church history, and I began to realize that the examination subjects were not merely punishment, but were exceedingly useful; they filled many empty hours of my monotonous life with something very valuable.

In spite of this new occupation I still had lots of time on my hands, and I spent a great deal of it playing chess. Many German POWs were remarkably good with their hands and could make chessboards and chessmen which they were willing to sell for a few chunks of bread. Card games, on the other hand, were strictly forbidden—the Russians called it "not culture"—but nevertheless, we played cards. The POWs made decks of cards from thin pieces of plywood and painted on the figures and numbers. Many hours went by playing cards, and I became quite good at playing several rather difficult games of patience.

A German officer from the Rhineland, Lieutenant Zinkhahn, claimed that he could tell fortunes by cards, and also read hands. He became very busy and knew exactly how to use his abilities in a businesslike manner. A slice of bread, for instance, or five grams of "mahorka"—Russian tobacco, if anybody had that kind of currency available—was his price for telling what the future had in store for each of us.

CHRISTMAS IN RUSSIA

On several occasions, I have spent Christmas with prisoners of war and refugees around the world. But the Christmas of 1945 in the prison camp in Russia was probably the most unforgettable I have ever spei..; never before or since did I experience a Christmas lacking so much in the good things of life, and in spite of this, I do not think that I have ever experienced a Christmas so intensely, so full of Christmas in the deepest sense of the word, as I did that year.

Dirty, cold, overcrowded huts, threatening watch towers, barbed-wire fences, guards with their ever-present machine guns dangling from their shoulders—this was the prison camp at Krasnogorsk at Christmas 1945. Hard labor, misery, loneliness, homesickness—these were our conditions. A chunk of sticky, coarse bread, soup with cabbage leaves—or rather water with cabbage leaves—and bugs, cold, diarrhea, weakness, illness, and death, even at Christmas time. No wonder we had a hard job getting into the right Yuletide spirit, and no wonder smiles only rarely lit up the faces of the German POWs. "Don't bother me with your Christmas," many said aloud, and many more thought to themselves. Nobody made any preparations because there was nothing to make preparations with. Somebody told me that some POWs had spent time in other camps where the commandants had turned a blind eye and allowed the POWs to hold a service on Christmas Eve. But other commandants had done all they could to keep everything that had the slightest connection with Christmas out of the huts and camps, because the celebration of the birth of Jesus Christ is not compatible with the Communist philosophy. A German chaplain had thus been sentenced to fourteen days of isolation because he had arranged a Christmas service in the camp in which he was a POW without having asked and obtained permission from the camp authorities in advance. There were two German chaplains in the Krasnogorsk camp, one Catholic and one Lutheran. They worked in a nearby factory under the same conditions as the rest of the POWs. Together, and well in advance, they applied for permission to hold a joint Christmas service, but were turned down with no reason given.

The days went by and nothing happened to give Edward and myself the slightest indication of us going home before Christmas. During one of our walks along the barbed-wire fence one week prior to Christmas, Edward remarked rather sarcastically that it seemed the colonel had once again promised more than he was able to deliver, and that therefore we had better be realistic and get used to the idea that we would have to spend Christmas and New Year and, he added pessimistically, "perhaps Easter, too," in this camp.

In order to make Christmas a little different from the rest of the year, we quickly agreed to put away a bit of our daily bread rations and keep them for Christmas Eve so that we could really eat our fill that night. Edward also suggested that we read the Gospel for Christmas Day together in Danish. The Russians had taken both my Bible and my hymn book, but two of the POWs had succeeded in keeping their New Testaments, and they were circulated among the rest of us, who made good use of them throughout the day. We had an unwritten rule that a New Testament was only kept for half an hour by any one POW, and after that it went to the next man. Edward wanted me to copy the Gospel for Christmas Day and translate it into Danish, so we could read it together when the time came.

One of the last days before Christmas Edward was lucky enough to get hold of a small spruce twig which one of the German POWs had smuggled into the camp, well hidden inside his large uniform cape on his return from work, and I had the opportunity to "organize" two small candle ends; it did not bother me one little bit to pinch them from the commandant's desk one day, when I was summoned for a conversation with the colonel from Moscow: I was left alone for a few minutes and the candles just happened to disappear into my pocket. Finally, on the very day of Christmas Eve, Edward traded a pair of socks with a Russian guard in exchange for a small bowl of cold porridge.

And so we were ready for the feast: With a bit of luck we managed to get the candles fastened on the "Christmas tree" and light them. We buttered the bread which we had put aside with porridge, and we stuffed ourselves and drank lots of water. The candles gave a bit of warmth and light in the large dark hut, and the German POWs sat around in their worn, dirty jackets and ragged shirts and watched us and our candles in complete silence. When we had finished eating, we read the Gospel of Christmas Day together in Danish. Then, suddenly, feelings began to get the better of the POWs; tears started to run down their bearded cheeks. Most of them had been at Stalingrad, where they had seen, suffered, and survived the bloodiest battles of the entire war—"The Stalingrad Hell," they called it. They had been capable of handling such horrible experiences, but the sight of Edward and me sitting around our spruce twig with two small candles burning, and the sound of us reading the Gospel of Christmas Day—which they, too, knew so well, and which they had been used to hearing together with their loved ones at home—was more than they could take. Despair and hope became one; the good memories of Christmas at home and the acute awareness of their present situation of filth and hopelessness merged. Tears could be restrained no more, and many of them were sobbing their hearts out. A few days later one of the POWs confided in me: "Never before have my wife, my children, and my mum and dad been so near and yet so far away as on that Christmas Eve."

Yes, spirits were low indeed. It was not often that I saw tears or fright on the faces of POWs. But on Christmas Eve in Russia I did and I felt infinite pain. So when Edward, who also felt ill at ease by this display of naked emotions, suggested that we go out for a walk, I did not hesitate but went with him immediately into the cold winter night to walk along the barbed-wire fence. We did not say much to each other—there was no need; both of us knew what the other was thinking about. Our thought set out on a long journey across the vast snow-covered landscape, far beyond the horizon to Sweden and Denmark, to our families.

Around midnight we finally decided to go back and get some sleep, and when we entered the hut I noticed that the Lutheran clergyman, Pastor Hesse, was sitting up busily engaged in, I presumed, the eternal bug hunt. I went over to wish him a merry Christmas and then I saw that it was not bugs he was concerned with—he was preparing a Christmas sermon. He told me that an hour earlier he had received word from the commandant that a service was to be held the next morning at eight o'clock, and so he was preparing the sermon.

Naturally there was no church in the camp, but there was a carpenter's shop with more space than in any other hut, and in no time the POWs had converted it into a provisional church. All the toolboxes and workbenches were pushed up against one wall except one, which was placed at one end to act as an altar, and a POW quickly nailed a couple of boards together and placed them on the "altar." When the service was about to begin, the shop was so full of people that not even a single standing place was available. The windows on both sides of the hut were pushed open and so were the two doors at both ends; outside, hundreds and hundreds of POWs had gathered to take part in the service, to sing the hymns and to listen to the sermon. I do not think I shall ever forget that sermon. True, it was about the infant Jesus who was born on Christmas night, wrapped in swaddling clothes and laid in a manger in a cowshed because there was no room for them in the inn. But the infant Jesus was not depicted in any sweetish or sentimental way. On the contrary. We were told that the infant Jesus grew up to become an adult who wanted to do something for man. He was the child, the pastor said, who later in life wandered all around Palestine and did good to all who needed it: He healed the sick and cleansed the lepers, restoring sight to the blind and hearing to the deaf. He associated with the despised and the unclean, proclaiming freedom to the prisoners, life to the dead. He was the child, Pastor Hesse emphasized, who in the end solemnly promised to be with his worshippers every day until the end of the world and, he added, "everywhere, no matter where in the world—also here in Russia!"

It was a Christmas sermon marked by the desperate situation in which we all found ourselves. As we stood there in our dirty rags, hungry and perishing with cold, without any connection with our beloved and without any knowledge of how long this was all going to last, I think we all felt that we could do only one thing: stretch out our empty hands and let them be filled with the Word of the almighty God, and His rich promise that He will be with us every day—everywhere. The Gospel was indeed preached with a vengeance that Christmas morning to the poor and the helpless, and Christmas came to the prison camp at last, because "God never forgets those who sit in darkness."

When the sermon was over, a Communion was held. The Lutheran pastor gave us the host, small bites of the ordinary Russian dark bread, and the Catholic pastor gave us the wine, water in metal mugs. Many hundreds of prisoners knelt in the sawdust and wood shaving scattered on the cement floor and took part in the solemn Communion, Catholics and Protestants among one another—but what difference did that make? In the common need we all shared we were one large community, part of God's church on earth.

Just as soon as the solemn service was over, we were back to normal: outside the shop, a couple of Russian guards ordered us to a medical examination in one of the huts. We had to strip naked and move in a single file past a pair of Russian doctors who pinched our buttocks to see whether our bodies contained water. With that concluded, the German POWs had to go to work; we had to make up for the service. "Dawai, bistré"—yes, Christmas was over!

The year of 1945 with its war, destruction, suffering, and death was nearing its end. I remembered the Christmas of 1944 which I had spent with twelve thousand British and American airmen in the prison camp STALAG LUFT IV at Gross-Tüchow in northern Germany. "Do you think that we will be home next year?" was the question I was most often asked that Christmas. At that time I did not fathom that I myself would be asking the same question a year later. The Allied POWs in Germany had their Christmas wish come true the following year. Would we be going home in 1946? In Krasnogorsk we were all concerned about this, but we were probably only a few who could hope for it. When the midnight bell sounded twelve in the loudspeaker on 31 December, Edward and I wished each other a happy New Year and—with doubts preying on our minds—an early release and repatriation.

THE LAST MONTHS OF CAPTIVITY

For some reason, the food got worse and the rations smaller when we entered the new year, and the consequences did not fail to show; hunger tormented us and we began to feel weak. Edward suffered from inflammation of the bladder; we were not nearly as inclined or eager to take our walks along the fence as before. Our spirits were affected and we were considering whether to start another hunger strike in an attempt to obtain better treatment. I was still wearing the same dirty clothes I had been wearing for the past five months, and I just could not understand why the Russians would not let me have my luggage with all my warm and clean clothes.

A hunger strike may seem a desperate act, and so it is, but apparently not in Russia. We did not fail to notice the enthusiasm with which the Russian news on the camp radio announced that Gandhi had begun a hunger strike in India as a protest against the British colonial policy, and we knew from experienced and tough German POWs that the camp authorities were instructed to immediately report to Moscow in the case that any of the Soviet Union's "guests" in the camp had died of hunger.

One day, however, before we had made the final decision concerning a hunger strike, a young major from the prison in Moscow whom I had not seen before came to visit us. He claimed that "your colonel" sent his best regards, and that he had come on the colonel's instructions to ask me how I was. I thanked him and asked him to return the colonel's regards, and then told him exactly how I was: weak, hungry, in low spirits! And I took the opportunity to ask for my luggage. Without hesitation, the major said that he would see to it.

Three weeks went by; nothing happened and no luggage arrived. The food was now worse and more scarce than ever before. The snowstorms and the frost grew in strength, and so did the bugs, so much so that one day at the end of February Edward had to let the German doctor operate on his right hand: Bug bites had caused a violent infection of his wrist. The wounds suppurated and Edward was in great pain. On 3 February I felt really terrible, to the point where, in my desperation, I sat down and wrote a letter to Colonel Lüttich. I still have a handwritten copy of the letter, which I succeeded in getting out of the Soviet

Union. I wrote the letter in German, and the English translation is as follows.

Camp 27, Krasnogorsk, 3rd February 1946

Dear Colonel,

We were very pleased to be able to talk to your representative from Moscow, the major, when recently he visited us. To us that was another proof of the personal care and kindness you show us.

Regrettably, conditions in this camp force us to approach you once again. The major was kind enough to grant us the following requests:

1. To have my luggage brought to me at once.

2. To see to it that Edward af Sandeberg—a citizen of a neutral country—and I—a citizen of an Allied country—no longer be forced to stay with prisoners of war, and that, as the major promised, a small heated room be placed at our disposal.

3. To let us have larger and better rations of food.

Unfortunately, we have to tell you that none of these promises have been kept to this day. The conditions in this camp are appalling: we are being harassed in many different ways, and without any right or reason we are being threatened with prison, because we refuse to be treated as prisoners of war.

It seems to us that the camp authorities are not concerned about us at all and even our smallest requests are brushed aside with a laugh and a shrug. They have completely forgotten or they will not recognize that we are not Germans or Hungarians, but citizens of a neutral and an Allied country. The fact that I am also an employee of one of the largest international relief organizations and have worked for more than three years among Allied prisoners of war in Germany seems to be of no interest at all.

Almost every day we ask ourselves: Why must we live under such miserable conditions? Why does my luggage not arrive? Has it disappeared? Or are the camp authorities sabotaging your instructions? Dear Colonel, every day we are treated wrongfully as prisoners of war, and in some cases even worse than that. We cannot bear this anymore, so if our treatment does not improve and if our requests are not granted, we have come to the decision that we shall commence a hunger strike on 11 February to demonstrate against the wretched and disgraceful treatment of us.

Therefore, Colonel, we beg of you to understand us. A possible hunger strike is not directed at you personally. We know that you are doing what you can for us, and we still have some hope that the camp authorities by the end of this week are going to grant us our requests, so that a hunger strike will become unnecessary. We know that you will not like the idea of a hunger strike, but at this time we feel much justified in taking this course of action.

Fleas, lice, bugs, filth, cold, darkness, humidity and commands like in a Prussian barracks, added to the German officers' never-ending discussions about the lost war—all these things influence us gravely and we simply cannot, neither mentally nor physically, tolerate this situation any longer.

When I think back to the first internment camp in which I stayed last summer, and the good conditions that prevailed, I feel my stay in this camp to be even more oppressive and the punishment which befalls both of us even more unjust.

Once again, we beg of you to expedite our repatriation and, until such repatriation can be carried out, to transfer us to another and better camp.

We remain your obedient,

Chr. Christiansen   Edward af Sandeberg

P.S. Sandeberg has had an operation on his right hand because of infectious louse bites, so he has had to sign his name with the left hand.

The letter served its purpose, because on 8 February I was told to pack my things, and a few moments later I was taken by jeep to the camp's zone 1, where I was quartered in a corner of the camp, referred to as "the Quarantine." I did not understand why Edward was not coming too, and this was a great and unexpected disappointment to me. However, one week later he did arrive, and so we were together again.

"THE QUARANTINE"

In "the Quarantine" conditions were tolerable. We lived in smaller rooms—ten to twelve persons in each—and with stoves installed. German prisoners of war kept the rooms clean, lit the stoves, and tended the fires. Conditions were almost like those in the diplomat camp where I had been detained the previous summer at the beginning of my forced stay in Russia. The food was better, although we still had the same amount of bread and cabbage soup. But for dinner we also had a spoonful of so-called "Kasha," a porridge-like substance which was made of either mashed potatoes, millet, or barley, and although you could not call it a delicacy, it was definitely nutritious and helped fill our empty stomachs.

Everybody in "the Quarantine" was an interned civilian. I knew four of them already because we had been together on the same transport in May 1945 from Berlin to Moscow, where we had been interned in Camp 20-B in Planiernaja. One was a Greek businessman, Mr. Akliros, from Berlin. In Camp 20-B he suffered the disgrace of having the Russians confiscate a great deal of his luggage, some very large containers which held 150 to 175 bottles of excellent wine. He was still very cross about it; however, he took comfort in eating pieces of toffee which he made of sugar and coffee. Mr. Akliros was the only one who had such a luxury as real coffee and he had it in great quantities. Unfortunately, he seemed never to have learned to share with others.

The Polish family Lejmanski, on the other hand, was an extremely likable family with a father, a mother, and a nineteen-year-old daughter. Czeslaw Lejmanski was born in Poland; he had lived in America for many years before returning and settling down in Warsaw as an American consul. When the Americans joined the war after the Japanese attack on Pearl Harbor, the Germans arrested Mr. Lejmanski and put him in a concentration camp outside Warsaw. At the end of 1944, when the Russians advanced on the Polish capital, the Germans brought the family westward and had them interned in a prison camp just south of Berlin. At the fall of the German Reich they succeeded in reaching Berlin and there, a few days after Berlin surrendered, the Russians took them prisoner and had them transported to Moscow on the same train as the foreign diplomats, newspaper correspondents, and the rest of us. When we reached Warsaw they tried to leave the train, but they were spotted and brought back, and thus ended up in "the Quarantine" in zone 1.

Then there was Sari Wein, a Hungarian journalist who had been a newspaper correspondent in Berlin. She had been married to a German officer who was killed during the battle of Berlin on one of the very last days of the war. Like other foreign citizens, she was transported to Moscow and interned in "the Quarantine," which was where I got to know her. Sari Wein had gone through a lot and she is one of the bravest people I have ever met. Soon after the fall of Berlin she realized that she was pregnant, and in November in captivity she gave birth to a boy under the most filthy, poor, and unhygienic conditions imaginable; it is a miracle that mother and son are still alive. Sari told me about the appalling shortage of all the things which are related to a child-birth under normal conditions—there was no hot water, no dia-pers, no swaddling clothes, no dressing materials whatsoever. "Old newspapers," she explained without a trace of bitterness in her voice, "can be used for lots of things, when there is nothing else at hand, and I'm quite sure that many Russian women in a similar situation made do with the 'Pravda'!" Sari named her boy Axel, and she longed for the day when she could bring him home to Budapest with her and have him baptized. It gives me great pleasure that I am still able to keep in touch with her and that she has been doing very well for herself and her son.

On 26 February my suitcase was finally returned to me, and for the first time since 2 August the year before, I was able to put on a clean shirt and a clean pair of socks. Colonel Lüttich personally returned the suitcase, which was carefully tied to-gether with a piece of string and sealed with a large wax seal. He wanted me to break the seal and open it in his presence, and when I did, I immediately noticed that much of its original con-tents was missing. The colonel asked me to acknowledge receipt of the suitcase, but how could I "when half of its contents is missing." He told me, then, to make a list of what was actually in the suitcase, give him a receipt, and finally write a letter to him stating what was missing; he would then do his best to re-trieve the things.

The month of March went by and nothing happened. The days became noticeably longer and brighter and the cold had to give way to the approaching spring. I walked around the camp for hours, sometimes with Edward, sometimes with Sari, and sometimes with Mr. Lejmanski. No matter what topics were brought up, we always ended up with the questions: "When are we going to go on from here?" "When do you think we'll be allowed to go home?"

On 30 March I was summoned to the office of the comman-dant to meet the colonel from Moscow. I do not remember what he wanted from me that day, but I took the opportunity to return to the question of my home journey and I asked him to tell me why on earth I was not allowed to go home; after all, he had been very liberal with his promises. For once, the colonel was very direct: Denmark and Sweden had refused to extradite certain persons whom the Russians wanted, and not until that matter had been settled to the full satisfaction of the Soviet Union could there be any talk about anybody going home.

On the morning of 2 April, Edward was unexpectedly told to pack his things, and shortly afterward he disappeared through the gate of the camp. We had no idea where he was going and he had hardly had time to say good-bye. Once again I was left behind, wondering why I could not go, too.

Now there was no one with whom I could speak my native language, and there was one less person in whom I could have complete trust and confidence. Two weeks went by, but then it seemed to be my turn: on 16 April the colonel returned for another visit and he told me that I would be going home soon, "but there is a small matter that prevents us from letting you go, and that is the list of the missing things from your suitcase. Your letter gives me the impression that you suspect us of having stolen your things." I answered that I certainly did not suspect anybody in particular, but I knew what was in my suitcase when I was arrested, and it was therefore easy for me to tell what was missing when the suitcase was returned to me. The colonel said flatly, "No matter what was missing, you just can't be allowed to go home before any suspicions on us have been removed, because we didn't steal your things!" He continued, "Couldn't you give me a written statement that indicates that you lost your belongings in Berlin in the last days of the war?" I told him no: "You always emphasized during your questionings that I must speak the truth, so how can I sign my name to a lie—I didn't lose my things in Berlin!" The colonel lost his temper: "You can do or not do whatever you want, but one thing is certain: if you want to go home you'll have to see to it that we are not under any kind of suspicion!" And so, in the end, I wrote, "In agreement with the camp commandant, I hereby certify that I lost my personal belongings in Berlin and therefore, I cancel my letter of

26 February." The colonel declared himself satisfied with this statement and I was sent back to my room.

RELEASE AND HOME JOURNEY

On 24 April my Bible and hymn book, my diary, and my passport were returned to me. This made me believe there would be a change in my situation and I naturally hoped that it was the beginning of the end of my stay in Russia and that, finally, I would be allowed to go home.

And so it seemed: at noon on 29 April the colonel arrived once more. I was told to pack my things while he watched, and before I closed my suitcase I asked him if I could have back my camera which had been taken into custody against a receipt. "Well," he said, "if you have a receipt, the camera must be in the store room. I'll get it for you." He returned almost immediately with empty hands and said, "It's in the car," so I closed the suitcase, bade a hasty farewell to my fellow prisoners, and followed the colonel. A car was waiting at the gate, but before I got into it I quietly reminded him about the camera. "There it is," he said, and pointed to a small parcel wrapped in gray paper on the back seat, the size of which could well suggest a camera. Later in the day, when I arrived in Moscow, I opened the parcel, and to my amazement I found that it contained a quarter of a loaf of white bread!

We stopped in front of the Commandant's headquarters and I was escorted to his office to say good-bye. He had only one remark to make: "It's customary for our guests when leaving the country to sign a statement to the effect that they have been well treated and that they have no intentions of putting any demands before the Russian authorities—but of course, it's quite voluntary." With these words he placed a piece of paper and a pencil in front of me and I naturally acknowledged the great hospitality of Stalin.

The car started off toward the city, and on the way I wondered what would be happening now. I gathered that there were three possibilities: either the Russians would take me to the legation, or they would bring me to the railway station, put me on a train, and escort me to the Finnish border, or they would take me to the airport and put me on an airplane to Helsinki. After some time, however, I realized that there must be a fourth possibility! We drove all over Moscow to different addresses, and at each address the escorting lieutenant went in with some papers and, after a little while, returned with some more. Finally we went back to the outskirts of the city and the car stopped in front of a long, red, four-storied building with guards at the main entrance. The lieutenant jumped out of the car and showed the large stack of papers to one of them. The gate was opened and the car proceeded into an enclosed yard. I felt myself stiffen noticeably, and I began to fear that something was terribly wrong— I was going back to prison! The lieutenant nodded for me to get out of the car, and when I asked him where we were, he said in a rough voice: "This is the Butyrka prison!" I said that it just couldn't be, "because I've been in the Butyrka prison before, and surely I would be able to recognize that prison." He did not bother to answer; he merely hauled my suitcase from the car, let it fall to the ground, got into the car, and left.

I do not think I was actually frightened, but I was certainly confused and I had absolutely no idea what was going to happen next. A few moments later, however, a soldier came up to me, hitched up my suitcase and demanded—"Dawai, bistré"—that I follow him. He led the way across the yard into the building, to the second floor and into a rather large room where about ten people were gathered, and then left without a word of explanation.

I felt terribly bewildered and looked at the other people in the room without recognizing any of them. A man immediately approached me and asked me where I came from; I explained that I had been in a camp in Krasnogorsk, and asked him why he was here. He told me that he was merely waiting to be allowed to go home. "For how long have you been waiting?" I asked him. "Tomorrow," sounded the encouraging answer, "I have been here one month." I sat down on the one available bed and began to ponder how long I would have to stay at this place, and the optimism which I had felt when we left the camp subsided completely.

After a time, however, I began to realize that this must be a step in the right direction. The building was not a proper prison; it was a barracks which was used as a transit barracks for Russian soldiers who had returned from military service in Germany and eastern Europe. In prison I'd had to sleep on the hard cement floor and in the POW camp on one of the wooden shelves. Here I found myself on a real bed—or at least one that used to be a real bed. It was very rusty and very unsteady, but it had a proper bedspring and a proper—if thin—mattress. And although there were no sheets or pillow it was still an enormous improvement.

The other occupants of the room were of five or six different nationalities—two from China, the rest from Poland, Romania and western Europe. Two of the Poles were Jews; they told me that they had spent three years in Auschwitz, and they showed me the marks of identification which had been burnt into their arms by the Nazis in the concentration camp. They related how the Russians had captured and liberated Auschwitz, and had brought all those who were still alive to the Soviet Union and put them to work as laborers. "We don't know what happened to our families," they sighed. "If only we could get to America—because we don't want to stay in Russia."

It did not really surprise me that no one told me what was going to happen to me. What surprised me was a young officer who appeared around ten o'clock in the evening and told me to get to bed, "because you aren't going anywhere until tomorrow," and then disappeared. But I had learned my lessons, and I knew by experience that "tomorrow" in Russia usually meant several days, even several weeks. I did not get much sleep that night, and not only because of the bugs.

As I had expected, nothing happened the following day, but shortly before midnight I was awakened by a young lieutenant who told me to prepare for departure. He did not know where I was going, only that I had to get ready. The two Polish Jews and one Romanian received the same brief order. A few minutes later we were brought down into the yard and told to get into an open truck, which then took off. It was the night between 30 April and 1 May, and all the streets of Moscow were decked out festively with large red flags and streamers, and large pictures of

Stalin and Lenin decorated the buildings from street level all the way up to the fourth floor; Moscow was ready for the celebration of International Workers' Day.

Finally we got to a railway station where we were met by a Russian captain who spoke excellent German and seemed very nice and helpful. An empty cattle truck was waiting alongside the platform, and around one o'clock in the morning we left Moscow. I was very anxious to know what direction the train was taking—west, or did we go toward Siberia? I did not sleep one wink, not because of the hard wooden floor, but because my mind reeled with thoughts of what would happen to me, and of what the terminal station would be. Not until morning, when I was able to determine that the sun was on my left, did I relax; now I felt sure that the train was going south and not toward Siberia.

It was a beautiful day, and as we proceeded further south the weather grew warmer and warmer and the day more and more beautiful. When I left Krasnogorsk the snow had only just disappeared, but when we reached the Ukraine we noticed blooming willows, anemones, and crocus by the thousand, and our spirits rose tremendously. May first was a day of festival and it was celebrated as such. Everywhere that the train pulled to a stop— and I am pretty sure that it stopped at every single little railway station—we saw red flags and large pictures of the political leaders, and of local people dressed up in national costumes—long, white shirts hanging outside the trousers for the men and beautifully colored dresses for the women. The train took three days to reach Odessa, and at every small railway station people crowded around it to try to sell some bread, boiled eggs, or fresh tomatoes to the travelers.

We reached Odessa at daytime in the most beautiful weather, and on an open truck we were driven to a POW camp, approximately ten miles from the town. The camp was a transit camp, where people stayed only as long as was necessary for the Russian authorities to assemble a group of POWs and interned civilians large enough to constitute a transport. The camp was beautifully situated some five hundred feet from the Black Sea and, as regulations were rather lenient, we could go there for a swim as often as we pleased. The food was more plentiful than at any other place I had stayed. Each day new groups of POWs arrived at the camp from all over the Soviet Union, and eight days after our arrival the number of POWs had apparently reached a point where a new transport could be arranged to go west. We returned to Odessa, again on open trucks, and proceeded from there in empty cattle trucks. There were no mattresses, no blankets, and no straw on the floor, so it was impossible to stretch out comfortably, but we did have a tin container placed in a corner in case a need for it should arise between the railway stations. I assume that we were about 150 men altogether: three Danes, a few Swiss, and the rest French, Poles, and Dutch. All—except myself—had served in the German forces, most of them as SS soldiers who had been taken prisoner by the Russians, but who were now being repatriated to stand trial in their home countries.

We were going west—there was no doubt about it. I was actually on my way home! We reached the river Dniester, the border between the Soviet Union and Romania, and there we were ordered out of the trucks and had to wait quite some time while the border police carefully checked the trucks—without, strangely enough, checking our luggage. While waiting, I looked around me and I noticed a large sign above the railway line which bore the inscription, "Welcome to the Soviet Union—Workers of the World, Unite!"

The waiting seemed very long, but finally we were told to get back into the trucks, and slowly the train started to pull out of the station and cross the river. I felt as happy and joyful as a child whose greatest wish had been fulfilled on Christmas Day. We were in Romania! A few hundred feet away I saw a small village, and I immediately caught sight of the building closest to the Russian border, which appropriately enough was a church. It was quite unharmed by the war, and in front of it the priest and some local villagers were standing, waving and smiling at us as we passed the village. At the next small railway station women were offering us wine and bread and chocolate in exchange for clothes. I bartered a couple of handkerchiefs for some bread and some homemade salami, well spiced. At the end of the day we arrived at a large town, Jassy, where some of the cruelest battles had been fought in August 1944. In spite of the extensive destruction, Jassy was still a beautiful town of distinguished old houses surrounded by green vineyards and numerous onion-shaped domes of the Orthodox churches, reaching toward the sky.

We had to spend the night on the cement floor of a Russian barracks in Jassy. So what! I was on my way home, wasn't I? The next morning, I woke up at the sound of a church bell accompanying the rising sun. So it was indeed true; we were not in Russia anymore! During the morning we could walk around in Jassy as we pleased, and at noon we made ourselves a hot meal on an open fire in front of the barracks. Many of the Dutch SS soldiers had brought with them oil cakes of a kind which were used to feed cattle. They claimed that they had eaten hundreds of them during their stay at collective farms in Russia where they had been put to work.

In the early afternoon we continued our journey through Romania to Bucharest, but we did not get the chance to go sight-seeing, because the train proceeded north along the river Danube to the Hungarian border and on, during the next few days, to Budapest. The train stopped numerous times and often we had to wait for several hours after having been shunted onto a side-track at some small railway station. There were lots of soldiers and military police on the train, and a railway official who spoke German explained to me that it was necessary to have guards on Russian military trains because of partisan operations. Apparently this was also true for our train, because one morning some of the notices "Reserved for Russians" had been replaced with "Long live King Michael."

In Budapest we had a stopover of more than twenty-four hours. I would have liked to have been able to spend a few of them taking a stroll through the capital of Hungary, but we were not allowed to leave the cattle trucks. So instead my thoughts went out to little Sari Wein and her Axel, both of them probably still in "the Quarantine" in Krasnogorsk. The next day the train crossed the Austrian border, and on 16 May at noon we finally reached Vienna, where the escorting Russians left us in the hands of the French occupational authorities.

I do not know what happened to my fellow travelers, but I myself was immediately taken to a French officer for a short interrogation, and when he had determined my identity he offered to have me brought to the American authorities at once. Already that same afternoon I was questioned by an American official during a two-hour session. He began our conversation by saying, "I have seen you before!" I was sure that there must have been some misunderstanding, but he went on and asked me: "Weren't you at Hammerstein? Aren't you the YMCA delegate who visited us at Hammerstein when we were prisoners of war?" He was right, because I had visited the prison camp STALAG II-B at Hammerstein numerous times. At the end of the interrogation, the American officer assured me that, "We know of the YMCA POW Aid, and I myself have personally experienced what the YMCA did to help us when we were prisoners of war, so now, I assure you, we will help you to get home as soon as possible." I thanked him and we said good-bye. Then I was brought to the office of the International Red Cross in Vienna and a room in Strudelgasse 10 was made available to me. It was a wonderful day; before it was over, I was deloused, had a luxurious bath, a much, much needed haircut, and a shave. The Red Cross generously provided me with clean underwear, a new shirt, socks, and shoes, and I began to feel like a civilized man again. I could move around quite freely, so I headed straight for a post office and sent a telegram to my parents. For the first time in twelve months I slept alone, and without being bothered by one single little bug. All these things were gifts and blessings which a man who has been a prisoner of war does not take for granted.

The following day, I was told that the Supreme Commander of the British forces in Vienna wanted to see me, and I had the honor of meeting him in his office at Schönbrunn Castle. By no means was this another interrogation; on the contrary, the general wanted to express his gratitude and appreciation for the work which the YMCA had done for the British POWs in Germany, and I told him that I would be very happy to pass on his regards to the YMCA World Alliance when I arrived at Geneva in another few days.

Ten days later the Danish Consulate and the American occupational authorities had arranged for my papers to be ready—an exit permit that would allow me to leave the Russian occupation zone and a permission to enter the other Allied zones. The Consulate General provided me with a courier certificate which confirmed that I traveled as an official courier from the consulate in Vienna to the legation in Bern. I got a train ticket to Geneva—a VIP sleeper—and on the evening of 26 May I was on the train going west. I arrived in Geneva the following morning. My Russian Odyssey had come to an end. I was with my own people again—a free man, able to put behind me a cruel, but nevertheless instructive period of my life.

A Danish Christian newspaper sent a journalist to Geneva to meet me and bring me home. The Copenhagen Church Fund had placed a car at his disposal for the purpose, but I hardly think that the fund even suspected at that time that the passenger in that car was to become the Secretary General of the fund eleven years later (1957–1962).

One last incident on my way home I shall never forget. When I arrived at the German-Danish border at Kruså, the gendarme scrutinized my passport very carefully, looked at me, and asked, "Are you the man who was in prison in Russia?" I nodded and his next words stunned me completely: "In that case, I have orders to arrest you!" I took one deep breath—what now? Enough is enough. Still, I managed to say, "That's all right, I don't mind, as long as I am being arrested by the *Danish* police." But then the gendarme proceeded to explain that his superior, the local chief constable, wanted to be informed the minute I arrived at the border, and that the gendarme had been instructed to detain me until the chief constable had the opportunity to meet me. Shortly afterward, Chief Constable Axel Bjerre and his wife arrived from Gråsten and they bade me welcome home with a large bunch of flowers and a superb dinner at the Grand Hotel in Aabenraa. In this manner, the chief constable wished to convey his thanks to the YMCA World Alliance on behalf of all

his colleagues, because the YMCA had visited the Danish police
officers in the German POW camps and prisons.

REFLECTIONS ON A PRISON STAY

People have often asked me what went on in my mind during my imprisonment in Moscow, and whether I consider the
twelve months to have been a complete waste. The answers will
of course be very personal.

What was most painful during my entire stay in Russia, I
think, was the awareness that my parents were desperately worried and did not know what had happened to me, whether I was
dead or alive. Week followed week, month followed month,
Christmas came and went and so did Easter. So much happened
outside the prison—nothing at all inside. No letters from home,
no opportunity to write home, nothing to read, nothing to do,
no news, removed from a world I had been part of. I was possessed by the same feelings that haunt any other prisoner of war.
I had been detached like a train carriage and shunted into a side-
track. I was a prisoner for a period of time that was indefinite.
The uncertainty of not knowing what was going to happen to
me and when was so great a mental pain that it sometimes seemed
unbearable. The Russian authorities would not allow me to pass
any messages to my home about where I was, whether I was
well, or when—if ever—I could expect to be released.

There were times when I was afraid, very much afraid, times
when I was haunted by thoughts that the Russians might intend
to forget me and have me quietly disappear somewhere in Siberia. No one, I was convinced, would be able to prevent them
from taking such an action. During these hard times, I realized
what a great strength it is to have a clear conscience. I had absolutely nothing to hide and I knew with unerring certainty that I
had never had anything to do with intelligence or espionage. The
Russian accusations were quite groundless. I also knew that the
work I had done among POWs in Germany was work I had been
employed to do by others; I myself had not searched for such
work; the Church of Denmark, or at least a branch of the Church
of Denmark, had asked me to be an employee of the YMCA

World Alliance POW Aid. And because I knew this to be true, worry and despair never got an upper hand on the hope and the belief that truth and justice would be victorious in the end. Such an implicit belief, together with a great deal of healthy—though at times somewhat tremulous—optimism were indeed of infinite value for surviving the fear, the cold, the filth, the lice, the poor and inadequate food, and the never-ending, brutal shouts of orders in the overcrowded prison cell number 92 in Moscow.

The good things in life—a warm bed, fresh clothes, a good meal, soap and a toothbrush—are things that I shall never again be able to take for granted. All the things that I had been used to thinking were there for the taking suddenly became priceless. Imagine being able to close your door, be alone, all to yourself, put out the light when you feel like it! Or imagine being able to go for a walk, wherever you want, whenever you want. These things have become like precious jewels.

In prison I learned to manage without a watch, without a belt, and without shoelaces. I learned to brush my teeth with my index finger, first the right finger, then the left. I learned to limit my toilet visits to twice a day—six o'clock in the morning and six o'clock in the evening—and to wear the same unwashed underwear and shirt for months. I learned the easiest way to kill bugs without getting blood on my fingers or clothes, how to sleep on a cement floor without a mattress or a pillow. I learned that the only way to keep warm during the night was to keep my clothes on and to move as close as possible to the men next to me. There were thirty-nine of us in the same cell and privacy was out of the question. I can confirm what I think is generally known: that common difficulties often bring either the best or the worst in human nature to the surface. Most of my cell mates were helpful and considerate, but some apparently thought only of themselves, and were willing to sell themselves to the Russians, to spy on the rest of us for a few slices of extra bread. "Judas" or "Iscariots," we called them.

I believe that my happiest moments during the imprisonment were when I could not fall asleep. Then I would close my eyes and everything around me—the ugly and filthy walls, bloodstained from thousands of crushed lice; the dirty clothes, and the soil tub in the corner—all of it faded away and I was back in my home country; I was walking down the so-familiar street from the railway station in Viborg toward my home, and I nodded in happy recognition to all the houses and buildings and squares I passed: the YMCA building with its happy memories of my childhood, the Building Society, the post office, the savings bank, the "Round Tree"; I passed the lakes at the banks of which people had settled more than twenty-five hundred years ago. I proceeded past the parsonage and my old school, and everywhere I saw people whom I had known for years; they came up to me, greeted me and embraced me and could not even think of all the good things they wanted to do to bid me welcome home. Night after night I was able to revive these precious moments.

All good things of this world can be taken away from a man by those in power, but memories of a happy childhood, a warm home, the spiritual heritage which he has been given—all of that can never be robbed from any man! Due, in large measure, to this mental ballast which I had been given and had taken with me when I left home, I sustained my stay in prison; it made it possible for me to learn to keep myself mentally occupied without the company of books, magazines, and newspapers, to spend Christmas without the church, Bible, or Hymn Book, without a Christmas tree and pleasant family reunions, without presents and seasonal greetings. I learned about patience, about freedom; I learned the value of what I had been taught in school and during my preparation for confirmation, and much, much more. I was lonely as I had never been before or since, but I was not alone, because I knew—with unwavering certainty—that my family and my friends at home were thinking of me every day and that they would never abandon me.

Those twelve months spent in prison were certainly a rough school to have to go through, but also an instructive one: when I resumed my work among POWs and refugees, including refugees from Eastern Europe, in different places around the world, I feel I was well equipped—I was able to put myself in their place, to understand their situation and reach out to them, to make them trust me and allow me to help them.

Part Three

AMONG GERMAN PRISONERS OF

WAR IN GREAT BRITAIN

THE CONQUERORS AND THE CONQUERED

DURING MY stay in Geneva, the management of the YMCA World Alliance asked me if I would consider continuing the POW work after a suitable period of recuperation. Genuinely pleased and without a bit of hesitation, I answered that I should be delighted to do so, and during a board meeting of the "Danish Inter-Church Aid Committee" on 1 August 1946, it was decided that, "Christian Christiansen is placed at the disposal of the POW Relief Aid in Great Britain." I was eager to start work again, but first I had to go through a six-week hospital stay in order to completely regain my strength after my experiences in Russia. At the beginning of November, I left for London and a new chapter of my life began, for this time I was to work among German soldiers in British POW camps.

The YMCA POW work in Britain was not much different from what I had been used to doing in Germany. In Britain it was also a matter of assisting POWs in initiating a variety of activities: training and education, individually or in groups; establishing libraries; procuring musical instruments, sports equipment, and so forth; in short, to help in whatever way possible to strengthen morale and lift spirits. It was work similar to and with the same aim as the work in prison camps in Germany;

the difference was in the conditions under which the POWs were held.

The relief work in Great Britain had its headquarters in London with an American, Mr. John Barwick, in charge. John Barwick was a former minister of the Evangelical Free Church of the USA and also a former director of an American travel agency. In 1941, the British YMCA had persuaded John Barwick to come to London to initiate relief work among the German POWs in Great Britain along the same lines as that directed to Allied POWs in Germany, in close cooperation with the British YMCA and the Church of England. At that time the number of German POWs had been moderate, and the prison camps therefore sparse and small. The POWs were mainly German airmen who had been shot down over British territory, submarine crew members who had been saved from drowning in the Atlantic, a number of high-ranking officers who had been taken prisoner during the Desert War in North Africa, and a few others who had lost their way and been taken prisoner separately. The many German soldiers who surrendered to the British in groups—for instance, entire detachments of Field Marshal Erwin Rommel's Africa Corps—had immediately been transferred to camps in Canada, Australia, and the USA due to limited accommodation and provisions in Great Britain. Not until after the Allied landing in Normandy in June 1944 did the number of German POWs in Great Britain increase substantially, and so did the workload of the YMCA relief work: already in 1943, the Swedish Pastor Birger Forell (who had been a pastor for the Swedish community in Berlin since 1929) had been assigned to the YMCA work in London.

In June 1945, more than 200,000 German soldiers were held in captivity in 130 different camps in Britain, 200,000 were in British captivity in Belgium, and approximately 135,000 were kept prisoner in the USA "at the expense of the British Government." At the end of the war, a total of 3.7 million Germans were held in British captivity all over the world, mainly in the western and northern parts of Germany. Keeping POWs in the USA at the expense of the British government was the result of an agreement between the USA and Great Britain which provided that half of the captured Germans were to be kept in prison camps in Britain, the other half in the USA, regardless of where and by whom they had been taken prisoner.

When I arrived in London, John Barwick immediately introduced me to the various authorities that handled matters concerning POWs—the War Ministry, the Foreign Ministry, and so on—just as had been done a few years earlier in Berlin. I was also briefed about my future work. John Barwick wanted me to be responsible for assisting POWs in an area stretching from the Scottish border in the north to a line in the south stretching from Liverpool in the west to Hull on the British east coast; my base was to be in Newcastle upon Tyne. Within my area of responsibility were twenty-seven prison camps, two field hospitals, and more than one hundred hostels, where German soldiers were put to work. I received a list of addresses, and during December 1946 and January 1947 I managed to visit all the camps, the two field hospitals, a couple of prisons, and twelve small hostels in my area. I found that a few visits were sufficient for me to get a reasonably good impression of the atmosphere in the camps and of the relationship between the POWs and the civilian population, and I realized that there was a great difference between visiting Allied POWs in Germany during the war and German POWs in Great Britain after the war. In a way, work in Germany seemed easier: the Allied POWs knew that if only they held out patiently, then some day they were bound to be released. They did not doubt that victory would be theirs and that they would return to their countries, if not in a triumphal procession, then at least in triumph. The German POWs were different—they had lost both the war and, most of them, the belief that they could look forward to a happy future; the most they could hope for were better times for their children. They were plagued by just about all imaginable concerns and worries and often found it difficult, not to say impossible, to keep up their spirits and the joy of living.

In Germany, it had been an exception to be allowed to have tête-à-tête talks with the POWs; we had always been accompanied by one or more German officers, often by the commandant himself. Not so in Great Britain: we were free to move about unaccompanied in the camps, hospitals, and even prisons, and a POW could ask for a private talk with a YMCA employee to discuss any matter which might weigh heavy on his shoulders, or to which he was unable to find a solution on his own. I have no recollection of the YMCA's work being impeded by the authorities at any time; on the contrary, we were always met with trust, helpfulness, and an understanding of the importance of the relief work. And besides, the YMCA was well known for having set up and managed soldiers' recreation centers—as they do to-day—all over the world where British soldiers were and are based.

It seems generally agreed that the German POWs in Great Britain were treated in accordance with the Geneva Convention, a copy of which could be found in all camps, usually on the camp bulletin board. And it is true that the Germans never complained to me about the food or about the housing conditions. The daily ration was based on a diet of 3,300 calories per person, which was more than the civilian population had, though a bit less than in British soldiers' diets. Many POWs were furthermore able to increase the nutritional value of their rations by cultivating vegetables; in almost every camp, an area had been converted into a vegetable garden. According to the Red Cross reports, the great majority of POWs considered their rations to be "adequate" and "good," and they also appreciated the fact that they received better and more ample food than did the British population, and definitely better than did their families in Germany. I was told that the POWs' rations had been somewhat reduced in the first months immediately following the end of the war; but as British housewives had had their allocations equally reduced, the reductions had not given rise to any complaints. The reason for the reduction was that during the summer of 1945, Great Britain had to provide food not only to its own population and POWs, but also to the civilian population in the British occupied zone in Germany.

Most of the POWs were housed in barrel-like huts made of corrugated iron, the so-called "Nissen-huts," named after the British engineer, Peter Nissen. However, although the Geneva Convention provided that the use of tents for POWs was only allowed during the summer, many POWs had to make do with them until the summer of 1946, when the last tents disappeared. The Nissen-huts were divided into rooms that could accommodate ten to sixteen men each and were equipped with bunks. Two to three woollen blankets were available for each bunk, sometimes more in cases of particularly severe winters. In spite of a national fuel shortage, the British authorities placed adequate supplies of coal at the disposal of the POWs, during the winter of 1946–47, one of the most severe winters in Great Britain in many years; in fact, in this the POWs were more fortunate than the British civilian population, who really felt the shortage of coal.

At their own initiative and in order to make amends for the conditions, the more understanding and humane among the British commandants had—already in the autumn of 1945, only a few months after the end of the war—seen to the removal of the much-hated barbed-wire fences around the prison camps. This was quickly communicated to other camps, and by Christmas 1946 official permission was granted to get rid of the fences, except for a single wire "to keep out cattle," as the saying went. Nevertheless, that one single wire remained a symbol of imprisonment, and the POWs often talked about "barbed wire" disease, thereby indicating that they longed for home and for freedom. The POWs suffered no physical but some psychological distress in Great Britain. They went through their own personal crises, a kind of "internal injuries" which tormented them and hurt terribly: What would they find once they got home? Would there be any home to return to at all? "Do you think my wife has been waiting for me? Has she remained faithful to me?" "Will my children be able to recognize me, do you think?" "Has my father returned from the eastern front, I wonder, or has he been reported missing?" "Are my parents still alive?" And so on, and so on. Such questions were asked again and again to the YMCA employees.

One day, a POW showed me the last three letters he had received from his wife in Germany; it was evident that she had become tired of waiting and had found another man. The prisoner was feeling terribly miserable at the thought of a divorce. I advised him to postpone any final decision on the matter until he had returned to Germany, and I also promised to write to his wife to explain the delay of his repatriation and to ask her to show understanding for the situation in which her husband had quite unwillingly been placed. I never received any reply and do no know how—or even whether—the matter was settled.

No POW could really imagine the tremendous changes which Germany had undergone since he was last there. Germany had become a withered shadow of its former glory. Every inch of land was occupied by foreigners; its leaders had either committed suicide, fled, or were in prison awaiting trial. More than four million Germans had been killed or reported missing, seven million were held in captivity in the Soviet Union, and several more million had been driven from their homes in Eastern Europe. There were indeed enough problems to make life painful for a German POW and to prevent him from believing in any decent future. And in the camp, he had plenty of time to envision the difficulties he would encounter when he returned, plenty of time to ache for home and imagine the difficulties he would have rebuilding his life.

Many POWs were well aware of the trial of strength it would be to adapt to postwar Germany. War invalids most certainly were not the only ones in need of rehabilitation and reeducation in order to make their livings in Germany. Every professional officer knew very well that he would have to start from scratch and undergo a complete retraining if he wanted a life in the new Germany. The older officers in particular worried about their prospects, and they—much more than the young officers—saw the defeat of their country as the most terrible of downfalls. Some gave up and simply accepted fate; others refused to do so, believing in themselves and confident that they possessed the capabilities and experiences which would be of value and could be utilized once they returned to Germany.

But what about their attitude toward the capitulation of Germany? Were they happy, relieved that the war was over? Who knows. To some POWs, the capitulation came as a relief: "Thank God, the madness has finally come to an end!" Others felt sorrow, because all their hopes had been scattered. But to most POWs, I think, the capitulation came as a shock; they were overwhelmed by a feeling of numbness, emptiness, and gloom, of having been let down and abandoned.

Calamities and misery generally bind people together in a common bond, but in the prison camps in Great Britain this was not so: most of the German officers persisted in thinking, feeling, and behaving as officers during their entire periods of captivity. And only on extremely rare occasions would the men dream of being critical of their officers, not to mention turning against them. This was especially true in the officers' camps: the men would continue to serve the officers, clean their huts, wash, iron, and cook—all in addition to their own hard work. Class consciousness and preconceived opinions flourished among the members of both groups, but it was accepted as quite natural: officers give orders, men obey.

There were other matters that gravely affected the general atmosphere in prison camps in Great Britain, matters over which the Germans had no control. The conquerors' attitude toward the conquered was sometimes difficult to understand, although the Geneva Convention was probably not violated. The British authorities had quickly made up their minds, based on interrogations of the Germans, that the airmen and the submarine crews were, if not fanatics, then at least National Socialists and still very loyal and devoted to their country. However, as long as the fighting had persisted, all efforts had been concentrated on winning the war, and the Germans had therefore been left alone politically. The importance played by preconceived opinions in the relationship between the conqueror and the conquered was clearly demonstrated in the camps. A few changed their opinion of the opposite party, but the majority nursed their preconceived conceptions, especially the Germans who seemed to continue to be loyal to Hitler and faithful to the national socialist ideology and the German militarism. But then, I do not think that the British authorities can be entirely acquitted of a certain amount of blame; they tended to generalize far too much and to see all Germans as Nazis who therefore deserved to be punished. To be a Nazi was a kind of contagious disease, almost like leprosy; German POWs should therefore not be able to associate with

others. National socialism was a moral evil that had to be removed completely prior to repatriating any large groups of
POWs. Reeducation became the keyword; reeducation, it was
said, was the best remedy. The war with its bombs and shells was
over and won; now was the time to win the conquered over to
democracy, and the British authorities believed that this was best
achieved by information, by reeducation.

A whole army of British interrogators swarmed into the
camps, this time not to ask questions about name, rank, and unit;
no, this time the questions concerned the POWs' background,
childhood, and youth, family matters, attitudes toward church
and Christianity, toward the state and its use of power. Based on
answers to these questions, the interrogators were to form an
opinion of the mental state and moral conduct of every single
POW, and then to subdivide them into three main categories, A,
B, and C. Category A consisted of the "White," the pure anti-
Nazis, category B included the in-betweens, the "Gray," and
category C consisted of the "Black," the convinced and fanatic
National Socialists.

At the same time, a couple hundred lecturers, mainly German immigrants and refugees who had come to Great Britain
shortly before the war started, were sent to the camps as "missionaries" for Western Democracy. The British authorities
hoped that lectures by such "missionaries," together with magazines and camp newspapers containing articles on British conditions, compulsory American films, and slides from Bergen-
Belsen and other concentration camps—all these kinds of "education"—would make it possible to reeducate the POWs and
convert them to true democracy, to "implant a new political
creed in their minds."

This political indoctrination and division into categories
gave rise to strong opposition. Regrettably, the political lecturers
and the interrogators were often confused with the YMCA employees; for a long time, we had been the only civilians who had
shown them any interest, and we had tried to give them assistance and help them in a natural way without lecturing them and
without behaving in a didactic manner. The political teachers
were considered to be "wolves in sheep's clothing"; what they

represented was "dogmatic tyranny." A German doctor once asked me: "Why do those who tour around and give their lectures all belong to the Labor Party? Wouldn't you agree that, if anything, that is regimentation? And that's exactly what we are accused of—regimentation!" There was no question about the need for the German POWs to be reeducated. The issue was not that—it was the way in which the reeducation was carried out that aroused antagonism and resentment; it was so easy for a German refugee to stand there and shout at the POWs, "It's your own fault that you're here, in a POW camp!" when he himself had been sitting comfortably in Great Britain at a time when the price for opposition in Germany was a man's freedom, perhaps even his life. Another problem was that you can accentuate crime and guilt only for so long before one day the culprit will stand up and protest: "Enough! Stop your blasted indoctrination!" Or, as somebody once said to me, "We have been freed from Nazism, we just cannot face one more liberation, so leave me alone; I won't have anything to do with it!"

The POWs were convinced that an "A-man" could expect to be repatriated rather soon, and a "B-man" might be allowed to work at farming. But a "C-man" was surely destined to remain in the prison camp indefinitely. For a while the POWs called themselves "A-mocrats," "B-mocrats," and "C-mocrats," thereby indicating in a subtle way that absolutely no one could ever expect to reach the level of "D-mocrat."

Lots of prisoners went berserk when former countrymen appeared in British uniforms and started to push them around, to interrogate them and tell them about the concept of justice and the philosophy of life in a didactic tone of voice. Many prisoners were tempted to answer untruthfully to the numerous tactless and unimportant questions, hoping to achieve a higher grade than they deserved and thus a speedier repatriation. The first transport of repatriates from Great Britain to Germany in July 1946 consisted of "A-men" only. Surprisingly, however, groups of "B-" and "C-men" were allowed to go home a few months later.

All the YMCA employees were in complete agreement that the POW Aid should be evenly distributed among all POWs.

The work should continue to be carried out with flexibility and, until this time, this had resulted in the YMCA being met with confidence and trust from POWs and the British authorities alike. A German officer summed it all up very well: "You let us have footballs, but you don't ask in return that we must attend religious or political meetings. You let us have books, but you don't ask in return that we say our evening prayers. If you continue this unselfish work, I feel that our antagonism and opposition against Christianity and the Church might well begin to break down."

As I said, a certain amount of instruction and information was indeed necessary. It would have been irresponsible for the British to close their eyes to the need to educate and train future leaders in a Germany which was in ruins and needed to be brought back on its feet again. The British authorities were definitely right about this. But the most favorable change of mind was undoubtedly the one to which the POWs were exposed indirectly at their places of work. From official quarters, a great deal of hesitation was expressed at the mere involvement of POWs in the work process. That was not how the civilian population felt: the demand that the POWs should take part in the general work grew stronger and stronger. "If we have to feed them, then at least let them give us a hand and work for their bread and butter," was one of the most frequently used arguments. Others pointed out that the German POWs had to help mend the extensive damage which the war had caused in Great Britain, and in fact this point of view was shared by the majority of the POWs; they were well aware that the German authorities had used slave laborers and Allied POWs in great numbers to supply cheap labor. Finally the British authorities gave in to the demands of the civilian population, and most POWs were gradually employed at industry, road building, unskilled labor, air bases, docks, minesweeping, and—in particular—at farming. Mornings and evenings they were taken in trucks to and from work. Some had bicycles at their disposal and were allowed to go to and from work without escort.

Many of the POWs soon began to impress the local population with their diligence, and the war psychosis which had characterized the British until the end of the war was now beginning to be replaced by a growing sympathy for the POWs. It was generally agreed that the Germans were usually well behaved; serious crimes were rare, and during the entire year of 1946, attempted escapes amounted to less than 0.5 percent. By the latter part of 1946, there was a clear indication of a change of attitude on the part of the British authorities; they began to show more fairness and understanding in their treatment of the German POWs.

Keeping in mind that it is the duty of every Christian man and woman to help the weak, the Anglican Church already in April 1946 encouraged all Anglican priests, wherever possible, to make contact with captured German chaplains, to cooperate with them, and to support them in their work in the POW camps. In several cases, British priests lent a hand in areas where there were no German chaplains. This was the case in a prison camp near Harwich, where the local priest held services in German on Saturday afternoons; after these services his wife, who also spoke German, arranged record concerts, followed by a one hour English lesson for those who were interested.

A number of clergymen who lived in and around Durham normally invited the twenty German chaplains who were held prisoner of war in the deanery to participate in their regular conventions. In one of the prison camps I met a commandant who was interested in religious matters and who often, together with his wife, took part in the Sunday services held for the POWs. Several politicians, members of Parliament, and other officials understood the value of all these initiatives and attitudes, and they recommended that a relaxation of camp and guard regulations be introduced. The motives for doing so were probably mixed: some people were prepossessed by a Christian mind, others were presumably afraid of West Germany becoming a hothouse for the spread of Communism. But no matter what the motives were, the attitude was communicated to the majority of the population. The POWs felt it and rejoiced over it: "At last," they sighed, "At last, we are treated like human beings again." To them, Christmas of 1946 came to represent the end of the quite severe regulations to which they had been subjected until then. The British government allowed the civilian population to associate with German POWs, and as of 20 December 1946, POWs could pay visits to private homes. In Bristol, a bilingual service for Britishers and Germans was held on Christmas Day, and hundreds of British families received German prisoners of war as guests in their homes on that day.

On 29 December 1946, the British newspaper "Sunday Pictorial" brought out the following article with the caption, "Let The Germans Go Back To Germany!"

Never would I have thought that the time should come, when a wave of sympathy for German soldiers would flood Great Britain and never would I have thought that I myself should share that sympathy for those men who bombed my home in London and whom I went after and shot at all the way from Monte Cassino to Coblenz. And if our Government had not had the idea of keeping 390,000 of these former enemies and soldiers here in Great Britain behind barbed wires for 18 months after the last shot was fired, then I doubt very much that I would ever have felt any kind of sympathy for them.

It has become the growing demand of all honest and ordinary men and women throughout our country that these POWs be repatriated as soon as possible and without hesitation. Their drab, mended uniforms have been giving us a feeling of discomfort for months; their gangs at our farms remind us too much of Hitler's own gangs of slave labourers.

During the Christmas holiday thousands of our countrymen had invited POWs to their homes. And what, then, did they discover? They discovered that the "Impersonal" POWs suddenly became individuals—lonely men—who experienced a rare happiness at playing with our children and helping us do the dishes after dinner. They discovered that these men have but one burning desire: to return to their wives and their children.

I implore our government: please let them go home—NOW. It is shameful that they should still be here. We British will never be able to raise our heads in a free world if any of them are still here in six months from now. "

Effective from December 1946, POWs were allowed to accept lifts in private cars; they were free to walk as they pleased up to eight miles from their camps unescorted; they were allowed to accept small gifts in the form of cigarettes and tobacco; they could play football against British teams. To use public means of transport or to go to pubs, however, was still forbidden.

The population's and the POWs' reaction to the relaxation of the regulations was overwhelming. It became more and more customary for British guards in the camps to be replaced by German POWs. From spring 1947, the POWs were allowed to stay at the farms where they worked "provided conditions were found to permit such stays." In this way, the relationship between the British population and the Germans grew much closer, and in fact this was a kind of reeducation of the POWs which was probably far more valuable than requesting them to watch didactic films and listen to political lectures. All over Great Britain, in the cities and in the country, a quiet reconciliation emerged slowly from what had been animosity not so long ago. The authorities began to realize that it was an unnecessary waste of time, effort, and money to continue reeducational programs, when in fact things were working so very well in a much more tacit way. The population seemed satisfied and the atmosphere in the prison camps was much better now that the POWs could make contact with ordinary people, and break out of the isolation they had endured for so long.

Not everybody, however, was equally enthusiastic about the relaxations, and so the atmosphere differed from camp to camp; in fact, I do not think the atmosphere in any two camps was quite the same. In a camp in northern England, I met a commandant who I think never spoke directly to a POW. His whole attitude was, "It's crazy with all these relaxations for the Germans. In another twenty years they'll attack us again without even thinking about the time when they were invited to spend Christmas in a British home!" In this particular case, however, I could appreciate his attitude: he had been a POW in Germany himself, had lost his home and his belongings during a German air raid on London, and related that "my only son fell during the invasion of Normandy and my wife is a nervous wreck."

It was in his camp, by the way, that I met fourteen German POWs who were Danish citizens, but who had entered into German military service. One of them came from Jutland, from the town of Esbjerg, and he was terribly worried about his mother: "She suffers so much, because I was stupid enough at the age of seventeen to sign up for German war service." He had only one wish—to go home, serve his sentence, and then start afresh. Another man was on the verge of tears because the Danish authorities would not recognize him as a Danish citizen, but considered him to be primarily a German soldier.

I often visited Camp 104 in the small town of Milnthorpe. This camp was known as a "bad" camp; the POWs called it "mini-Belsen." It was looked upon as a convict camp, and perhaps rightly so: the commandant did seem at times to be rather unbalanced and uncertain, presumably due to his young age. He once said to me that he wanted to treat the Germans "just as they treated our men!" I tried to explain to him that if the British started to act like the Germans, then obviously we would be well on the road to becoming Germans ourselves. The commandant did not answer, but when I proceeded to tell him that I had noticed several Germans walking around in the cold wearing socks full of holes, he got very angry and led the way to a couple of huts. There he ordered the Germans to unpack their luggage, and I could see for myself that they had lots of socks without any holes. I realized then that the POWs wanted to bring them home to their families; most of the socks had been bought during their captivity in the USA.

Under the auspices of the same camp was a hostel in the village of Borwick; it housed eighty-five men who were employed at farming and who lived in a former horse stable—clean, well-furnished, and cozy. During one of my visits, I saw a POW return from work leading a calf which the farmer had given to him. Another POW had been able to procure two sacks of potatoes. The delight was great because now, "our Sunday dinner will be served," as they said.

In Haltwhistle, a town near the Scottish border, three thousand German officers lived in a prison camp, the commandant of which was convinced that what the POWs needed the most was to be shown confidence. On his first day of duty, he told them: "Gentlemen—During World War I, I was in German captivity and was treated like a gentleman. It is my intention to treat you likewise." He proceeded by having the barbed-wire fences and watch towers removed, together with the fences that divided the three categories of POWs—the "White," the "Gray," and the "Black"; finally, he changed the official name of the camp to "Camp of Confidence." This camp was to become one of the best prison camps in Great Britain.

One day, returning from a visit in Haltwhistle, I had problems with the fuel supply of my car, and it was beyond my abilities to fix it; but before I had the chance to get hold of a mechanic, an AA man on his yellow motorbike stopped and helped me repair the car. I wanted to pay him, but he interrupted me and said: "That's the least I can do. I got so much help from the YMCA when I was a POW in Germany." He told me that his name was Davies and that he had spent his period of captivity in STALAG XX-A, in Lamsdorf.

THE CONTRIBUTION OF THE CHURCH

As early as in the autumn of 1944, the YMCA employees recognized that the reeducational work among German POWs, which the British authorities deemed so very essential, would hardly prove worth the effort. Through many camp visits and numerous conversations with German Men of Confidence, chaplains, and others, John Barwick and Birger Forell could not but notice the strong opposition and apprehension that prevailed among the majority of the POWs. Because of these sentiments, and acting in the spirit of its policy, the YMCA POW Aid very sensibly refrained from taking part in any kind of public reeducation programs; any other initiatives which aimed at educating and training POWs for useful work in their home country were fully encouraged and supported, but such education and training should be for those interested and willing, and without an eye toward political and religious affiliations.

The YMCA was well aware of the poor possibilities for getting an education in Germany right after the war, and of the importance of training and educating the German people. Consequently, at the time when the discussion about reeducation was at its height, the YMCA proposed that a training and education center for POWs be established in Camp 174 in the small village of Norton, in Nottinghamshire. This was Pastor Forell's idea and it was strongly supported by Mr. Barwick, as well as by the other leaders of the British YMCA and the Anglican Church. What Pastor Forell had in mind was the establishment of a special camp for students of theology, beginners as well as those who had to interrupt their studies due to conscription. He also had in mind a teacher-training preparatory college, in which they could finish primary and secondary school and proceed with a higher education. The theological school would provide a most valuable support to the chaplains in the prison camps, and the teacher training college would act as a useful incentive to POWs who wanted to become teachers in the new Germany. Both schools would be financed and managed by the YMCA.

Norton's British camp commandant supported the proposal wholeheartedly, and the German camp leadership recognized its enormous benefits, so the War Ministry approved the proposal and declared its willingness to cooperate in its preparation and implementation. The difficulties of getting started, however, were huge, and the preparatory work lasted ten months.

Pastor Forell was untiring in his efforts to procure the necessary material: he went to France and collected books from the deserted Wehrmacht libraries; he combed antiquarian bookshops in London to find books on German literature; and he went all over Great Britain to dig out books of interest. His efforts paid off. A priest's widow in East Anglia donated her deceased husband's book collection on theology; the University of Oxford let him have a large part of the college's stock of books of German literature on theology, and the World Council of Churches in Geneva shipped sixty-five boxes of German books to the Norton camp. It was pointless to try to get books from Germany; The war and its purge of literature had seen to that, and the leftovers were not nearly sufficient to cover Germany's own need. Moreover, due to a paper shortage, new books did not leave the print. In spite of these generous donations, books remained a great demand, so the YMCA set up its own printing house at Luton, just north of London. The House employed fifty to fifty-five POWs, who produced and distributed more than one million books not only for Norton Camp but for camps all over Great Britain.

Through these persistent efforts, Norton Camp gradually created a reasonably well-supplied library for its two schools of education and training. But setting up the library was not the only major problem. Getting teachers was obviously very necessary before the entire project could commence at all. It was really no surprise that not one single German professor of theology was to be found in the British camps, so instead the YMCA had to search for and recruit teachers among German chaplains and other academics. John Barwick and Birger Forell went to work to prepare a list of names of POWs whom they judged could be—for lack of better ones—taken into consideration as teachers, and they forwarded an application to the British authorities for approval and permission to have the candidates transferred to Norton Camp. The authorities rejected all but two, but it was probably just as well, because many German chaplains were under suspicion of remaining loyal to the Nazi regime—and with good reason. Pastor Forell, however, was exceedingly persistent, and after numerous applications to the authorities, the YMCA finally succeeded in getting the necessary teachers. On 8 August 1945, "The YMCA Training Center of Norton Camp" was inaugurated at a festival service in the camp church. Everybody was present: POWs and representatives from the authorities, the Anglican Church, and the YMCA.

A few days later, the first group arrived. A total of 179 German theologians acting as chaplains in the British prison camps; they were to attend a course aimed at inspiring them to renewed efforts, and at brushing up their professional knowledge. It must not be forgotten that for many chaplains, their ecclesiastical and theological work had been interrupted because of the war. Most of them had had to do military service as active soldiers, not as chaplains, and they had thus been removed from their usual fields of work. And now, those who had been officers had to be taught not to be officers, and those who had been warrant officers and men, not to be warrant officers and men; this task was made infinitely more difficult by the inherent German discipline. A refresher course at Norton meant renewed inspiration, renewed energy, and renewed encouragement to a lot of lonely and dispirited men who were facing general standstills. In this regard lectures did a lot of good, but getting together with colleagues who experienced similar problems, and having discussions with teachers, employees of the YMCA, and others were even more valuable tools for encouraging the students to attempt to tackle the tasks and problems which were waiting for them in the camps where they would be working.

Soon Norton became an important educational institution, where hundreds of future clergymen and teachers received an education that would prove to be a valuable foundation upon which to build when they returned to Germany to carry on their work in schools and churches. All over the country, POWs were relieved of their duties and sent to Norton to concentrate on their studies. From spring 1947, the YMCA was able to invite scientists from other countries to come to Norton as guest speakers and teachers; I remember, for instance, the Swedish professor Anders Nygren, and the Norwegian bishop Bjarne Skard, the German bishop Hanns Lilje, the Danish professor Niels H. Søe, and the Dutch missionary historian Dr. Hendrik Kraemer. They all came to the camp and stayed for at least a couple of weeks, during which time they gave numerous lectures.

The main office of the YMCA POW Aid was still situated in London, but the Norton camp gradually developed into a center for activities in Great Britain. A large sign at the main entrance told people that here was the "YMCA's Education and Training Center Norton." A small printing works operated here in close cooperation with the printing house near London, and it produced more than one million books of scientific as well as vocational literature, religious writing, works by the best German writers, and so on, which were all reprinted and distributed from there to all the POW camps in the entire country.

The British authorities requested that the YMCA take over the overall organization of entertainment activities for the prison camps. The Norton camp became the center for this organization—films were bought in large numbers and, as more than one hundred projectors were available, every camp had the opportunity to show a new film to the POWs once every two weeks; the projectors simply moved from camp to camp. Norton also housed the YMCA's "theater wagon": it looked like a giant moving van, but it was designed for the specific purpose of being converted into a theater. It was on the move almost constantly with its load of POW assistants, equipment, actors, chairs, and bands, and by this means of transport, members of the theater group were able to tour from camp to camp to set up a diversity of shows and performances.

Shows, pictures, concerts, books, lectures, and education were excellent ways to divert POWs from depression. But there were still many POWs who were not satisfied by mental work, music, or sports, and for whom books held no interests at all; these were the unskilled workers. They seemed to have the greatest difficulties appreciating their situation and getting something useful out of their lives; they felt that they were wasting their time and they could not grasp why on earth they had not been repatriated long ago. Fortunately, however, some of them had sufficient initiative and ability to throw themselves into other activities such as woodwork, drawing, painting, and the like, and with a bit of help from the YMCA to further enhance their abilities, it often happened that one POW could set an example for others to go do something similar. In Norton a number of small workshops were established for the benefit of such POWs, a kind of technical school, where all those who wanted to could get basic training and exercise in precisely those hobbies in which they had developed an interest. "Reeducation"? Sure, but most definitely not a compulsory one!

The main objective of the YMCA's activities in the Norton camp was education, primarily in theology and pedagogics. But other subjects were also offered to the POWs. It is impossible to measure or evaluate the importance of the activities which originated from the Norton camp and what they meant to German POWs, and thus to postwar Germany. More than six hundred POWs received education as teachers and became useful members of a teaching staff in German schools; 120 prisoners of war—Catholics as well as Lutherans—were given basic knowledge about theology and ministration, and 125 POWs were trained to become future leaders of different youth organizations. A couple hundred POWs prepared themselves and sat for school-leaving certificates. The YMCA did right when it decided to prepare and introduce its own mammoth reeducation program, and the British authorities were indeed quick to admit this, to appreciate its enormous value to the POWs, and to give it their wholehearted support.

During visits to the camps, emphasis was placed on supporting and encouraging ecclesiastical work. Talks with the chaplains, Protestant as well as Catholic, were a fixed item on the agenda—preferably a personal talk in the chaplain's own room, not in the office of the commandant or the Man of Confidence. Most chaplains had a great need to talk to somebody from the outside, someone who came from a church organization, about their difficulties, problems, and possible complaints. And it became customary that we enquired into church matters and needs without waiting for the chaplains to bring up the subjects themselves. How frequently were services held? Were the men interested? Did the camp run any Bible study groups? What about Christian literature? Were there enough hymn books and Bibles available? Many chaplains worked in loneliness and under very difficult conditions, and questions such as these would sometimes serve as an encouragement for them to open up; besides, such questions could bring valuable information to light. It was important to the YMCA to find out whether captured chaplains actually did enjoy the privileges normally associated with the position of chaplain. Did a chaplain have his own room? Did he receive the pay to which he was entitled? Did he have the opportunity to minister to his countrymen in the hostels on a regular basis? Were the necessary means of transportation made available to him? If such matters were not in order, the problems might often be solved during the routine conversation with the camp commandant prior to leaving the camp.

These questions normally were also put to the German Man of Confidence or to the camp leader. Although a lot of camp leaders were quite indifferent to Christian activities in the camp, it was still important to ask the questions to make clear that the YMCA and the YMCA POW Aid placed just as much empḥ sis on the ecclesiastical conditions in the camp as on its genɛral welfare.

CHRISTMAS 1946

On the day of Christmas Eve 1946, I visited sixty German POWs at their hostels, and it appeared that as many as forty of them had been invited to spend Christmas Eve in British homes. Christmas Eve itself I spent in the Norton camp. The camp had been decorated for the occasion, just as the POWs would have done it had they been at home in their own country. I went by all the huts during the evening to say hello. Photographs of wives and children had been produced from their secret hiding places, and they stood in long rows on the tables among cakes and coffee mugs. The atmosphere was the same throughout: music, Christmas hymns and Christmas songs, recited poems, Christmas stories—all of this provided a traditional Christmas atmosphere in spite of the circumstances. At midnight, a joint service was held to conclude the evening.

All through Christmas Day and Boxing Day I acted as a driver to the bishop of Berlin, Dr. Otto Dibelius, who had taken this opportunity to visit his countrymen in Great Britain. Thousands of German POWs gathered in front of the pulpit in the Cathedral of Bristol, in village churches, and in the camps, where he held sermons and spoke to his fellow citizens.

The Bishop's name was well known and respected by most people, as were the names of Martin Niemöller and Lilje, all because of their anti-Nazi position and their importance to the German Confessional Church since 1933. The POWs listened to Bishop Dibelius in the Cathedral of Bristol as he went on to describe the conditions in Germany after the war. He spoke candidly about the tremendous difficulties and tasks—economic as well as ethical—which the German people were facing at that time. I could see from their faces that they were listening, and that they understood every word he said. The Bishop conveyed greetings from home, he told them about the petitions which the Church of Germany had forwarded to all the nations in the world with an appeal to release and repatriate the German POWs, and he continued: "Five million Germans are still held in captivity. It means that half of the German men between the age of twenty and twenty-five are not in Germany." He raised the question whether Germany had a future at all and answered it himself: "It all depends whether our people has the urge to live a decent life or not." He went on: "God doesn't go for the great masses, but for the minorities, always. Today in Germany, we find a minority which bravely and without complaint carries the sufferings which are placed upon our country's shoulders. But this minority mustn't become as small as the one in Sodom and Gomorrah, where not even ten just men could be found, because if so, then God will let our people perish." The Bishop concluded his speech by once again conveying greetings to the POWs "from home and especially from the minority of which I just spoke, and I invite you to come home and take part in our community."

Shortly after Christmas I was asked to move to London. I really did not understand the meaning of taking me away from Newcastle and "my" camps in northern England so soon after I had started work there. I felt that I had not even started yet, and already the management wanted to replace me with a newly arrived young Swedish staff member. However, as John Barwick was of the opinion that "we need you more in London," I complied and went there. By the beginning of 1947, I had settled and begun my work at some of the prison camps in the south of England.

John Barwick had offered me accommodation in his family house in the northern part of London, and my almost daily presence in the offices of the POW Aid in the city resulted in my quickly getting to know the other staff members, and familiarizing myself with the administrative and economic problems. Barwick often asked me to accompany him to meetings in the Foreign and War Ministries, and to meetings with other authorities about POW matters. It was very instructive, but I still did not quite see the reason for it—all the meetings took me away from my customary camp visits.

Finally, at the end of April, John Barwick disclosed the reason: the YMCA World Alliance intended to send me to Egypt "as soon as possible" to assist German POWs in North Africa. And so, on 19 June 1947, I arrived at the airport in Cairo, and yet another chapter of my life among prisoners of war was about to begin.

Part Four

AMONG GERMAN PRISONERS OF

WAR IN EGYPT

THE ATMOSPHERE IN THE PRISON CAMPS

WHEN THE war ended and Germany collapsed in 1945, German troops in Greece and on Crete and the remaining Greek islands surrendered to the British unconditionally, and, together with the troops who had fought and surrendered in Italy, they were shipped to Alexandria and Port Said over the months of May, June, and July and put into prison camps in the northern part of Egypt, mainly in the desert along the Suez Canal between Port Said and Suez.

Not many preparations had been made prior to their arrival. They had to build the camps themselves in an area which had served as a depot and assembly area for Field Marshal Montgomery's Eighth Army. In only a few cases had they been fortunate enough to be able to move into barracks which were no longer occupied by the British forces. The POWs lived mainly in tents, eight to twenty-five men in each, and considering that there were almost one hundred thousand POWs it is easy to imagine that the prison camps were a dominant feature in the landscape along the canal from Port Said toward the south. The camps were usually surrounded by double fences of barbed wire, not so much for fear of attempts at escape as for protection from thieves and robbers who were on the loose in the desert. If a POW would even begin to think about escape, his chances of success were very slim, because he would have to stick to the marked roads and paths to avoid mine fields. Germany was a long way from Egypt, and in between was the Mediterranean.

The climate was one of intense heat—95–105 degrees Fahrenheit in the summer—and shade was in short supply. In the spring, occasional sandstorms raged over the area, turning day almost into night for a couple days, and causing the fine desert dust to penetrate everything and everyone—eyes, ears, nose, and throat. During the summer, the hot desert wind whistled across the tent camps, and without the wind the hot air was like a heavy cloud. Shade could only be found in the tents, and there the heat was even more overwhelming.

The POWs slept on sacks of straw, or on willows or reeds. Blankets were unnecessary, but they were available in case somebody wanted one. Each man got at least two thousand calories per day of bread, rice, and beans, and they were quite happy with this diet; you do not work up a hearty appetite in hot weather, and the Red Cross reported the daily rations to be "adequate." The majority of the POWs also had the opportunity to earn some money by disarming land mines, disposing of other explosives, carrying out surveillance services, building houses for the British soldiers, constructing runways, repairing cars and armored vehicles, and other tasks. The pay was not much, but it was sufficient to add to the daily ration in the forms of bananas and other kinds of fruit, tinned meat, lard, chocolate, cheese, eggs, and so on; they could also spend it on cigarettes, or save it for later purchases to bring home to Germany, where there was a general shortage of most necessities.

Not all POWs were allowed to work and make money to spend in the canteens. Just as in Great Britain, the German Africa warriors and their Italian colleagues in Egypt were interrogated and classified as "White," "Gray," and "Black" POWs. The "Whites" could work without any restrictions, so they were always able to earn a little extra. So, too, could the "Grays," as their opinions changed for the better. But the "Blacks" who, according to the British experts—the reeducationalists—would never stop thinking and acting in accordance with their National

Socialist convictions, did not get the opportunity to work. As a rule, and in most cases with good reason, the British were suspicious of those who suddenly declared themselves to be advocates and supporters of democracy. In December 1946, fourteen thousand German POWs in Egypt were considered "Whites," more than twenty-four thousand "Blacks," and the remaining fifty to sixty thousand "Grays." Already by then, the "Whites" enjoyed the privilege of moving around as they pleased, going to and from work without escort. Sometimes they were employed in surveillance service, including keeping an eye on those of their countrymen whom the British regarded as "ultraorthodox."

The atmosphere was very much like that in Great Britain: the POWs were worried about the future, they had difficulties keeping up their spirits, and they could not understand why their repatriation had to be delayed for so long. However, around Christmas 1946 the atmosphere grew better when the first group of POWs—about six thousand—was repatriated just a few days before the Christmas holiday. This group consisted of "Whites" only—"anti-Nazi" and "Nazi-persecuted" men; most of them were probably Communists. Among these fortunate men was also Pastor Reinhardt Wester, who later became Bishop of Schleswig; he was known as the leader of the Confessional Church in Schleswig-Holstein and thus considered to be "anti-Nazi," and qualified for repatriation. Bishop Wester later told me how the POWs spent Christmas on board a ship in the middle of the Mediterranean: "We held a service and sang our Christmas hymns, but we were constantly outsung by other men who sang the 'Internationale.'"

At the time of this first repatriation transport, the British announced the schedule for future repatriations intended to take place during 1947. But unfortunately it did not go according to plan; no transports were sent off in the following months and on 30 September, the British authorities issued a statement to all prison camps that "due to lack of vessels," the repatriation of POWs had to be delayed, and that the "Whites" would be the first to be repatriated, the "Blacks" the last. It was further stated that "the 'Blacks' do not yet qualify for repatriation." The POWs who now found themselves sentenced to stay indefinitely in Egypt might, however, be able to expedite their repatriation, provided they changed their political convictions. "Category Black," it was stated, "will be abolished as soon as all 'Blacks' have been investigated and—depending on the result of such an investigation—moved to category "Gray minus," "Gray," or "Gray plus," or have been placed in the lowest category, that of the "Ultra-Blacks."

The British were not satisfied with a system of colors only; they also invented a subtle system of points, whereby decisions could be made as to the order in which the POWs would be repatriated. Such considerations as the age of the POWs, the size of their families, the period of time spent in captivity, their general behavior in camp, and so forth were now taken into account. Furthermore, POWs who had been working at mine-sweeping for a period of at least six months would occupy a privileged position because of the danger connected with such work. In other words, the "Blacks" were able, through work, to wash themselves "white."

This announcement did nothing to improve the general at-mosphere among the POWs. No one seemed to believe that "lack of vessels" was a true reason for the delay of their repatria-tion, and few understood that at that very time the British des-perately needed all the boats they could lay their hands on to get their own soldiers home from Palestine and India. The reac-tion was a completely empty auditorium the next time a political lecturer arrived in Camp 380, and he could read the reason why from the blackboard in the tent: "We are absent due to lack of vessels," an unmistakable sign of the POWs' feelings. From then on, lectures were terminated. Through newspapers and letters from home, the POWs were rather well informed about the situation in Germany—about the hunger, the cold, and the short supply of almost everything. Why could they not be al-lowed to go home and be united with their families, to suffer with them and to help get their daily bread? Again and again, they compared their own situation with that of their coun-trymen who were held in captivity in Great Britain.

The conditions in Great Britain and in Egypt were indeed different. The climate in England was more or less like that of Germany; in Egypt—at least for half of the year—it was unbearable to have to work even six hours a day, with the burning sun and a temperature near 105 degrees Fahrenheit. The air would often be extremely dry and suffocating and it would drain all the energy a man might possess.

In Great Britain, the POWs were allowed to accept invitations to visit private homes, and many days of the week such invitations were extended and accepted with great pleasure to guests as well as hosts. In Egypt such opportunities did not exist. The POWs were allowed to walk away from the camp areas wherever they wanted as long as they had returned by eleven o'clock in the evening—but where could they go? Nothing but desert sand surrounded them, and the few Arabs who lived along the Suez Canal certainly did not extend any invitation to any POW.

In Great Britain, the public opinion that POWs ought to be repatriated at the first possible opportunity was expressed in the media; several members of Parliament stood up and spoke in favor of the POWs. No one in Egypt stood behind the POWs, no public opinion was backing them, and they often felt that they had been deserted and forgotten.

Letters from POWs in Great Britain reached their destinations within a few days, whereas they took six to eight weeks from Egypt: air mail was not allowed, so the letters had to go by sea. The worst case was mail to and from the Russian occupied zone in Germany; a POW with his home in East Germany could consider himself lucky if he managed to receive a reply within four months.

No restrictions prevented POWs in Great Britain from sending parcels containing food and rationed goods, such as clothes, chocolate, and tobacco, to their families in Germany. In Egypt, where there was no rationing at all, and where everything could be had for money, the POWs were not allowed to send parcels. The YMCA made several futile attempts to change this situation, but the Egyptian authorities were unbending and would not permit it.

All these minor and major problems were pulling things in the wrong direction. And not only that; always, always, you kept seeing the same faces around you; you would meet the same fellow prisoners on the sports fields, and across the chess boards. Everywhere it was the same crowded tents, the same never-ending discussions about the lost war, the same dissatisfaction with the complete lack of privacy, the same uncertainty about the fate of their families, the same longing for their families, the same constant debates about how long this was going to last. All of this occasionally resulted in one, then another making the decision to put an end to it all. They just could not find a way out or see any solution to their problems and, finally, they took their own lives; most often, they would hang themselves in the darkness of night from a pole in the barbed-wire fence. The number of suicides grew alarmingly during the autumn of 1947, and so did the number of POWs who had to be admitted to British military hospitals due to shattered nerves.

PROTESTS FROM THE CHAPLAINS

The situation became so serious that the twenty German chaplains held captive in Egypt felt called upon to do something quite extraordinary. Pastor Norbert Rückert was a chaplain in the largest officers' camp and had recently been appointed Dean for the German POWs in Egypt by the leadership of the Evangelical Church in Germany, following a unanimous nomination from the other chaplains in Egypt.

On 1 October, Pastor Rückert forwarded a letter to all thirty-eight prison camps and hostels in the canal zone; his main purpose was to appeal to everybody to be sensitive to fellow prisoners in distress and to try to help them. The second step he took was to make, on behalf of all the chaplains in Egypt, a statement to the British authorities explaining the situation from the chaplains' point of view. The statement was copied and distributed to all camps in Egypt, to the World Council of Churches in Geneva, and to the Evangelical as well as the Catholic church leaderships in Germany.

The letter and the statement tell us something very important, I think, about the Church's contribution to POW camps, and therefore, they deserve to be quoted in their entirety.

The content of the letter addressed to the POW camps was as follows:

Dear friends and comrades,

Within a short period of time, two of our countrymen have committed suicide, they resorted to the rope and we carried them to their graves. What impelled them to take such an action, I cannot know. But I do know that there are enough burdens here and in our home country to weigh us down.

It is terrible when a man says: "I cannot stand it anymore—I will not," and then takes his own life. Suicide is the only act in the world that does not change anything to the better or to the worse; suicide puts an end to a life, a life that can never be restored. Suicide has no meaning—suicide can only be committed by those to whom life has become meaningless.

But does that mean that nothing has a meaning? We cannot determine the meaning of life—that is for God to do. And now, some of you will probably say: "God is but an empty word. We have never met Him." But it is God who gave us our lives. And it is God who knows why we so often find everything so very hopeless. He does not want suffering, hardship, death. He is our Father, and He wants only that we be helped, when we are in need of help. If we have faith in Him, then we shall know that when He closes a door, He always leaves a window open. That is why it is not right to throw away in desperation the life that God has given us. That is why it is not right to let a fellow man be alone with that strain, that burden which has brought him to despair. That is why we must help each other and go to Him in unison. God never deserted us in our captivity—not in the past and not now.

Dear friends—please help each other. Pray to our Lord if you are able. Ask Him to help you and to lead you and your fellow men to the church in your camp.

My warmest regards,

Norbert Rückert

The content of the very detailed statement, dated 11 October 1947 and addressed to the British authorities in Egypt, is as follows:

Caused by the extraordinary critical mental situation in which our fellow prisoners find themselves, and in obedience to the official duties that are incumbent on us, the Lutheran chaplains held in war captivity in Egypt hereby wish to submit the following statement to the British authorities, to the German public, to our fellow prisoners, and to Christianity all over the world:

For two and a half years—in many cases much longer than that—60,000 Germans have been held prisoners of war in Egypt and continue to be so; they have been put to work in a climate which, for at least six months of the year, is extremely difficult to tolerate.

The inordinately long separation from their families, bad news from home, the fact that they are unable to help those close to them, and the complete uncertainty as to how long they shall have to remain prisoners of war, all these things have caused a mental strain on the prisoners of war so grave that there is cause for serious concerns regarding the future. The symptoms which have emerged already are in themselves very frightening: the number of POWs who suffer mental breakdowns and who are declared insane is growing at an alarming rate. In camp Number 2719, for instance,

6 POWs out of 5,000 have been admitted to the British military hospital, to the ward of the mentally deranged, during the past six months. Growing in numbers, too, are those POWs who take their own lives, because they find life utterly meaningless; only last month, five suicides were committed in the Southern Canal District, one of the three British military districts in Egypt.

The majority of the POWs are without any faith or confidence in British promises and announcements, and the mental strain which they suffer is becoming more and more serious. The most important reasons for this critical situation are as follows:

1. The scheduled repatriation—published at the end of 1946, more than 18 months after the capitulation—and supposed to commence in 1947—has hardly begun.

2. On 30 September 1947, the British authorities announced that, due to lack of vessels, it had become necessary to limit the repatriation of POWs to a mere fraction of the anticipated quota. You will appreciate that the POWs have their doubts as to the truth of such an announcement, and that they think that the true reason behind the slow rate of repatriation of POWs is rather the wish for and use of the POWs as a labour force.

With sincere gratitude, the POWs have noticed that numerous people—in particular bishops and ecclesiastical leaders—in Great Britain have publicly declared themselves in favor of an amelioration of the conditions of the POWs. The impact of such ameliorations, however, is barely noticeable to POWs in Egypt and has greatly increased their feelings of bitterness, hopelessness, despair, and resignation.

3. Another very serious strain on the POWs is the recently issued order, directing them in future not to bring home more than 10 pounds of food when they are repatriated. Germany is facing another cold winter which will cause its population to starve and freeze. For many months, yes, even years, thousands of POWs have been saving money from their hard-earned and modest pay, they have deprived themselves of almost everything, with the sole purpose of being able to bring home as much food as possible to their starving families. Many have resigned themselves to the fact that their repatriation had been postponed again and again, because they have found comfort in saying to themselves: "Never mind, at least I can ask some of my mates to bring my family some food, especially lard, as a small contribution to ease their conditions." The new order renders this impossible. The kind of food we are talking about is readily available in Egypt, it can be bought in the camp canteens and consumed by the POWs in whatever quantities they wish. Why then, are they not allowed, when they have saved the money for it, to bring home something which is so desperately needed in their own country. No one gets harmed and the money stays in Egypt. It seems especially destructive and it has embittered the POWs that the treatment of the POWs, which was supposed to get better and gentler with the passing of time after the end of the war, in reality is getting stricter when orders such as the above are being introduced.

The prisoners of war simply cannot understand why—on top of the delay of their repatriation—they must suffer even further hardships by the introduction of the order in question, while fellow prisoners who were so fortunate as to be repatriated at an earlier time were allowed, without any restrictions, to take a few kilos of food back to a starving Germany.

4. Yet another severe mental strain on the POWs is the treatment of those who are suspected of being war criminals, but whose identities have not been completely clarified, or those who will be needed as witnesses in cases against such war criminals. These POWs are detained indefinitely without being told the reason why and without having stood trial. In spite of the fact that the British authorities have had at least two years and often longer to determine the identities of the men concerned, they have been unable to do so, and the result has been that the POWs in question in numerous cases have been taken off the repatriation transports only a few hours prior to departure and have been placed under "automatic arrest." In two specific cases they were even taken off the repatriation ship as it was ready to leave harbour in Port Said; to talk about "mental cruelty" in this connection is certainly no exaggeration. To detain, indefinitely, a POW who has been through numerous interrogations and tests and who has been declared eligible for repatriation, is nothing less than psychological torture.

5. The POWs are very grateful that the prevailing majority of camp and hostel commandants are making every effort to relax the conditions of the POWs by enlarging the canteens and establishing new canteens, and day rooms, by improving the provisioning, organising film shows and sports events, and giving the POWs the possibility of enhanced training and education. The POWs understand perfectly that owing to the special peculiarities in Egypt, they cannot have quite the same relaxations as are possible in Great Britain.

What the POWs cannot understand, however, is that even the smallest offence is often severely punished. The most severe sentence—28 days in prison—is in numerous cases passed immediately and does not compare at all to the size of the offence: a POW, for instance, was sentenced to 14 days of prison and loss of points, which prolonged his captivity for several months—just because he failed to notice and therefore to salute a passing British military vehicle's flag of the commander.

Till this date we—the Evangelical chaplains—have kept silent about cases of brutality, some of them even involving physical maltreatment in the short term prisons; instead, we have personally approached the British camps or prison managements responsible, to seek immediate termination of such incidents. In the present situation, however, we have had to seriously ask ourselves if we really have the right to remain silent; we think that perhaps we and our Evangelical Church might be blamed, and rightly so, for keeping quiet when, in fact, we ought to have spoken.

We have finally come to the conclusion that, if we are to act responsibly in our positions as clergymen, and unless we wish to become a party to the wrongs which have been committed, and still are being committed against POWs in Egypt, then surely we must now speak up.

If our former adversaries in the war had threatened us with revenge and retaliation if we dared to speak up, then we would have had to keep quiet; we would have had to say to our fellow prisoners: "Look, this is what lawlessness and godlessness lead to; this is what the law of retaliation carries with it." We would have had to silently defer to the judgments of God and would have deserved it. However, our former adversaries have made no such threat; on the contrary, they have solemnly declared that they went to war in the name of justice and humanity to put an end to all evil and that, in the spirit of Christianity, they will now lead our people onto a new road. This is a great encouragement and in all urgency, because we feel it to be our sacred duty as priests and spiritual advisors to our fellow prisoners—we dare implore all leading men and women and all responsible authorities in all of Great Britain to stop being passive spectators to the wrongs that have been and are being committed against POWs in Egypt, and instead, through practical, efficient and expedient measures, to remedy the mental sufferings and the despair among the POWs which are spreading day by day.

We entertain the greatest and most serious concerns that our fellow prisoners in Egypt shall lose—and many already have—the very last and most precious of what we, in the spirit of Christ, have wanted to impose on them—the faith and confidence that it is not power, not revenge, not retaliation and not the justice of the strongest which will have the final word, but that it is indeed possible for peoples and nations to live together and be together in a spirit of justice, fairness, reconciliation and brotherly assistance.

On behalf of and at the request of
the Evangelical Chaplains in Egypt.

Signed Norbert Rückert, Dean
Camp 380, 11 October 1947

Copies of this statement were forwarded to the Church of Germany, the International Red Cross, and the Lutheran World Federation in Geneva; it was distributed to a number of distinguished men and women in Great Britain: for instance, Bishop George Bell of Chichester, Mr. Victor Gollancz, one of the most fervent advocates of a united Europe, and several prominent members of Parliament; it was circulated in every POW camp and hostel, it was read out from the pulpit, and it was broadcast over many camp radios.

In the British headquarters, this unexpected initiative on the part of the chaplains caused great consternation and a good deal of annoyance. Some commandants simply forbade the reading of the statement and threatened the chaplains with punishment if the statement were read out during a service. Nevertheless, it was read out by all the chaplains and no commandant ever carried out his threat of punitive measures.

The POWs sensed great relief: "Finally, we have someone who has the guts to say openly what all of us think and feel!" Some of them said, with wonder in their voices, "It was the Church, not the politicians, that spoke up for us!" The public reaction was certainly not long in coming: shortly after the issuing of the statement, a British member of Parliament arrived in Egypt to find out whether the statement was speaking the truth. And in February 1948, a representative of the German Evangelical Churches, Dr. Reinhold von Thadden-Triglaff, stayed in the Middle East for three weeks. In close cooperation with Dean Rückert, the YMCA POW Aid escorted Dr. von Thadden to all POW camps, where he briefed the POWs on the situation and conditions in Germany and answered countless questions. Bishop Bell and Mr. Gollancz also paid a visit to Egypt.

But the most important consequence of the statement was that toward the end of the year, it seemed that the "lack of vessels" was over: already, from February 1948 onwards, the repatriation transports were resumed and quickly increased in number. Regulations about searching the returning POWs' luggage were eased, if not revoked. From that time on everybody was allowed to bring with him just as much as he could carry, provided it had been acquired in an honest way.

ECCLESIASTICAL AND CULTURAL ACTIVITIES

In London I was rather given the impression that the POWs in Egypt were left to their own devices, and that I was therefore to break entirely new ground. However, this impression proved to be somewhat inaccurate.

Already at the end of the war, the YMCA World Alliance had requested the Egyptian YMCA to initiate relief work among the German POWs in northern Egypt, along the same guidelines and principles as was done in other countries. The necessary funds had been transferred from Geneva to Cairo to cover expenses. Furthermore, boxes of such materials as books, sports equipment, and musical instruments had been dispatched and distributed to the various camps. However one rather serious problem remained: No one on the Egyptian YMCA staff had any experience in POW work, or—what was more important—any knowledge of German. At the beginning, and as an interim solution, an American missionary living in Cairo had offered to spend part of his time visiting the prison camps. He went from camp to camp and distributed the goods which the World Alliance had dispatched, but he could only make himself understood through an interpreter and he did not have too much time to spare, so the number of POWs he was able to talk to was rather limited. Furthermore, there were so many camps—twenty-eight in all—spread out over so large an area, that one single man—working part-time, mind you—could not possibly handle such a mammoth job adequately.

A turn for the better occurred in August 1946, when the YMCA in Cairo employed a fifty-year-old Austrian, Edward Morgan, to be responsible for the aid to POWs. Edward Morgan had lived in Egypt for more than twenty years and was fluent in English, French, German, and Arabic. Furthermore, he had excellent connections to Arab businessmen in Cairo, so he was able to procure, locally and at fair prices, the things most coveted in the camps: things like exercise books, books on all subjects, and sports equipment, and then to travel to all the camps in the canal zone to deliver his goods. Edward Morgan was the first YMCA representative who really succeeded in making contact with all the POWs, their Men of Confidence, and their leaders.

The reason why the YMCA World Alliance, toward the end of 1946, considered employing yet another staff member was that several POWs, independently and from different camps, wrote letters to the Geneva office asking for the YMCA to visit them and help them in the same manner as they knew was being done for their countrymen in camps in Great Britain. Another reason was a request from Colonel Fraser, a British officer and a former commandant of one of the large prison camps near London, who had been transferred to Egypt to be in charge of the

British Ministry of Foreign Affairs' department of POW matters. He knew John Barwick and Camp Norton, and he recognized from personal experience the favorable influence the
YMCA would have on the morale and welfare of the POWs. In
a letter to John Barwick he explained that in Egypt he had seen
only few and sporadic traces of the YMCA, and he asked him
to consider expanding the relief work in Egypt and making it
more efficient.

The final reason was that the Egyptian YMCA asked for
further financial support, due to their increased expenses in connection with work among POWs. The World Alliance was unable to raise more money—it was not as easy as during the war—
and consequently, it was decided that an employee be sent to
Cairo. The aim was to try to build up the relief work in such a
way as to make it self-supporting. And so, at the end of June
1947, I came to Egypt.

The men in charge of the YMCA in Cairo were a great help
to me with their guidance and advice. Edward Morgan immediately offered to accompany me on camp visits, and within one
week we had called on all twenty-eight camps and on the British
headquarters. Of course, with such speed, the visits were limited
to brief conversations with the camp commandants, the German
camp leadership, and, once in a while, with the German chaplains. During the rides from camp to camp, I had the opportunity to tell Edward Morgan how the POW Aid operated in Great
Britain. He said that many things regarding the POWs in Egypt
were in need of improvement, but he doubted that it would be
possible to introduce any such improvements, due not only to
the British but also to the Egyptian authorities.

In Fayid, halfway between Port Said and Suez about eighty-
five miles east of Cairo, the British had established their headquarters. I was issued a pass which authorized me to visit all the
prison camps and field hospitals, and I met Colonel Fraser, the
man who had approached John Barwick concerning aid to the
camps in Egypt. As I have already mentioned, he was in charge
of the Foreign Ministry's special department for POW matters,
and he was particularly interested in the German POWs' political
pasts. He was also at the head of British propaganda and of the

courses of lectures in the camps. Not everybody took to Colonel Fraser; some found him too "radical," too "socialistic" in his efforts to reeducate the POWs. But his critics were not always possessed by pure motives or sentiments, because although he often aired his political views, he never hesitated to intervene on behalf of a POW against a colleague if he found out that the POW had not been treated correctly.

I spent the months of July and August familiarizing myself with the area in which the POWs were staying, and after numerous talks with German Men of Confidence, camp leaders, and chaplains, I soon realized that if we wanted the relief work in Egypt to reach the same high level of efficiency as in Great Britain, then we would have to establish a YMCA center similar to the Norton camp at one of the camps in the canal zone. In the middle of March 1947, the British forces in Egypt had been moved east, away from Alexandria and Cairo in the cultivated and densely populated Nile delta to the wide, almost unpopulated desert stretches along the Suez Canal. Camp 380 was situated in the middle of this huge area, and there were several reasons for choosing that camp to be the center of the YMCA's work in Egypt.

Camp 380 was the largest POW camp in Egypt; the majority of German officers were held prisoner there and, as they were exempt from work, it was very likely that suitable employees could be found among them. Furthermore, Camp 380 held far more leisure-time facilities than any other camp. It was centrally situated not far from the British headquarters, and the British authorities intended to establish a transit camp in one of the wings, a wing for POWs waiting to be repatriated. A YMCA center in Camp 380 would ensure assistance to all POWs; from there, YMCA employees would be able to follow them and help them in all practical matters right up to the moment when they reached the harbor in Port Said and embarked the transport ship bound for Europe. Additionally, the camp's commandant— Colonel T. Shirley—was a man most interested in the work of the YMCA, a man whose advice and help were to prove extremely valuable to all of us.

It was Colonel Shirley who suggested to me that I move out

of Cairo and into Camp 380. He would arrange for me to have a tent to live in, and he would make further tents available to the YMCA for storage space and offices. He said that I would be most welcome to take my meals in the British officers' mess, and that "you can count on my full support, whenever you need it. "

Colonel Fraser and his staff in the British headquarters were delighted by this suggestion; so was the YMCA in Cairo, because they could see the advantage of Edward Morgan and me sharing the work between us: Edward was to be in charge of procuring in Cairo and dispatching to Fayid all of the necessities for the prison camps, and I was to be in charge of further distribution from the new offices in camp 380. The fact that this system would also be very cost-effective to the YMCA because of my free board and lodgings was naturally a second advantage; at any rate, it was decided that effective on 1 September, I should move to the canal zone.

Colonel Shirley welcomed me in a most kind and helpful manner, and he invited me to attend his staff meetings, which he held in his office every Saturday morning. At the first meeting I attended, he officially welcomed me and introduced me to his staff members. He asked them to be of assistance to me if and when I approached them for help, and he expressed his pleasure at "having the new center of the YMCA POW Aid placed at our camp. "

I suppose that as a commandant, Colonel Shirley was in many ways conservative in his methods and views, and he was probably not as wholehearted in his attitudes toward the democratization and reeducation of the POWs as were Colonel Fraser and other officers in the headquarters. But he was impeccably correct in his treatment of the POWs, and on several occasions he proved that he was most capable of showing concern for individuals. To him a POW was an individual human being, not a number in his files. Everybody in the camp knew where the commandant's office was, and that he could always come and see him during office hours. And if the colonel found out that a man needed his help in any way, that man could be sure of his support and understanding. I remember one such incident, where a POW had received a letter from home telling him that his wife had attempted suicide in despair that her husband had still not returned. In his great need he turned to the commandant, who immediately made investigations and, when he had received confirmation that what the POW had told him was quite true, he arranged for him to be included in the very first shipment for Europe; he did this even though this POW had been classified as category "C," or a "Black." Thanks to Colonel Shirley, he came home several months earlier than he could otherwise have hoped for.

It did not take me long to realize the advantage of living among the POWs in Camp 380. Not only did I make very good contacts, but I did not have any difficulties finding qualified POWs to assist me as my workload grew. But my job as a POW field delegate naturally remained the same here as anywhere else: to do all I could to keep up the POWs' courage and spirits by supporting them in whatever sound occupations I could think of, and, to the widest extent possible, to be at the disposal of any POW who wanted to talk to me on whatever subject he wished.

It seemed natural to begin work by finding out what kinds of activities the POWs themselves had already initiated in each camp, such as education, church services, libraries, sports, music, theater, wood carving, and then, through the office in Cairo, to procure things necessary to expand the on-going activities in order to benefit more POWs.

Right from the beginning, there had been churches and congregations in the camps. More than twenty chaplains, twenty students of theology, and a few deacons had been taken prisoner and transferred evenly to all camps and hospitals. Naturally the religious work had been forced to begin from scratch, and Camp 380 was an excellent example of how a congregation of POWs came into being and gradually became larger. At the beginning, the chaplains had gone from tent to tent and invited the POWs to attend services, which were held without any kind of ceremony. Before long, study groups on the Bible had been formed and soon they, too, grew in number. The subject for discussion was mainly Saint Paul the Apostle and his Epistles. Saint Paul became quite a personality to many POWs because he himself had been a prisoner, and the POWs found renewed courage by getting acquainted with him through his Epistles.

The services were held in tents, sometimes in churches which the POWs had built. Communion tables, pulpits, and decorations were made, often from very modest means. The churches were used by Catholics as well as Protestants. The YMCA assisted in procuring Bibles, hymn books, and altar wine and wafers, and the services and other church activities were announced on the camp's notice board. The atheists and the indifferent respected what the church did and recognized that it was something very special to many POWs; no one, as far as I know, ever tried to interrupt a service.

During 1946 and the beginning of 1947 many YMCA associations were set up, reaching a total of eleven hundred members. The very first association was founded by some officers, mainly older ones who knew of the YMCA in Germany, before Hitler had the associations forbidden and dissolved. One of the officers was transferred to another camp shortly after the first association had been founded, and he immediately set out to establish another one. The initiative was catching, and it spread such that by Christmas 1947, eighteen associations with a total of two thousand members had been formed in the camps. It was among these members that I was able to find the most faithful and hardworking employees.

The associations differed a lot from one another. In some camps they were identical with the Protestant congregation; in other camps, they included Protestant as well as Catholic members. Some associations were pure Bible study groups and seemed somewhat self-contained, important only to the few members without any significant contact with the large masses of POWs; often the Man of Confidence and the commandant did not know of their existence. In other camps, the associations were open to and important to everybody. Here too emphasis was placed on the study of the Bible, and the members would probably claim that this subject was indeed the most important one. But they arranged numerous other activities and took part in most of what went on in the camps. They put their mark on different study groups, initiated language courses, arranged well-frequented lectures, during which a POW would often be asked to discuss some nonpolitical topic. Some associations published their own periodicals and posted newspaper clippings on the notice board—pictures and short notes that informed the readers about the work of young Christian men and women all over the world.

Any active and well-managed YMCA association would always do numerous things to heighten the general well-being of the POWs, and it would always be possible to persuade members to take charge of things. Several YMCA associations were fortunate enough to have their own tents, which the British camp management had willingly placed at their disposal, and in which reading rooms had been set up with newspapers, small libraries, games of entertainment, and the like made available to everybody who wanted to make use of these facilities. Occasionally these premises were used by chaplains for preparing POWs for confirmation: twice a week young POWs under the age of twenty-five met to be taught Christianity, a tuition which in many cases continued beyond the ceremony of confirmation in so-called "Jugend-Kreise"—youth circles. In some camps, the YMCA associations offered to maintain the German war cemeteries, and even had photographs taken of each grave and sent to relatives as a memento of a dead husband, father, brother, or son.

Camp 380 had a well-managed YMCA association with 150 active members, or 13 percent of the total number of prisoners. The chairman, a 28-year-old lieutenant named Peter Heyde, had become acquainted with the German YMCA just prior to its abolishment and his own draft for service. The Lutheran chaplain, Pastor Rückert, had been a secretary in the YMCA in Erlangen, and he possessed a rare quality of being able to talk to all sorts of people; he was a man of unfailing good spirits, quick-witted, and an excellent athlete. His advice was always sound and he would always have the time to listen when somebody wanted to talk to him about personal problems. These two men became my closest colleagues in Egypt and our warm friendships lasted as long as they both lived.

Pastor Rückert could congratulate himself on being able to hold services in a real stone church instead of in tents. One day he had made up his mind that Camp 380, being situated so close to the British headquarters and the garrison church, must have a "proper" church. He would name it "St. Martins in the Sands," and it was to be built on the most central and conspicuous spot in the entire camp. He discussed the matter with his congregation, and the great majority supported his idea wholeheartedly and promised to help build the church. Volunteers were of course necessary if this ambitious project was to be a success. The pastor submitted his proposal to the commandant, who approved it and gave his permission for the church being built on the desired spot, just inside the main entrance to the camp. And so, work could commence.

The ground was leveled and an artificial rise was made of gravel and sand. Everybody was welcome to lend a hand, after they returned from their own work, and lots of POWs did so, digging, wheeling stones and sand to the building site, and making bricks—for these, a mixture of sand and clay was poured into special forms, and after a couple days in the sun they were ready for the bricklayers. Experts supervised the work, and about thirty to forty POWs would be sweating at the site each afternoon. "Just as the Israelites were slaving for Pharaoh, so are the POWs slaving for their 'desert bishop'," some claimed. But the "desert bishop" did his own share of work: every day he could be seen stripped to the waist and bare-legged, handing bricks to the bricklayers. When the walls had been completed, they were roughcast with liquid cement inside and outside. Then it was the carpenters' turn to start work: Timbers and woodwork were made from old poles which had been used for the barbed-wire fences. Finally, eight large tents were stretched out above the walls and fastened to the woodwork to provide the roof. Two POWs were busy shaping yellow sandstones, roughcasting them and building a beautiful and stately altar, and with that finished the men began to build the stairs to the main entrance of the church, also from shaped sandstones. Pastor Rückert had been lucky enough, through the British chaplain at headquarters, to come by a wide double door, and that made a very impressive entrance to the church. The windows presented a problem, because window panes were almost impossible to get hold of, but

Pastor Rückert found the solution: bottle bottoms! Very carefully, the bottoms were knocked out of some twelve hundred bottles and put together in pairs, one bottom turned inward, the other outward. Putty to stick them together was made from a mixture of sand and clay. Each window required six hundred bottles—brown and green ones in some pre-arranged pattern. Finally, the British authorities provided benches to accommodate four hundred people.

After two months of hard work, "St. Martins in the Sands" was ready for its inauguration. The church was an amazing accomplishment, something very unique in the POW camps in Egypt. The site chosen for it was immediately named "Church Square," and the mammoth work of building it—done by numerous volunteers, who received no pay for their efforts—compelled people's respect and admiration, including that of those who were less interested in the activities of the church.

The church was much frequented—the number of churchgoers grew slowly but surely—and the greatest loyalty and faithfulness to this camp church was shown by those men who had sweated and worked the most to complete it. Pastor Rückert may have named it "St. Martins in the Sands," but soon after its inauguration the POWs began to refer to it as "our cathedral," or simply "the cathedral."

Concurrently with the building of the church, the YMCA POW work had expanded and strengthened. Through regular and frequent visits, circulation of briefings in the camps, and lectures before the POWs, the purpose and policy of the work of the YMCA were thoroughly explained and disseminated. It soon became general knowledge that the YMCA had established a center in Camp 380 and that, whenever they wished, POWs could approach the center about any matter. The camp commandant placed ten tents at the disposal of the YMCA. They were pitched in a horseshoe shape, and three of them acted as library and reading rooms. The remainder were necessary for storage space and offices. As in Great Britain, we maintained a reasonable stock of the things most in demand, so that the POWs could get what they wanted immediately. The Cairo office procured large quantities of sports equipment, musical instruments,

games, pencils, toothbrushes, and other articles for everyday
use, and they took care that these stocks were always replen-
ished. Much was given away, but in most cases the POWs paid
for what they wanted. The principle of having to give something
to get something is a healthy one, and besides, the World Alliance
wanted the work to become gradually self-supporting. We normally allowed ourselves a profit of 5 percent on what the POWs
bought. This was adequate to cover expenses incurred for paper,
postage, a duplicator, a calculating machine, a typewriter, and
gasoline for and maintenance of our car; and after these expenses
had been met we would still have a surplus, which enabled us in
hundreds of cases to provide repatriating POWs with a rucksack
full of food. Many POWs had not been able to earn their own
money due to such factors as illness or a prison stay, and this
rucksack meant that they were not left in a worse position than
other POWs once they got back to Germany.

The daily administration of purchases and sales in the
YMCA did not take up much of my time, because two POWs,
a merchant and a banker, took care of that part of the business.
And because of the conditions in Egypt—everything could be
bought and there was no rationing at all—the YMCA POW Aid
was much better equipped to provide material assistance, and to
do so quickly, than was the case in Great Britain, where restrictions and rationing often set rather narrow limits to what the
YMCA was able to accomplish.

After the completion of the church, the POWs decided to
start work on a building near the church to accommodate the
YMCA. There was really nothing wrong with the tents which
the commandant had made available to us, but the chaplain and
his congregation felt that it would look better and more inviting
if the YMCA could strike the tents and move into a real building.
The commandant had no objections as long as "you do it your-
selves and it doesn't involve any expenses to the administration
of the camp." And so another building was erected, from the
same materials as the church, and some of the rooms were turned
into library, reading, and writing rooms. Tables and chairs—
including easy chairs—were provided by the British YMCA,
chairs which could no longer be used in the soldiers' recreation

centers because they were too worn. German POWs repaired them, made bookshelves and reading lamps, and covered the floor of the entire building with strips of coconut matting. The home of the YMCA became the most favored rendezvous in the camp, and it was in constant use. "At last," everybody seemed to think, "we have a place where we can sit quietly and peacefully, without having to listen to the never-ending flutter of the tent canvas, or to the never-ending talks and rumors and discussions about 'when are we going home?'"

From then on, there were two impressive buildings on Church Square, the church right in the middle and the YMCA to the right. To the left we pitched the three largest tents and turned them into table tennis rooms, and that proved an enormous success. Within four months the center of the camp had completely changed its look and was now quite dominated by the church and its work. Though the greatest amount of credit must be given to the German chaplain and his active congregation, we would never have achieved this much had it not been for the commandant's kindness and his generous permission to allow us to build on the best spot in the entire camp. And he was indeed pleased with the result; every time he received visitors who had not been there before, he invariably had to show them the interior of the church.

I myself had not participated much in the building of the YMCA center—my colleagues had done that. Instead, I had concentrated on visiting all the other camps in the canal zone to make myself useful where the POWs were not so fortunate as to have a YMCA center. I had long conversations with the respective commandants, Men of Confidence, chaplains, and others. I was often invited to attend theater performances and concerts in the evenings, to watch football matches between POWs and British soldiers on Saturday afternoons, and to speak in front of the POWs about my impressions of prison camps in Germany, and about my experiences in Russia. Of similar interest were topics like "the co-operative movement" and "the folk high schools" in Denmark; the audiences were large—from 150 to 900 men, depending on the size of the camp. Due to such visits and lectures, and to circular letters which were usually read aloud over the camp radio, it was possible to constantly disseminate knowledge of the existence and mission of the YMCA.

At the beginning of November 1947, we started an action aimed at helping the many hundreds of POWs who had turned to us for help because they had lost their homes and jobs in the Russian occupied zone in Germany, and therefore had no idea what to do when they were repatriated. We worked in close cooperation with the YMCA and the church of the three western zones in Germany on this matter. We forwarded all the relevant information about the POWs in question—their age, education, political past, religion, family relations, and so forth—to the German YMCA, and in many cases the YMCA succeeded in locating individuals, associations, or congregations who would be willing to take care of the homeless POWs, to support them during the initial difficult time after their repatriation. This operation gave all of us a lot of work during the last months of 1947, so much so that we were unable to handle it ourselves and had to ask for volunteers; however, the importance of this task was easily appreciated by everybody, and it was no problem getting enough volunteers to help us.

There was another matter which took up a lot of time toward the end of that year: in the middle of October, a POW had suggested that the YMCA POW Aid arrange a prize competition "to lift up spirits and make people think of something else." This suggestion was found good, and we immediately circulated letters to all the camps inviting the POWs to compete for the prize by submitting any poems, short stories, or articles which they might have written during their captivity. If they had not they were encouraged to do so, about, for instance, "Advantages and Disadvantages of being Prisoners of War." They were told that just about everything would be of interest—poetry or prose, short or long, and that any contribution should be submitted to the YMCA office by 15 November. Friends and business acquaintances donated three wristwatches, one camera, two fountain pens, and ten new German books as prizes for the competition.

The competition aroused a great deal of interest and enthusiasm, and we received several hundred poems, short stories—

even novels, plays, and travel books. The amount of work that went into the evaluation of this huge quantity of written material was indeed large; a committee of six judges, elected from among the POWs themselves and representing officers as well as men, did the evaluations. A German professor was appointed chairman. In the end, the committee had to work around the clock to complete the evaluations before Christmas. They barely succeeded and, on 23 December, the result was published and the lucky winners were presented with their prizes during a get-together in the YMCA building. The competition attracted so much attention from the British authorities that after Christmas they had the sixteen winners' works published in a book with "Published by the YMCA POW Aid in Egypt" printed on the cover.

MY FOURTH CHRISTMAS WITH
PRISONERS OF WAR

At the beginning of December 1947, the POWs in Egypt did not feel much like celebrating Christmas. Many of them were unable to be with their families for the sixth time at that time of the year. Many of them felt depression and self-pity; they moaned and were unable to hide their disappointment that the repatriations had been brought to a standstill due to "lack of vessels." But nevertheless, as Christmas drew nearer, one, then another began to make small preparations, and soon more and more joined them. As we know, trees—especially firs—cannot grow in deserts, but the POWs found a way to circumvent this fact and made Christmas trees out of very modest means—a bit of wire and some discarded sacks. Two or three pieces of thick wire would be twisted together to form the trunk of the tree, then the branches would be made in the same way, only with thin pieces of wire, and fastened to the trunk. Threads of sackcloth were cut into small pieces and pushed carefully between the wires until the entire tree was completely covered, and the whole thing was sprayed with grass-green paint and dried. After that, it was ready for use.

On the day of Christmas Eve I called on a military prison

which housed, among others, about twenty Germans. Some of them were suspected of having committed war crimes in one or more of the formerly occupied countries. Others had stolen British property, such as weapons, food, and clothing, and sold it to the local population—an offence which was severely punished. Nevertheless, I had been given permission, prior to the visit, to bring a small parcel to each of the POWs, containing a few of the most necessary toilet requisites, a bit of chocolate, and twenty cigarettes. I could walk around unescorted, so I went by all the cells and spoke to each of the POWs. It is my impression that most of them were very happy and grateful to receive such a visit; at least, several told me that they had not expected any kind of visit on Christmas. A few seemed rather apathetic and indifferent, or even distrustful and suspicious. But a change of heart occurred when they realized that I was not a representative of the authorities, but of the Church, and that I came from a small country, Denmark. Then they began to question me about conditions outside the prison walls. There were also those who were more interested in complaining about this and that and all the rest of it, but I soon found out that I could have sensible conversations with all of them when I told them that I knew perfectly well how it felt to spend Christmas in captivity, and that I myself had been in that position not so very long ago. All of them—with no exceptions—took my hand to bid me farewell, wished me a Merry Christmas, and thanked me for coming to visit them.

I returned to Camp 380 and spent most of the afternoon in the hospital. The patients were perhaps those in most need of having someone look in on them and bring them greetings from outside the hospital. Small Christmas trees were placed in all the rooms, and over the loudspeaker they could listen to the Christmas service later in the afternoon. Christmas chimes were sounding over the camp radio and at five o'clock when the service was about to begin, not one standing place was available in the "cathedral." Two large "Christmas trees" were placed at each side of the altar, decorated in the traditional fashion and with lots of candles. The church had its own eminent choir of thirty-five singers, and the church echoed to the sound of the first hymn—"Silent Night, Holy Night." Everybody knew the hymn and everybody joined in.

After the service it was time for Christmas Eve celebrations in the many tents. I had only time to go by a few of them, but there was no mistake about the atmosphere. At about nine o'clock, I left the camp and drove to a place approximately fifty miles north of Camp 380 to be with forty-three young Danish soldiers who had served as volunteers with the British forces in the Middle East. Hundreds of my countrymen had volunteered for military service with the British after the liberation of Denmark on 5 May 1945, and after having been trained in Great Britain they had reported for duty in India, Palestine, and Egypt. I had already visited these Danish soldiers once before, so when I received an invitation a few days earlier to be with them on Christmas Eve, I gladly accepted. We had a very nice, typically Danish Christmas Eve, where we sang Christmas hymns and made speeches. At midnight we sang the Danish and British national hymns, and then I drove back to Camp 380.

On Christmas Day, the YMCA POW Aid helped arrange Christmas festivals in several camps. I and three of my staff members spent the day in a remote camp, where 450 German soldiers were occupied with the surveillance of British ammunition depots. Those who could be spared were allowed the afternoon off to participate in the Christmas festival, and it was an excellent festival, prepared by the Germans themselves and characterized by a combination of seriousness and cheerfulness. In the middle of it all we had coffee and cookies, compliments of the nearby British soldiers' recreation center. On our way home to Camp 380, I had to agree with a colleague who spontaneously said, "Thanks to the YMCA, hundreds and hundreds of POWs have been able to celebrate Christmas this year in a dignified and festive manner."

Shortly after Christmas, the YMCA's stock of books was increased considerably due to a donation of two thousand books from the relief committee of the Danish Church, and of eight thousand books of German light literature from ecumenical circles in Geneva. These were a much-valued contribution to our stock of fifteen thousand books. They were sorted and divided into fifty small libraries, packed in strong "circulation boxes," and distributed—one or two boxes for each camp. The boxes "wandered" from camp to camp and two POWs were responsible for cataloging and circulating them.

Apart from fiction and other light literature, the library had a significant collection of factual books available to all interested, especially students who wished to improve their knowledge and proficiency. The library contained a multitude of classified medical books—in particular up-to-date Swiss professional journals—which enabled the YMCA to circulate a number of circulation boxes among twenty-five to thirty doctors in captivity, who were very grateful for the books.

A main task of the YMCA was to assist the various studies in the camps, especially in Camp 380, which housed a large number of officers. Because officers were not allowed to work, these were among the most eager to participate in courses or to study on their own accord. The camp had a faculty of law headed by a lawyer, a man who presumably had an easy time of his captivity because he was always fully occupied by lectures and classes. He came from East Prussia and had therefore lost everything; his wife and young son were in the Ruhr area as refugees.

The faculty of theology, with its twenty students, was originally headed by Pastor Wester, later bishop of the federal state of Schleswig-Holstein. Upon his repatriation a young theologian, Wolfgang Arnold, D.D., took over. Obviously, these two faculties could not be compared to any faculty in, for instance, Denmark, but they represented an admirable effort to achieve something meaningful in the midst of hardships, and the YMCA sought always to lend a helping hand by procuring necessary books and other study materials. The six brightest students of theology were repatriated at the same time and enrolled in the same school of theology, and their studies in Egypt were acknowledged as equivalent to two terms in Germany, proof enough that the efforts of the YMCA were worthwhile.

As regarded music and theater, the situation was much the same in Egypt as in Germany. Camp 380 had six large orchestras and three jazz bands. A former conductor of the Berlin Philharmonic Orchestra, Dr. Hörner, headed the camp's best symphony orchestra.

One would not believe it, but there was actually a fantastic richness of fauna and flora in the desert, and this encouraged some POWs who were interested in nature to arrange an exhibition in Camp 380. They approached the YMCA to borrow premises for such an exhibition, but what we could offer proved far too small for the numerous fossils and species of plants, animals, birds, fish, and insects; besides, the exhibitors also wanted to include fish and squids from the Suez Canal and the Great Bitter Lake, and it became necessary to ask the commandant for three more tents. The exhibition was officially and ceremoniously opened in the presence of guests from the British headquarters and from Cairo, and it aroused a great deal of interest: twelve thousand people came to visit it, mainly POWs from the surrounding camps. After awhile, at British request, it was moved to two soldiers' camps in the area, so that British troops would also get the opportunity to see such an interesting collection of fauna and flora under the expert guidance of the exhibitors. Finally, the entire collection was packed into wooden boxes with the greatest care and dispatched to Germany, where it was placed at the disposal of the Bonn University.

The POW camps in Cyrenaica, Libya were administered by the British headquarters in the canal zone and were thus, very naturally, under the auspices of the YMCA POW Aid in Egypt. Seven or eight small prison camps were scattered in and outside the cities of Tobruk, Derna, and Benghazi, housing about three thousand men altogether. Over the years, the YMCA had sent parcels of books, German newspapers and magazines, sports equipment, and the like when the POWs had written and asked for them. In the spring of 1948, I set out to visit these camps on a two-week trip.

In several ways, POWs in Libya were much better off than their countrymen in Egypt. The climate was more tolerable; a moderate breeze from the Mediterranean meant that the weather was not as hot as in Egypt. There were green fields everywhere and gardens, flowering in every color, surrounded the houses. The POWs could go where they wanted and were often invited to visit the local Italian and French populations. Many POWs earned an extra income by working for the civilian population during their free time, and many houses which had been seriously damaged during the war were thus repaired and made habitable again. POWs in Libya also had the chance once a month to send parcels of up to five kilos of food to their relatives in Germany. All this helped lift their spirits and caused less moaning and friction, and fewer bitter questions.

I spent some hours in the afternoons and evenings in each camp—after work, when everybody had returned to camp—to give me ample time to talk to the POWs individually and, if they wanted me to, to address them all. They were very interested in being told about the treatment of the POWs in Egypt so that they could make comparisons. The interest increased when they found out that I could also tell them about the circumstances of POWs in Germany during the war, and when we began to discuss the conditions of German POWs in Russia, the last little bit of self-pity disappeared completely.

One day I paid a visit to the military prison, but to no avail; when I asked the British commandant if he had any German "guests," he answered: "Yes, I have one, but I don't think he is at home. A little while ago I saw him leave, so he's probably gone to the movies." And so he had!

A small incident of a different kind occurred in one of the camps in Tobruk. A commandant greeted me with the following words: "Hello—how nice to see you again! You probably don't remember me, but when you last visited me, I was a prisoner of war in Germany, in Torgau. You are most welcome." And he did indeed make me feel very welcome.

THE LAST DAYS IN THE DESERT

The repatriation of German POWs from Egypt had been suspended from January 1947 to February 1948, but in the spring and summer of 1948 the transports were rapidly picking up. The long period of suspension, however, made most POWs question the validity of the British official announcement that everybody would be repatriated before the end of September. The men had their doubts, and the general attitude was: "We can't believe it! Our hopes have been dashed before." Nevertheless, during the month of March no fewer than eight thousand POWs were able to turn their backs to the desert, and in spite of past experience, the doubts gradually began to give way to the conviction that, this time, the British authorities would keep their promise. In the following months, five to eight thousand men per month were repatriated, and the conviction was strengthened. The transports caused a noticeable lifting of spirits in all the camps. A kind of excitement began to possess everybody; the interest in studies, sports, and entertainment diminished. One thought seemed to occupy everybody's mind: "We're going home. And it's important that we get as much food, clothing, and other necessary things as we can possibly carry home with us." Every spare moment was spent sewing strong and capacious rucksacks and bags, or making large suitcases. The deft POWs had the advantage of being able to make such fashionable items as work boxes, cigarette cases, frames, and bookends, which they sold at a fair price to British soldiers who wanted to bring such things back from German POW camps in Egypt as souvenirs.

This exodus of the prisoners of war also influenced the YMCA POW Aid: sports equipment, exercise books, and classified books were no longer in demand. Now it was a matter of getting things which could not easily be had in Germany. The YMCA was also asked to procure tens of thousands of envelopes and writing pads, and the demand for warm underwear grew steadily. The YMCA in Cairo secured large quantities of underwear at a very favorable price, and the POW Aid resold them in Camp 380 with the usual profit of 5 percent.

Effective from March, the British authorities had three transport ships available which maintained regular runs between Port Said and Hamburg with the sole purpose of transporting POWs back to Germany. The passage usually took eleven to twelve days, and this time seemed long because there was nothing for the POWs to do; very soon, therefore, the YMCA POW Aid found out that a library on board each of the three ships would serve as a remedy against having POWs go nuts in their anticipation and excitement about going home. We got hold of twenty-four hundred books and a number of games to divert their attention. When a ship was about to leave port, we would find a POW willing to be a librarian during the voyage; a librarian was necessary because of the demand on books and games. He had to handle book loans and games in a fair way and, just before reaching Hamburg, to collect the books and games, put them into specially made boxes, lock the boxes, and hand over the keys to the captain of the ship. The contents of the boxes would thus be ready for the next group of repatriates. This system functioned very well and gave much pleasure and satisfaction to the POWs during their long voyage back to Germany.

All the POWs had to spend the last few days prior to being taken to Port Said in the "repatriation wing" of Camp 380. The idea was to equip them with new uniforms—chocolate brown battle dress—new underwear, socks, and boots, two towels, two woolen blankets, and forty German Westmarks. The transport ships left Port Said once a week, and I made it a habit, together with two or three colleagues, to accompany the men to the harbor, in case I could be of assistance during the last hours before their departure; sometimes I acted as an interpreter or as an intermediary between a POW and the military police right on the pier in Port Said: the military police would invariably pick out about twenty POWs each week and check their luggage very thoroughly—not to try and find any dutiable goods, but to find things which were British property. And it often proved advantageous if a civilian was present at such "delousings," as the Germans called these checks. If the police discovered a couple of khaki shirts or soldiers' towels, a quiet remark on my part usually put things in order. Of course it was wrong what the POW had done, but because I knew the man and his circumstances—that he was one of those who had lost just about everything he had owned due to the war, or that he was a refugee from the former eastern German territories—then perhaps his act was understandable and excusable, and most police officers did indeed forgive such acts and say, "All right, then, you can close your suitcase."

I also made a point of going on board the ships in Port Said to say hello to the captains, to explain to the temporary librarian how the system worked, and to check if the books and games were in order and in their proper places. Whenever a German chaplain was among the repatriates, I would introduce him to the captain, who usually offered to help arrange the services on board the ship. Gradually I got to know the three captains and a few of their crew members rather well, and most of the time they were all very cooperative, and also interested in having the church on board their ships. One of the captains even told me that he had introduced crew prayers on Sunday mornings after the German service.

I usually stayed on board until the ship was due to sail, and this gave me ample opportunity to say good-bye and wish a safe journey to the POWs I knew best. Sometimes I could not help feeling sad standing on the pier and waving good-bye when the ship left harbor. I knew for certain that I should never see them again, or at least only very few of them. But I also knew that when they disembarked twelve days later in Hamburg, the West German YMCA would be there to welcome them back to Germany and to show them around the large transit camp, from where they would be discharged after a few days to continue their journey—as free men—back to their families. A returned German POW once wrote to me: "The YMCA was with us in our captivity. The YMCA was the last we saw in Egypt and the first to bid us 'welcome home' in Germany."

The growing number of repatriates also meant that chaplains were beginning to leave Egypt. Pastor Rückert, however—the "Desert Bishop"—chose to prolong his captivity by six months, and at his request the Evangelical Church in Germany sent eight chaplains to Egypt in the spring of 1948 to replace some of those who were to be repatriated after several years of captivity. The ecclesiastical work in the prison camps thus continued to the very last, and if a chaplain was no longer available in a camp or hostel, then we were normally able to get hold of a couple of laymen who were willing to carry on the work of the chaplains as long as was necessary and possible. Thus, in Camp 380, twenty to thirty POWs continued to assemble in the church for morning and evening prayers, and many more than that on Sundays.

From the middle of July the repatriations assumed such proportions that one camp after another could be closed down. For the YMCA this meant collecting all the books, musical instruments, surplus sports equipment, and so forth, and having it all carefully packed and dispatched to Germany, where it could be of good use to the associations of the German YMCA in their reconstruction work. We were given 150 strong metal boxes, formerly used by a British ammunition depot for shells. In the middle of September they were dispatched to Hamburg, where the German YMCA immediately took action to have them distributed to the associations.

Before I conclude this chapter about the last days in Egypt, I should like to mention a number of people and institutions in that area, with which the YMCA POW Aid enjoyed a friendly relationship and close cooperation, and to which a lot is owed.

First, the International Red Cross. I was very pleasantly surprised when I realized that the International Red Cross representative in Cairo was an old acquaintance of mine, a Swiss named de Cocatrix. I met him in Berlin and we developed a very close and mutually profitable relationship. The same applied to his two colleagues. When Berlin fell, de Cocatrix was arrested by the Russians, accused, as I was, of espionage, and taken to the prison camp in Krasnogorsk near Moscow, where I too had been a prisoner for several months. The joy at seeing each other again was mutual and we started once more to work closely together: if de Cocatrix happened to come upon deficiencies or requests in the POW camps which he felt ought to be taken care of by the YMCA, he would immediately inform me; and vice versa if I happened to learn about deficiencies or maltreatment of POWs which the Red Cross could point out and have corrected.

In Berlin and London it was a great help to be able to approach the Danish representative and to feel that you were met with trust and an understanding of the special nature of the relief work. This was also the case in Cairo, where the Danish consul took a great interest in the YMCA work because he himself had been a prisoner of war in France for quite some time during World War I. He came from south Jutland, a part of Denmark which, following a war in 1864 between Denmark and Germany, had fallen under German sovereignty and remained so until 1920; he had been one of about thirty thousand Danish-minded citizens who had been forced to fight on the German side against the Allies in the Great War.

The American Bible Society in Port Said deserves mention, too. It arranged for the necessary amounts of Bibles and testaments to be made available to the POW camps. The man in charge of the society was an American who spoke fluent German, and he and his family opened their home in great hospitality to the POWs in the Port Said area.

There were thirteen soldiers' recreation centers in the canal zone, and a close relationship developed between us and all of the centers. Even though the main task of the centers was to be of service to the British soldiers, German POWs were nevertheless most welcome, and many of them made use of the canteens and received the same service as the British soldiers. Furthermore, the British YMCA helped us on several occasions to get furniture and equipment to YMCA premises in the camps, and once a month they arranged for a movie to be shown in Camp 380, free of charge.

About fifteen German Catholic nuns and two deaconesses from the Kaiserswerth Deaconess Institution had their work in Cairo. They were extremely well liked by the POWs because of their dedicated and unselfish welfare work to help the Germans. They often visited the prison camps and were always allowed to enter, even though no women had ever had access to the camps. Usually, they carried loads as heavy as they could manage of warm clothes for women and children, lard, rice, and other essential articles which were in short supply in Germany. They gave it all to the chaplains for further distribution among the POWs who were sick or imprisoned, because those POWs, as I mentioned, had the least possibility of obtaining a full rucksack to bring back to Germany.

GOOD-BYE TO THE PRISONER OF WAR CAMPS

On 23 September 1948 I went to Port Said for the last time to see off a transport of repatriates. Now only 1250 men remained in Egypt. In Camp 380, expectations were high and everybody was as happy as a crowded railway station the day before Christmas. Everybody was hurrying around, spending their last pennies on small purchases and getting the last things stowed away. The day when I myself would have nothing more to do in Egypt was approaching, and I had no problem getting the British authorities' permission to accompany the last prison transport to Europe. It meant a free return passage, at least to the transit camp in Hamburg, and it gave me the opportunity to be together with those POWs who had been my most loyal companions from the beginning to the very last. Several of these men could have left Egypt a few months earlier, but they had volunteered, without receiving any economic advantage, to stay behind in order to help me during the final stages of my work in Egypt.

On one of the last days in the camp, we let the British soldiers' recreation centers have all our furniture. Curtains and tablecloths and the like were packed away and, upon arrival in Hamburg, handed over to the German YMCA for use in one of the eighteen convalescence homes which the YMCA managed at that time to help POWs who had returned from Russian captivity.

On the last evening we gathered at half past six, as we had so many times before, for prayers in the church. It became a memorable evening, an evening which I believe not many of those present will ever forget. The passages for daily morning and evening prayers had been selected several months before, and it was really a coincidence that on that particular evening, the selected passage was about Peter's release from the prison in Antioch (Acts, chapter 12), but the topical interest was indeed striking, even though the chaplain emphasized that he had not really looked upon the prison camp as a prison as such. Finally, we sang "A Safe Stronghold our God is Still," and then the chaplain quietly removed the crucifix and the holy things from the altar. The church in Camp 380 had fulfilled its mission, and could now be transferred to the British chaplain for those troops who were to remain on Egyptian soil.

The next morning at four o'clock everybody was on the move. With a couple of colleagues I took the last rounds of the premises, before we closed down forever and handed over the keys to the commandant. At seven o'clock we all left the camp for Port Said.

Several high-ranking officers from the British headquarters had appeared to be present when the last POWs left Egypt, and so had the Secretary General of the YMCA in Cairo together with some of his colleagues. One of the deaconesses had even traveled all the way to the canal zone in order to say good-bye. And on this occasion, there was no military police escort and no POWs were "deloused."

In the middle of the afternoon the ship weighed anchor, and soon we could see only dimly the minarets of the mosques of Port Said in the distance. The ship was old, with a tonnage of 16,500, especially fitted as a transport ship for troops; everything was clean and well-maintained, and the three decks were fitted with hundreds of hammocks. On board the ship were about 800 British soldiers in addition to the 1250 repatriating POWs. I was the only civilian.

The POW library was in constant use, and it functioned quite well during the long passage. We had three orchestras on board and once a day they gave performances on all three decks. On Sundays, Catholic as well as Protestant services were held. The weather was as fine as it could possibly be—calm and warm—and the passage was very enjoyable. We wore light clothes as we had done in Egypt. But as soon as we anchored in the harbor of Trieste, the weather turned to rain and wind; we were back in Europe, and many of us caught colds.

The reason we ended up in Trieste and not Hamburg, as was the original plan, was that the passage to Trieste was only half as long, and the British authorities had therefore decided on Trieste because it meant that the three ships were able to manage three passages a month instead of only two, as had been the case before.

From Trieste we continued the journey by rail, twenty men to one train car. The cars had been supplied with a thick layer of straw to make a softer floor. In a downpour and in autumn cold we proceeded through north Italy and Austria without the opportunity to see any of the beautiful landscape. Twice a day the transport would stop for a couple of hours at some small railway station. We would then be able to stretch our legs, and have a wash and a big hot meal. At each stop, crowds of hungry children immediately surrounded us, and they were happy and grateful when we gave them some dry soldiers' biscuits from Egypt. Everywhere we went, the local population was standing at windows and in doors, waving a "welcome home" to the returning "Egyptians," easily recognizable by their white caps. Some were drying their eyes with their handkerchiefs—were they happy? Or did they mourn a lost son, husband, or brother?

Many of the POWs had not set foot on German soil since 1943, and they were quite unable to recognize their homeland in all the bombed and destroyed towns we passed on our way. But they were not taken by surprise. They had no illusions about the conditions to which they were now returning. Letters from relatives and former POW friends had informed them about the situation and they were acutely aware that they would have to readjust, from the fleshpots of Egypt to the destruction of their homeland.

AT HOME AT LAST

The transit or repatriation camp for the POWs who had been in British captivity was situated in Munster, a village not far from Hamburg. From this camp the POWs who had their homes or families in the British occupied zone of Germany were discharged in singles, and from here, collective transports of the POWs who lived in either the American, French, or Russian occupied zones, or in Berlin, were dispatched. The POWs had to walk from the railway station to the camp, a walk of about two miles, but their heavy loads of luggage were transported on trucks, together with the sick POWs.

The main street of the camp led to a big square with lots of signs bearing the names of the individual towns and counties in the British zone. For the other three zones there were no such signs, because the POWs who had their homes in these zones were taken there in a collective transport. The many signs helped each POW find the right box. Once this had been done, the POWs were shown their quarters in the camp. Everybody bedded down in huts—fifty men in each—and everybody had to take care of his own luggage and get it installed in the huts. Then the repatriation procedure could begin: registration, medical examination, payment of allowances, and so forth. Everybody entered the floodgates at one end of the camp and forty-eight hours later they could exit as free men, with discharge papers in their hand and a train ticket, to whatever railway station they wished, in their pocket. POWs going to the other occupied zones, however, had to wait a little longer; transports were dispatched once a week to the American or French zones, and once every ten days to the Russian zone.

One of the huts was marked "CVJM," the German name for the YMCA, and here members of the staff would help repatriated men sort out all the different formalities they had to take care of, and to discuss problems and difficulties any man might have concerning his future. The POWs who didn't know whether they had a home or a family anymore were the ones most in need of talking to somebody who would listen to them and try to give them some advice. A representative of the German Job Center had his office in the YMCA hut. Also available were books, games, a modest stock of sports equipment, and, twice a week, movies. A hospital with doctors and nurses was ready to take care of the sick and the weak, to nurse them back to health before they proceeded on their journeys.

The Munster Camp was in many ways an interesting place—and also an instructive experience for many of the "Egyptians": shortly after their arrival, they met thirty-eight POWs who had returned from captivity in Russia and it was impossible not to make a comparison. While the POWs from the Middle

East were generally in good health, suntanned, and full of energy, with a rucksack and a couple of suitcases bursting with all sorts of good things, the POWs from the Soviet Union had nothing but a self-made wooden spoon and a similar metal bowl. Some of them did wear wadded jackets and trousers of the usual Russian kind, but not even a rag dealer would touch them. Most of them came stumbling into the camp without socks, and wearing shoes with numerous old patches and strips of sackcloth around their legs and feet, fastened with pieces of string. They were starved, hollow-cheeked, unshaven, and filthy, numbed with cold and suffering from lice; they did not say much, full of mistrust against everything and everybody. When the "Egyptians" saw these poor men, one of them could not help exclaiming, "Thank God, we didn't end up with Ivan!" And nobody contradicted him! When the German YMCA delegate in the camp encouraged them to let the Russian POWs have a little of their own abundance from Egypt, they did so most willingly and generously—food, clothes, cigarettes, and money.

I stayed in the Munster Camp until all the "Egyptians" had had their matters sorted out, and I was thus able to wish them all the best for their continued journey. One of the last POWs I said good-bye to heaved a big sigh of relief: "God be praised and thanked that I'm now a free man." And he expressed his gratitude towards the YMCA and told me in German, "Gott befohlen"—commit your soul to God. I never saw the man again, but I think he meant what he said; it seemed to come from the bottom of his heart. And I suddenly realized that a new chapter of his life had just begun—and of my life, too. My seven years as a YMCA field delegate working among prisoners of war in Germany, Great Britain, and Egypt were over.

Appendix

LIST OF PRISONER OF WAR CAMPS

IN POMERANIA, MECKLENBURG,

BRANDENBURG, AND SAXONY

STALAG II	—	A	— Neubrandenburg
STALAG II	—	B	— Hammerstein
STALAG II	—	C	— Greifswald
STALAG II	—	D	— Stargard
STALAG II	—	E	— Schwerin
Luft I			— Barth
Luft IV			— Gross-Tüchow
OFLAG II	—	A	— Prenzlau
OFLAG II	—	B	— Arnswalde
OFLAG II	—	C	— Woldenberg a.d. Warthe
OFLAG II	—	D	— Grossborn
OFLAG II	—	E	— Neubrandenburg
STALAG III	—	A	— Luckenwalde
STALAG III	—	B	— Fürstenberg a.d. Oder
STALAG III	—	C	— Alt Drewitz
STALAG III	—	D	— Steglitz
STALAG IV	—	A	— Hohnstein
STALAG IV	—	B	— Mühlberg
STALAG IV	—	C	— Wistritz b. Teplitz-Schönau

STALAG IV — D   — Torgau
STALAG IV — E/Z   — Annaberg
STALAG IV — F   — Hartmannsdorf
STALAG IV — G   — Oschatz

OFLAG IV — B   — Königstein
OFLAG IV — C   — Colditz

POW Camp Hospital   —   Elsterhorst b. Hoyerswerda
POW Camp Hospital   —   Königswartha
POW Camp Hospital   —   Schmorkau

REFERENCES

Eva Berthold. *Kriegsgefangene im Osten, Bilder, Briefe, Berichte.* Athenäum Verlag, Königstein/Ts., 1981.

Paul Carrell & Günter Böddeker. *Die Gefangenen, Leben und Überleben deutscher Soldaten hinter Stacheldraht.* Ullstein, 1986.

Arthur A. Durand. *Stalag Luft III.—The Secret Story.* Louisiana State University Press, Baton Rouge and London, 1988. (The pages 192–253 comprise a detailed description and an appraisal of the YMCA POW Aid).

Theo Findahl. *Lange Skygger. Dagbok fra Krigens Berlin 1939–1945.* Dreyers Forlag, Oslo, 1964.

Helmut Gollwitzer. *". . . . und führen, wohin du nicht willst." Bericht einer Gefangenschaft.* Chr. Kaiser Verlag, München, 1952.

Paul Guinness. *I was in Prison.* The World Alliance of the Young Men's Christian Associations, Geneva 1947.

Wanda Heger. *Hver fredag foran porten.* Gyldendal, Norsk Forlag, Oslo, 1984.

Clarence Prouty Shedd. *History of the World Alliance of Young Men's Christian Associations.* S.I.C.K., London, 1955.

Axel B. Jeppesen. *Blandt fjender og venner.* Viborg Domkirkes Forlag, 1987.

R. W. Kimball. *Clipped Wings.* The United States Air Force, 1948.

Stefan Kotarski. *Oflag II-C, Woldenberg.* Kaiqza i Wiedza, Warszawa, 1984.

Jacob Kronika. *Berlins undergang.* H. Hagerup, København, 1946.

Erhart Kästner. *Zeltbuch von Tumilat.* Suhrkamp Verlag, Frankfurt am Main, 1967.

Hans Pfahlmann. *Fremdarbeiter und Kriegsgefangene in der deutschen Kriegswirtschaft 1939–1945.* Wehr und Wissen Verlagsgesellschaft, Darmstadt, 1968.

Edward af Sandeberg. *Nu kan det sägas.* Saxon & Lindstedts Förlag, Stockholm, 1946.

Didrik Arup Seip. *Hiemme og i Fiendeland.* Gyldendal, Norsk Forlag, Oslo, 1946.

Christian Streit. *Keine Kameraden. Die Wehrmacht und die Sowjetischen Kriegsgefangenen 1941–45.* Institut der Zeitgeschichte, Deutsche Verlagsanstalt, Stuttgart, 1978.

Matthew Barry Sullivan. *Thresholds of Peace.* Hamish Hamilton, London, 1979.

Henry Söderberg. *Över gränser gennom spärrar.* P. A. Norsted & Söners Förlag, Stockholm, 1945.

We Prisoners of War. Sixteen British Officers and Soldiers speak from a German Prison Camp. Edited by Tracy Strong, Association Press, New York, 1942.

The YMCA and the Italian Prisoners of War: A Report. The British YMCA, London, 1945.

Zur Geschichte der deutschen Kriegsgefangenen des zweiten Weltkrieges, Band XV, bearbeitet von Kurt W. Böhme und Helmuth Wolf. Verlag Ernst und Werner Gieseking, Bielefeld, 1974.

Diaries and personal letters of Chris Christiansen.

The YMCA and YWCA in the Danish National Archives—Numbers 255, 633, T 2, T 3, T 4, T 5.

Sammelmitteilungen des OKW, Abteilung Kriegsgefangenenwesen, datiert am 21. Mai, 1944, Militärhistorisches Institut, Freiburg in Breisgau.

The Danish Ministry of Foreign Affairs Archives, dossier No. 6. U. 338: "KFUMs arbejde blandt krigsfanger."

The Danish Ministry of Foreign Affairs Archives, dossier No. 17. Tys.10/1006: "Christiansen, Christian + avisudklipspakke."

A NOTE ABOUT THE AUTHOR

CHRIS CHRISTIANSEN is a Danish citizen, born in 1914, who after his graduation from Copenhagen University in 1940 with a degree in Theology served for seven years as an international YMCA worker among Allied prisoners of war in Germany. After his release he continued to work with the World's Alliance of the YMCAs—first among German prisoners of war in Great Britain and later in Egypt—until the last prisoners of war were repatriated. He later worked for the Lutheran World Federation and assisted refugees in western Germany and the Middle East. From 1962 to 1980 he served as the Head of Division in the Ministry of Foreign Affairs, Copenhagen. After retiring from goverment service in 1980 he has served as Acting Director to the World Council of Churches Service to aid refugees from Cambodia and Palestine and as Acting Director to the Lutheran World Federation Service to aid refugees in Swaziland.